AN INTRODUCTION T

This is the first comprehensive introduction to Quakerism which balances a history of the theology of the Quakers or Friends with an overview of present-day practice. It charts the growth of the Quaker movement through the 1650s and 1660s, its different theological emphasis in the eighteenth century, and the schisms of the nineteenth century which resulted in the range of Quaker traditions found around the world today. The book focuses in particular on notions of 'endtime', 'spiritual intimacy', and what counts as 'the world' as key areas of theological change. The second half of the book uses extracts from Quaker texts to highlight differences in belief and approach between the different traditions and analyses their future prospects. The book is generously illustrated and includes numerous diagrams to help the reader. Undergraduate and graduate students will find this an essential introduction to the Quaker movement.

PINK DANDELION is Programme Leader, Centre for Postgraduate Quaker Studies at Woodbrooke Quaker Study Centre and Honorary Reader in Quaker Studies at the University of Birmingham. His publications include *The Liturgies of Quakerism* (2005) and *A Sociological Analysis of the Theology of Quakers: The Silent Revolution* (1996).

AN INTRODUCTION TO QUAKERISM

PINK DANDELION

CAMBRIDGE
UNIVERSITY PRESS

CAMBRIDGE UNIVERSITY PRESS
Cambridge, New York, Melbourne, Madrid, Cape Town, Singapore, São Paulo,
Delhi, Dubai, Tokyo

Cambridge University Press
The Edinburgh Building, Cambridge CB2 8RU, UK

Published in the United States of America by Cambridge University Press, New York

www.cambridge.org
Information on this title: www.cambridge.org/9780521600880

First published 2007
Third printing 2010

Printed in the United Kingdom at the University Press, Cambridge

A catalogue record for this publication is available from the British Library

ISBN 978-0-521-84111-5 hardback
ISBN 978-0-521-60088-0 paperback

For Wendy, Jennifer, George, and Florence

Contents

Illustrations

FIGURES

Tables

Boxes

Acknowledgements

This book is based only in part on my own primary research. It also builds on and synthesises the work of numerous other scholars, in particular the proliferation of theory about Quakerism since the 1980s (Dandelion 2004b). I am particularly indebted to the work and colleagueship of Douglas Gwyn and Timothy Ashworth in helping my thinking. Also to Margery Post Abbott, Hugh Barbour, Peter Collins, Catie Gill, Thomas Hamm, Larry Ingle, Thomas Kennedy, Pam Lunn, Rosemary Mingins, Esther Mombo, Rosemary Moore, Rachel Muers, Elizabeth O'Donnell, Brian Phillips, Gay Pilgrim, John Punshon, Arthur Roberts, Jackie Leach Scully, Carole Spencer, and Michele Tarter. I have particularly valued the friendship which has run alongside the exchange of ideas.

The friendship and support of a host of other scholars also need to be mentioned. Roger Homan has been a supervisor, mentor, and friend for two decades. The company of scholars at the British Sociological Association Study of Religion Group and the Quaker Studies Research Association has been invaluable in my scholarly formation. Hugh Pyper at the University of Sheffield, Paul Anderson at George Fox University, and Janet Ross at McMaster have all expanded my sense of Quakerism. Max Carter and Deborah Shaw at Friends Center, Guilford College, North Carolina, have provided ample and generous opportunities to rehearse new ideas.

Kate Brett at Cambridge University Press has been unstintingly supportive and empathic. Finally, but not at all least, I thank all those many friends who kept me on track with the writing and the colleagues who gave generously of their time in reading drafts. That companionship is a rare and valuable thing.

Introduction

Quakerism is often misunderstood. Images of the eighteenth-century Quaker costume, or a focus on pacifism (or even porridge oats!), predominate in the popular imagination, as do confusions between this group and other sects. All too often, Quakers (or 'Friends') are confused with Jehovah's Witnesses or the Mormons or Shakers for example, or are believed to have died out. Equally, within Quakerism, only a minority realises the complexity of the worldwide picture, each of the branches seeing its own version of Quakerism as normative; or caricaturing or conflating Quakerism elsewhere as simply 'other'.

This book, divided into two parts, one of history, one of present-day practice, presents a clear and accessible outline of the history of the Quaker past, as well as clarifying the diversity of the Quaker present. Unlike other books on Quakerism, this volume mixes these two aspects equally. It also dwells less on the lives of individuals. Informed by a sociological approach to theology, the book blends the theological claims of the various types of Quaker encountered with the everyday consequences of these ideas. Thus Quaker history sits alongside the attempt to show how present-day Friends express their interpretations of context, tradition, and corporate vocation.

This introduction outlines the historical context for the beginnings of the Quaker movement (see Box 1 for the variety of academic interpretations of the beginning of Quakerism), describes the three theoretical threads used in this volume, and outlines the contents of the book.

QUAKERISM AND THE RADICAL REFORMATION

When Henry VIII created a national 'Church of England' separate from papal authority in 1534, it was a political reformation as much as a theological one. Indeed, the religious history of England in the following century and a half can be viewed as an attempt to settle the true nature and extent of the Reformation, theologically, and of campaigns to achieve a full

Box 1 Quaker Studies

Modern Quaker Studies began with the work of Robert Barclay of Reigate
with his unfinished 1876 publication *The Inner Life of the Religious Societies of
the Commonwealth*. Barclay was an evangelical Friend who used his own
reading of the early history to justify the form of Quakerism he most preferred
(Hamm 2004, pp. 11–18). However, his history was also to prove seminal for
Friends of other persuasions, as they came to review the past (2004, pp. 11–18).
Liberal Friends such as J. W. Rowntree believed an understanding of Quaker
history was the key to a (Liberal) Quaker revival (Hamm 1988, pp. 154–5).
When Rufus Jones and W. C. Braithwaite took on Rowntree's vision for a
comprehensive and complete history of Quakerism as a means to this revival,
the Victorian Barclay was the author they used as both a foundation and a
departure point for their own interpretation of the essence of Quakerism.
Rather than posit Quakerism as essentially evangelical, with George Fox and
the early missionaries as proto-pastors, as Barclay had, Jones in particular
presented Quakers as essentially, and foremost, mystical (Braithwaite 1912,
p. xxxiv).

Jones' view has since been much challenged. Wilmer Cooper is lucid on the
history of ideas of Quakerism and Jones' place within it (1994) and Melvin
Endy concisely summarises the competing interpretations of Quakerism in his
article in *Quaker History* (1981), between Jones' view which located the beginnings of Quakerism with church mystics and the Geoffrey Nuttall/Frederick
Tolles/Hugh Barbour (1946, 1948, and 1964 respectively) view that Quakerism
can be best understood as a wing of puritanism (though Tolles also suggested
that Quakerism was neither Protestant nor Roman Catholic but a third way:
1948). This view of a Quakerism rooted in puritanism, the 'Puritan School',
gathered pace in the middle of the twentieth century and Hugh Doncaster
wrote a new introduction to replace Jones' for the 1955 edition of Braithwaite's
Beginnings of Quakerism (1955).

A third strand of interpretation emerged in the 1950s when Lewis Benson
began a lifetime's work of trying to communicate a more prophetic understanding of what Quakerism was about. Drawing on the writings of George
Fox, Benson argued that to see Friends in terms of mysticism alone was
insufficient. Quakerism, Benson argued (1968), was about the inward experience of the Light of Christ *and* the universal mission which was led and fed by
this experience. His prophetic Christianity was about a dialogical relationship
with God, of hearing and obeying, and he framed Quakerism within a more
biblical sense of history than Jones.

In the seventies and eighties, in counterpoint to previous 'insider' accounts
of Quakerism, Christopher Hill (1972) and Barry Reay (1985) presented
Quakerism from a Marxist or materialist perspective.

Richard Bailey established Fox's concept of 'celestial flesh' as a way of
describing divine indwelling. Bailey also offered a theory of the divinisation
of Fox in the 1650s and 1660s and the de-divinisation of Fox after 1670. Fox was

brought down to the level of an Apostle, other Friends to the state of believers (Bailey 1992). His work has been partnered by that of Michele Tarter who has looked in particular at the experience of early women Friends (1993, 2001, 2004). In this, she is part of a movement which has rightly placed the experience of women at the heart of Quaker history. Other scholars in this vein include Maureen Bell (1988), Patricia Crawford (1993), Catie Gill (2001, 2005), Elsa Glines (2003), Elaine Hobby (1989, 1995), Sandra Holton (1994, 1996, 2005, and with Margaret Allen, 1997), Bonnelyn Kunze (1994), Rebecca Larson (1999), Pam Lunn (1997), Phyllis Mack (1989, 1992), Elizabeth O'Donnell (1999), Sally Padgett (2003), and Christine Trevett (1991, 2000). Together with Hobby and Gill, Margaret Ezell (1993), Elspeth Graham (1996) (see also Graham *et al.* 1989), and Hilary Hinds (1996), Tarter engages literary theory, significantly bringing those tools of analysis to the study of Quakerism.

If Jones, the 'Puritan School', and Benson were the key Quaker theorists of the first half of the twentieth century, Douglas Gwyn has emerged as the fourth main Quaker theorist of Quakerism in the second half of the century. His doctoral work on 'apocalyptic' and his complementary and contrasting approaches to understanding the nature of Quakerism (1986, 1995, 2000) have been seminal to most of the more recent scholarship. Gwyn alone, though with later agreement (Dandelion *et al.* 1998; Moore 2000), argues that early Friends felt they were living out a 'realising eschatology', i.e. an unfolding endtime. In all of his work, Gwyn is similarly trying to understand how Friends compensated for the defeat of the 'Lamb's War' and how they sustained themselves following those early years.

Not all scholars agree with this view of early Friends and few place the same emphasis on eschatology. Most argue that Friends were talking *not* about the second coming when they claimed 'Christ is come to teach his people himself' (Nickalls 1952, p. 107) but rather about a mystical experience appropriate to (one of a number of) Christian revival movements. John Punshon, for example, claims that early Friends' use of Scripture was symbolic and that 'millennial speculation has never been a prominent feature of Quaker thought' (2001, p. 309). Additionally, Punshon sees the early Quaker experience as individualised rather than an unfolding of global change (2001, p. 311). Carole Spencer is another of those who wishes to play down the central emphasis Gwyn gives eschatology and the apocalyptic. For her, this is only one element of seven which characterise early Friends' theology, a collective group of characteristics which she sees as unmistakably 'Holiness' in character. Spencer argues that early Friends preached a radical Protestant holiness which in time was imitated by Methodism (although Barbour (1994) identifies five distinct ideas of perfection and distinguishes Wesley's from Friends'). Spencer claims that this Holiness theology is a thread which runs throughout Quaker history (2007). The Holiness Revival of the 1880s is not foreign to Quakerism, as Hamm suggests it is in his *Transformation of American Quakerism* (1988), but rather an explicit return to essential Quaker beliefs. Only the outward form is different but, she argues, form is of secondary importance in Quaker tradition. Her work rewrites the family tree of Quakerism as she places the Revival as central in the genealogy of the Quaker traditions. Carole Spencer's work is exciting because of this consequent and latest rewriting of Quaker history. However, Gwyn's framework is compelling, particularly when laid out across time to explain the current challenges facing Quakerism, and is the one adopted here.

or radical reformation (Gwyn 1995, p. 68). Catholic Queen Mary, and the reigns of episcopalian Elizabeth and James, sent many reformers overseas but to return all the more zealous (Gwyn 1995, pp. 70–4). The availability of the Bible in English, particularly after 1611, democratised the interpretation of Scripture and diminished the authority of the clergy and the rule of expertise. The advent of the printing press and the unprecedented sense of possibility brought on by the English Civil War raised hopes in every theological direction. Groups that had separated from the national church or who had set up as independents, such as the Grindletonians, Levellers, Diggers, Ranters, Seekers, Fifth Monarchists, and Baptists, all pursued their own vision of the coming kingdom that would surely emerge from the interruption of earthly monarchical rule. They were largely to be disappointed, partly in that their own views of religious settlement would not be more widely adopted, but also by Cromwell's moderate alternative (Gwyn 1995, pp. 82–8).

Read Fox's *Journal* (Nickalls 1952), the account of the life and work of the early Quaker leader George Fox, and you could be forgiven for thinking that there had been no Civil War. George Fox was a part of the debates of the 1640s, but it was in the 1650s that Quakerism as a movement emerged into this arena of disappointment as a fresh and powerful dynamic that was to become the most popular and successful sect of the decade. Timing and, as Moore argues (2004), the depth and quality of the leadership were critical to this Quaker success.

With their open 'unprogrammed' liturgy based in silence, the free ministry of all, and the primary authority of revelation over Scripture, these early Friends can be seen to be both an alternative to Protestantism (Tolles 1948) and the logical consequence of the impulse to complete reformation (Barbour 1964). However, the passing of time, and their own sense of eschatological disappointment, would temper and formalise the movement (Dandelion *et al.* 2004, chapter 2). In the nineteenth century, theological dispute would become internalised, and Quakers, in all their varieties, took their place amidst Christianity rather than as its vanguard.

THE APPROACH OF THIS BOOK

In this volume, three over-arching frameworks are used to approach the history of Quakerism. The first is to do with 'time', the second with 'spiritual intimacy', the third with the definition of 'the world's people', that is those outside of Quakerism, and in particular those seen to be in need of Quakerism.

Christianity was created as a religion of waiting. Founded on the promise of the second coming of Christ and the end of the world (the endtime), the history of Christianity, as Schweitzer noted (1968, p. 360), has been about delay. Similarly the history of Christian diversity can be charted as a story of differing perspectives on the timing of the end of waiting (what I will call the culmination of God's plan for the world), or on the best ways in which to wait. Christianity has seen itself as a temporary institution, helping humanity remain faithful in the meantime, in the interim.

Liberal Christian groups often have a particularly non-literal reading of Scripture. The book of Revelation may be no more than a coded political apocalyptic, rather than a prophecy of Christ's second coming. The 'mean-time' may be the *only* time for these kinds of groups. This is true for at least present-day Liberal Quakerism. However, early Quakerism, I argue, as per Gwyn, was built upon an understanding/experience of an unfolding second coming (experienced inwardly), and the history of Quakerism is best understood in terms of its changing relationship to this founding experience of endtime and the necessary internal shifts which take place as a sense of endtime is replaced by one of meantime.

The second theme is one of spiritual intimacy, of direct intimate relationship between humanity and God and Christ. The sense of endtime experienced by early Friends was founded upon a more fundamental experience of spiritual intimacy and direct divine revelation. This experience continues to run through all six Quaker traditions today even though it no longer accompanies an immediate sense of endtime. The way notions of intimacy are negotiated and presented is a running theme of the book.

The third theme around which the history and current practice of Quakerism is organised in this volume is the sense each Quaker group makes of the non-Quaker world and the criteria used to define what counts as 'the world'. Sectarian groups such as early Friends typically talk of the apostasy (the falling from the faith) of other believers and of 'the world'. For early Quakers, everything which was not Quaker had fallen from the faith and was part of 'the world', thus requiring redemption. Over time, what constitutes this pejorative sense of 'world' shrinks and this change is charted alongside the Quakers' changing relationship to endtime and meantime.

The first half of the book, 'The history of Quaker theology', is itself divided into three sections: 'The single Quaker theological culture', 'The beginnings of Quaker diversity', and 'Quakerism and modernity'. In turn, each section is divided into sub-sections to aid accessibility and readability.

'The single Quaker theological culture' charts Quakerism from its origins in the post-Reformation bid for full reformation in England, through to the 1820s when Quakerism ceased for some Friends to represent the one true church, and began to schism in a major way. Three main periods of Quaker theology are considered within this section, following a sub-section on the origins. These are: 'The first Friends, 1647–1666', 'Restoration Quakerism, 1666–1689', and 'Quietism, 1690–1820s'. 'The first Friends' concentrates in particular on the number of grand claims made by the first Quakers and by George Fox, an early leader of the movement. These Friends claimed an intimacy with God and acted as if they were co-agents with God over and against 'the world'. Many had undergone a powerful 'convincement' experience. This involved a conviction of the erstwhile sinful life, repentance, being born again, being gathered into community, and the consequential mission work which accompanied the clarity and certainty these Friends felt about being part of the only true church. Direct revelation, the inward Light of Christ, had replaced scriptural authority and these Quakers claimed they had been set free from sin, a vanguard people heralding the global transformation that would follow when all had experienced the inward second coming of Christ as they had. The eschatological understanding underpinning the radical message is brought to the fore, as are its consequences, particularly for liturgy (early Friends worshipped in silence and claimed communion was inward) and ecclesiology. The 1660s was a time of persecution and a need to negotiate with the authorities. As the sense of unfolding second coming diminished, Quakerism needed to organise and re-present itself to the world. Robert Barclay (1648–90) systematised (and altered) Quaker theology during this period. The third period, Quietism, is framed within a further development of how Quakers thought about their place in 'the world' and a more anxious spirituality. Empowering eschatological understandings were replaced by fearful anxiety about missing the possibility of salvation which Barclay claimed came only once (2002, p. 119).

The children of the first Friends knew their hope for salvation lay in the kind of convincement experienced by their parents. All lay in faithful waiting. 'Peculiarities' of dress and speech and rules about marriage and outward life in general acted as visible signs of difference between the faithful and 'the world'. Meetings disowned those who broke the 'discipline'.

'The beginnings of Quaker diversity' charts a nineteenth century characterised by schism and innovation. Evangelicalism was to bring new energy and new ideas to a Quakerism much depleted owing to disownment and voluntary departure. Evangelicalism was also to challenge traditional Quakerism with its emphasis on scriptural authority. In 1827, the 'Great Separation' began in Philadelphia, eventually affecting 'Yearly Meetings' throughout the USA. The two parties were called the Hicksites and the Orthodox Party, the latter representing the new evangelical persuasion. British Quakerism was clearly Orthodox by this time and was frightened by the spectre of Hicksism. However, the evangelical elements of British Quakerism were themselves divided, and in 1836 Isaac Crewdson led 400 'ultra-evangelical' Friends out of British Quakerism. Crewdson wanted to drop the idea of the 'inward Light' as unscriptural and in this parted company with other evangelical Quakers. This latter group remained and in the next thirty years opened British Quakerism up to a wider Christianity of which it began to see itself as a part. The peculiarities were largely abolished, resulting in a small conservative schism in the late 1860s. In the USA, Orthodox Friend John Wilbur led a campaign against the teachings of Joseph John Gurney, leading British evangelical Quaker. When Gurney toured the USA between 1837 and 1840, there was a further set of schisms along Wilburite/Gurneyite lines on the role of the inward Light and the degree to which its authority was equal to or greater than Scripture. Gurneyite Yearly Meetings suffered further internal divisions in the 1860s and 1870s, between 'renewal' and 'revival' tendencies. Holiness revivalist influence led to experimentation with forms and a new emphasis on expression. Silent worship had become formulaic or legalistic and an influx of new converts created the need for a teaching ministry. This led to pastoral committees and eventually the adoption of pastors. In turn, this led to 'programmed' worship with hymns and altar calls as well as the silence of inward communion. This innovation sparked further conservative separations. For some Revival Friends, only the outward ordinances separated them from other Christians and David Updegraff led a bid for 'water-toleration'. This was generally unsuccessful, and in 1887 the Gurneyite Yearly Meetings drafted the 'Richmond Declaration' maintaining the historic testimony against outward baptism. For the Hicksite tradition, the years following the

Great Separation had also seen some schism, not in terms of doctrine, which was not definitional for them, but in terms of form and testimony, which was. The 'Progressives' were more politically radical than many Hicksites, were more prepared to work with the world's people, and were congregational in ecclesiological terms. Beanite Quakerism was a Gurneyite offshoot in the 1880s, but modernist in tone, and symbolised an approach which allowed some Hicksites and Gurneyites to regroup in the twentieth century.

The third section of 'The history of Quaker theology' focuses on the twentieth century and on Liberal Quakerism and mission in particular. Liberal Quakerism in Britain was the fruit of the opening up of Quakerism to the world by evangelical Quakers in the 1850s. Fuelled by Darwinianism and biblical higher criticism, John Wilhelm Rowntree and others led the campaign for a modern and progressive Quakerism in which experience rather than Scripture was primary. This form of Quakerism claimed to be open to new Light, and in time it would cease to be a wholly Christian group. Today, this branch, which is the dominant one of the 'unpro-grammed' tradition, is permissive in terms of belief, centred rather on a conformist attitude to forms, worship style for example, as well as a distinctive approach to the nature of theology. A historic meeting between Rowntree and American evangelical Quaker Rufus Jones in Switzerland in 1897 converted Jones to this modernist approach. In the ensuing fifty years, Jones worked hard to spread this modernist interpretation of Quakerism and to forge unity between Hicksites and Gurneyites on the basis of it. In the twentieth century too, Conservative Quakerism, comprised of Wilburites and conservative schisms since, emerged as a unified body. The renewal/revivalist tendencies within Gurneyite Quakerism eventually led to two main evangelical traditions within Quakerism, one more modernist than the other. Mission work by both groups has led to a huge expansion of Quakerism, particularly in Kenya and Bolivia, whilst the interpretation of the degree to which church life is distinctively Quaker varies enormously, with some churches now practising outward communion and seeing them-selves more as a community church than as a Quaker one.

A 'family tree' of Quakerism is included to help the reader follow the complexities, as well as a chart giving numbers for the different kinds of Quakerism worldwide, leading into the second part of the book, 'Worldwide Quakerism today'. This part is in three sections: 'Theology and worship', 'Quakers and "the world"', and 'The Quaker family'.

'Theology and worship' is itself divided into three sub-sections: 'Authority', 'Belief', and 'Covenant and practice'. In 'Authority', the rela-tionship of the different branches to the first Friends is considered as well as different systems of legitimising divine authority. Different approaches to the nature of theology are also considered. 'Belief' includes ideas of God and Christ and eschatology, as well as consequent ecclesiology. The third sub-section considers the theological basis and understanding of the different forms of worship within worldwide Quakerism.

'Quakers and "the world"' has three sub-sections: 'Testimony', 'Mission, membership, and diversity', and 'Ecumenism'. Each of these looks at the contrasts between different branches of present-day Friends. How separated should Friends be and how do they mark any differences today? How is Quaker identity constructed and maintained within different branches? What emphasis is placed on mission, what is the understanding behind it, how is church membership approached and what are its limits? How do the various Quaker groups see themselves in relation to other churches and other faiths? Who is kin, who is part of 'the world'?

The final section, 'The Quaker family', considers the relationship between different kinds of Quakers, and the challenges and opportunities facing the movement. Thirteen key differences between Liberal and Evangelical Friends are set against three historic and ongoing commonalities. Numerical prospects are discussed for Evangelical and Liberal Friends. A chronology of Quaker history, suggestions for 'Further reading', and a full list of references complete the volume.

SUMMARY

In summary, this book offers a comprehensive history of ideas of worldwide Quakerism and a digest of present-day statements of faith on key issues both to amplify and to nuance the differences between different types of Quaker. Three themes are followed throughout, that of the relationship to endtime, spiritual intimacy, and notions of 'the world'. Scholarship from all over the world is used to draw out the clearest understandings possible of Quaker history and thinking but also to outline debates in this area of the academy. Boxes elucidate key concepts in greater depth and diagrams are used to help convey critical ideas. The aim of the book is to increase the understanding of Quakerism, its varied history, and its fascinating and unique set of theological complexities.

NOTE

All biblical quotations are from the Authorised Version.

PART I

The history of Quaker theology

CHAPTER I

The single Quaker theological culture, 1647–1827

This chapter charts the period in which worldwide Quakerism, mainly transatlantic, functioned as a single community and in which Quakerism was largely a single theological entity. This period is divided into three distinct theological phases.

THE FIRST FRIENDS, 1647–1666

FORMATION OF THE MOVEMENT

So much happened so quickly for Friends in so many locations in the summer of 1652 that if you visit a Quaker 'Meeting House' in the '1652 country' of southern Cumbria and the north-east of Lancashire in England, you may well be told that the Quaker movement owes its origins to the events that happened there in that year. It was in 1652 that George Fox (1624–91), itinerant preacher, travelled westward from Yorkshire where he had found much support in the Doncaster area amongst the Yorkshire Seekers (Gwyn 2000, pp. 223–4) (see Box 3).

Fox was travelling with Richard Farnworth westward from Bradford but Farnworth had a bad leg and, like Fox, had not eaten for many days. Fox wrote in his journal (see Box 2) that he felt 'moved by the Lord to go atop' of Pendle Hill near Clitheroe (Plate 1), a hill previously associated with the witchcraft trials of 1612 (Nickalls 1952, p. 104). Farnworth said he would see him round the other side. Thus Fox ascended alone that week of Pentecost, 1652: 'when I came atop of it I saw Lancashire sea; and there atop of the hill I was moved to sound the day of the Lord and the Lord let me see a-top of the hill in what places he had a great people to be gathered' (Nickalls 1952, p. 104). At the foot of the hill, on the other side, Fox had a further vision of a 'great people in white raiment' (Rev 3:5, 18; 10:8, 14).

This was a critical moment in Quaker history. It was at this point in Fox's spiritual journey when it became clear that his call was to gather a

---

Box 2 The journal of George Fox

Fox's journal was dictated, initially in 1664, with a longer version in 1676 years after the events described (Fox had lexical agraphia and could not write easily or sensibly – Ayoub and Roeltgen n.d.). The 1676 version was later edited by Thomas Ellwood prior to publication. As such, its reliability as a source has been questioned. Whilst Douglas Gwyn has claimed that Fox's message remains consistent throughout his life (1986), Rosemary Moore chose only tracts published in the year of her research for her painstaking analysis of Quaker theology through the 1650s (2000). For example, the language of the later version is toned down in places. There is a debate about whether Fox really climbed Pendle Hill as he said he did in 1652. Sue Bell argues that the geographical chronology does not make sense, that some of the descriptions do not, and that maybe Fox really climbed Pen-y-Ghent but preferred to list the less anti-royalist area of Pendle Hill in his memoirs, crafted at a time of ongoing persecution for the movement (1995). David Boulton disagrees on each of these points (1995). The Ellwood journal is now commonly available as the Nickalls 1952 edition; the 1676 manuscript forms the basis of Smith 1998.

Box 3 The Seekers

The Seekers were a group who eschewed the outward forms as part of worship, convinced they were trappings of apostasy. They met in silence until their minister addressed them. Many early Friends were part of the Yorkshire and Westmorland groups, including Francis Howgill and Edward Burrough. Burrough was later critical of them for merely waiting and for not waiting at 'the true door' (Burrough 1656, p. 29). Douglas Gwyn has identified two types of Seeker, A and B. Seeker A types wished to restore primitive Christianity, awaiting a prophet to help achieve this. Seeker B types believed God would not take humanity backwards, especially to a faith which had been so easily corrupted before, but that they were living in a new and distinct age (Gwyn 2000, pp. 93–4). Simple analysis suggests more women Friends and more of those in London subscribed to this latter view, one also favoured by Nayler. Part of Fox's genius was to meld the two types together.

---

movement. This was a fresh revelation and set Fox off with a new mission, one very soon to be realised. Two weeks later, again alone, Fox arrived in Sedbergh at the time of the hiring fair. Flax workers, dressed in white, thronged the streets hoping for work. Here was a people dressed in white raiment. Fox preached in Sedbergh churchyard and at private meetings of the like-minded: he would have come to this area knowing that he would find support and companionship. He wrote in his journal that he was asked

Plate 1 Pendle Hill, from the north (taken from Downham, Lancashire in 1971 by
G. Bernard Wood)

on his way there whence he had come: 'From the Lord', Fox replied
(Nickalls 1952, p. 106).

As Fox had met theological allies amongst the Yorkshire Seekers, such as
James Nayler, Farnworth, and William Dewsbury, so he also met future
leaders of Quakerism amongst the Westmorland Seekers, notably Edward
Burrough, Francis Howgill, and Richard Hubberthorne. On a June
Sunday, Howgill was preaching to a Seeker congregation in a small chapel
on Firbank Fell north of Sedbergh. Seekers, in their critique of the apostasy
of the rest of Christianity, had minimalised their services, stripping away all
that was outward. The group met in silence, with a minister speaking when
led by the Holy Spirit to do so. They did not have a formulated theology
outside of their critique of the falsehood they saw around them.

The same Sunday, people stayed on and listened to George Fox (and
probably competing preachers) on the fell next to the chapel. Some
questioned why Fox did not preach in the chapel:

I was made to open to the people that the steeplehouse and the ground on which
it stood were no more holy than that mountain, and those temples and 'dreadful

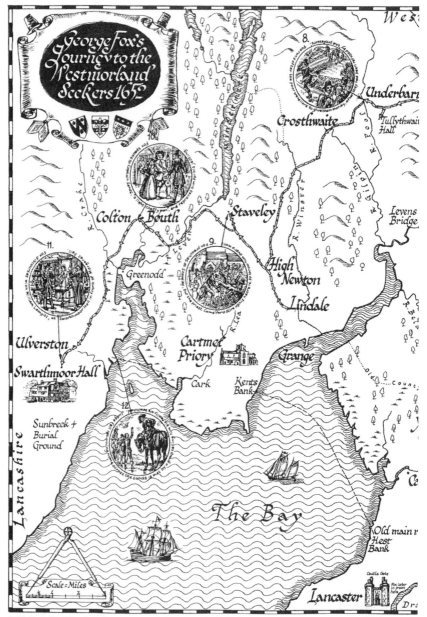

Fig. 1.1 Map of Fox's route through Westmorland in summer 1652

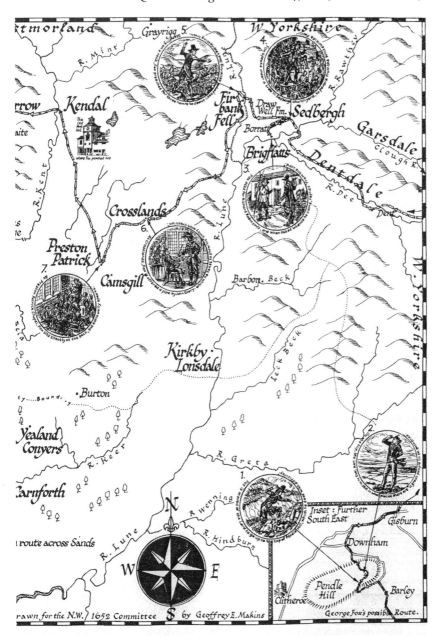

houses of God' (as they called them) were not set up by the command of God or Christ; nor their priests as Aaron's priesthood; nor their tithes as theirs was. But Christ was come, who ended the temple, and the priests, and the tithes, and Christ said, 'Learn of me', and God said, 'This is my beloved Son, hear ye him.' For the Lord had sent me with his everlasting gospel to preach, and his word of life to bring them off all those temples, tithes, priests and rudiments of the world, that had gotten up since the apostles' days, and had been set up by such who had erred from the spirit and power the apostles were in; so that they might all come to know Christ their teacher, their counsellor, their shepherd to feed them, and their bishop to oversee them, and their prophet to open to them, and to know their bodies to be the temples of God and Christ for them to dwell in. (Nickalls 1952, p. 109)

Fox emphasised the apostasy of the church and the integrity and legitimacy of his own message. He claimed that Christ was available personally and directly, as we shall see below, and that he, Fox, had been given the authority to remind people of this truth. This was the first mass meeting at which Fox was so successful: his journal claims that there were perhaps a thousand gathered that day and that many hundreds were 'convinced' (see p. 23 below). Fox was twenty-seven years old.

From Sedbergh, Fox moved on to Preston Patrick, then to Kendal, and later to Ulverston (Fig. 1.1). Here he met Margaret Fell, wife of Thomas Fell, the local circuit judge, and part of the gentry of the region. Born Margaret Askew at Marsh Grange near Dalton-in-Furness in 1614, Margaret Fell (d. 1702) was left an inheritance of £3000 and in 1652, at the time she first met Fox, presided over two estates, Marsh Grange and her husband's home, Swarthmoor Hall (Plate 2) (Kunze 1994, pp. 29–32).

Judge Fell was away working but Fox and Nayler managed to 'convince' Margaret Fell, her daughters and her household at Swarthmoor Hall, within days of arriving. At the parish church the following Sunday, Fox interrupted the local minister, William Lampitt, and Fell prevented Fox being thrown out. Fell was moved by Fox's preaching: 'This opened me so, that it cut me to the heart, and then I saw clearly, we were all wrong. So I sat down in my pew again, and cried bitterly, and I cried in my spirit to the Lord' (Kunze 1994, p. 15).

This was a key convincement. The Fell household offered protection to an embryonic Quaker movement and Fell was to become an administrative and inspirational backbone to Quakerism throughout the world in its early years. Her prolific correspondence, often with complete strangers, gave pastoral support and theological insight to those working in isolation. It was Margaret Fell who in 1660 penned the first comprehensive outline of the Quaker 'testimony' (i.e. expression of witness) against bearing arms.

Plate 2 Swarthmoor Hall (watercolour by Constance D. Pearson, c.1954)

Thomas Fell was met by Lampitt as he rode back to Ulverston across the sands of Morecambe Bay. He was told his wife was bewitched, a claim which if proved could have resulted in hanging. However, Nayler and then Fox spoke with Thomas Fell and he was persuaded to continue the protection and toleration initiated by his wife. Swarthmoor Hall was to become the headquarters of the Quaker movement for the next few years until the centre of Quaker activity moved to London in 1657.

EARLY QUAKER THEOLOGY

Quakerism, in terms of its theology, began in 1647 when the twenty-three-year-old George Fox (Plate 3), born in Fenny Drayton in Leicestershire but already much travelled, had reached a low point in his search for true spirituality.

Now after I had received that opening from the Lord that to be bred at Oxford or Cambridge was not sufficient to fit a man to be a minister of Christ, I regarded the priests less and looked more after the dissenting people . . . As I had forsaken all the priests, so I left the separate preachers also, and those called the most experienced people; for I saw there was none among them all that could speak to my condition. (Nickalls 1952, p. 11)

Plate 3 George Fox woodcut (taken from a late seventeenth-century broadsheet)

Fox had already become clear that the university-trained priests were not of any particular or necessary help to him in has spiritual quest. Consequently he had spent time with the dissenters, a year with his uncle, William Pickering, a Baptist, in London, and time moving around the army camps which were where the most radical religious ideas of the day were circulating (Ingle 1994, pp. 34–40). However, no one he had met had been able to respond adequately to his soul's search. Only when thrown onto the inward as opposed to the outward did the young Fox feel met in his struggle.

And when all my hopes in them and in all men were gone, so that I had nothing *outwardly* to help me, nor could tell what to do, then, oh then, I heard a voice which said, 'There is one, even Christ Jesus, that can speak to thy condition', and when I heard it my heart did leap for joy. (Nickalls 1952, p. 11) (my emphasis)

This was not simply an adequate answer. It was a radical and revolutionary experience which cut across much church teaching of the time. It became foundational for the emerging Quaker movement and remained central even in its later, multiple and diverse forms. Fox discovered that one, even Christ, could speak to him directly.

'How do we know what is of God?' is a key question for all religious groups. Here, Quakers had their answer. It was in their experience of Christ's direct revelation that authority lay. Fox claimed that this revelation never contradicted Scripture for he always found it confirmed by Scripture even when he was neither looking for it nor needing it (Nickalls 1952, p. 33).

The reference to 'outwardly' is significant. Creasey highlights the use of spatial terms in early Quaker writing, in particular distinctions between 'inward' and 'outward' (1962). Creasey claims that Fox used the term 'outward' to refer to formal and conventional Christianity and 'inward' to refer to 'a transforming and creative personal acquaintance with and relation to Christ in the Spirit' (1962, p. 3). Graves finds this pattern in early Quaker sermons as well (1972, p. 253): 'Let us not be Outward but also inward Christians' (*Harmony of Divine and Heavenly Doctrines*, 1723, p. 197). The inward was the authentic, the mode of true spirituality. The outward was connected with 'the world', the human, the material.

Fox continues:

Then the Lord did let me see why there was none upon the earth that could speak to my condition, namely, that I might give him all the glory; for all are concluded under sin, and shut up in unbelief as I had been, that Jesus Christ might have the preeminence who enlightens, and gives grace, and faith, and power. Thus, when God doth work who shall let [i.e. hinder] it? And this I knew experimentally. (Nickalls 1952, p. 11)

In other words, the fact that Fox had drawn a blank with human teachers was no accident. Rather, it was the logic of the truth of a more interior spirituality, one of direct revelation ('faith's inner voice': Dandelion *et al.* 1998, pp. 27–32), and of the apostasy of humanity, all 'shut up in unbelief'.

Critically, this experience of direct revelation was not to be limited to Fox. This was not a revelation akin to Paul's who was the last to have encountered the risen Christ, 'out of due time' (1 Cor 15:8). Rather, this was a revelation available to all. Significantly, whilst Fox and others founded and led the movement in the 1650s and 1660s, the egalitarian nature of this foundational insight, the priesthood of all believers, was to allow him to make himself redundant before his own death. When Fox died, Quakerism was not plunged into a crisis of leadership. Quakerism was to model a *collective* apostolic succession, requiring neither priests nor the primary authority of text.

It was this experience of 1647 which was the foundation stone for what was to become the Religious Society of Friends and all else was a subsequent interpretation of context and experience deriving from this intimacy with Christ. In other words, this intimacy with Christ, this relationship of direct revelation, is alone foundational and definitional of the movement. It does not describe any period or branch of Quaker theology sufficiently – for example, it is not an adequate way to characterise early Quakerism as Rufus Jones tried to do in the early twentieth century (Braithwaite 1912, Introduction) – but Quakerism has had its identity constructed around this experience and insight.

The 1648 experience which Gwyn says completed the outlines of Fox's theology (1986, p. 23) is described by Fox as follows:

Now I was come up in spirit through the flaming sword into the paradise of God. All things were new, and all creation gave another smell unto me than before, beyond what words can utter. I knew nothing but pureness, and innocency, and righteousness, being renewed up into the image of God by Christ Jesus, so that I say I was come up to the state of Adam which he was in before he fell . . . But I was immediately taken up in spirit to see into another or more steadfast state than Adam's in innocency, even into a state in Christ Jesus that should never fall. (Nickalls 1952, p. 27)

Here, we have the return to Eden through the flaming sword of Genesis 3, into a state of all things being new (Rev 21:1), but also the passage to a higher state, the sinlessness prophesied by Paul (Dandelion *et al.* 1998, p. 83), a clothing of humanity in Christ. This is the power to resist temptation rather than not be tempted at all but it puts Fox and the other early Friends who reached this state into a space of spiritual evolution beyond Adam, and indeed beyond all those yet to experience this process.

The claim of perfection was based in part on Matthew 5:48, Romans 6:14 and 1 John 3:9. Fox wrote that the Lord told him that his name was 'written in the Lamb's book of life' (Nickalls 1952, p. 33). This sense of being part of a vanguard elect led to one of the grand claims of Quakerism and the one which was most to bring them into dispute with others. In 1660 Fox outlined this doctrine in Bristol: 'He who was perfect comes to make men and women perfect again, and bring them again to the state God made them in' (Nickalls 1952, pp. 367–8).

We believe that the saints upon earth may receive forgiveness of sins, and may be perfectly freed from the body of sin and death, and in Christ may be perfect, and without sin, and may have victory over all temptations by faith in Christ Jesus. (Burrough 1657)

Whilst the whole of humanity would be brought to this state, some had been already whilst others were still shut up in unbelief. When Fox was on trial at Derby, he was asked whether he was sanctified. 'I said "Sanctified? Yes" for I was in the Paradise of God. They said, had I no sin? "Sin?" said I, "Christ my Saviour hath taken away my sin, and in Him there is no sin"' (Nickalls 1952, p. 55). William Dewsbury, like Fox, felt a cleansing aspect to his convincement: 'through the righteous law of life in Jesus Christ I was made free and clean from the body of sin and death, and my garment is washed, and made white in the blood of the Lamb' (Dewsbury 1689a, p. 51). Fox criticised the hireling ministers for 'preaching up sin' (Nickalls 1952, p. 688) whereas the anti-Quakers criticised the spiritual arrogance of this position. Richard Baxter wrote: 'the devil himself has less pride or less ignorance' (1655). What is interesting is that this perception of being beyond temptation did not lead to a relaxed life. Gwyn has made the point that one of the attractions of Friends was their strict moral line (Gwyn 1995, pp. 111–18). Another of the 1650s sects, the Ranters, also claimed a regenerated life, an intimacy with God, and a state beyond sin. For them, though, this meant that even those activities perceived before regeneration as sinful were now permissable and accounts of their worship mention drunkenness and orgies (Gwyn 2000, p. 167). This can be called a 'practical antinomianism', that nothing can count as a sin (Moore 2000, p. 100). In contrast, Fox taught that convinced Friends could resist sin and his view is not antinomian in a doctrinal sense as such. Fox's sense that the perfected life was visible to all as such was misinterpreted by some, and on one of his travels to America he stayed with two Quaker couples who had abstained from sexual relations for years believing it to be part of Quaker practice (Mack 1992, p. 227).

These two experiences of Fox can be seen to characterise his 'convincement' experience. Using Nikki Coffey Tousley's carefully researched work on this process (2003), we can identify six key stages in early Friends' narratives. Technically, convincement meant literally conviction (Pickvance 1989, p. 63), the experience of the day of visitation. However, I am using convincement here to refer to all of these processes. Convincement then, in the sense I am using it, was about (a) a powerful in-breaking of God, (b) a sense of conviction of sin, (c) a choice, repentance, and (d) being born again into perfection, or a measure of perfection. These stages are clear in the case of Francis Howgill.

My eyes were opened, and all the things that I had ever done were brought to remembrance and the ark of the testament was opened, and there was thunder and lightning and great hail. [a] And then the trumpet of the Lord was sounded, and then nothing but war and rumor of war, and the dreadful power of the Lord fell on me: plague, and pestilence, and famine, and earthquake, and fear and terror, for the sights I saw with my eyes: and that which I heard with my ears, sorrow and pain. And in the morning I wished it had been evening, and in the evening I wished it had been morning and I had no rest, but trouble on every side. [b] And all that ever I had done was judged and condemned, all things were accursed; whether I did eat, or drink, or restrain, I was accursed. Then the lions suffered hunger, and the seals were opened, and seven thunders uttered their voices ... I became a perfect fool, and knew nothing, as a man distracted; all was overturned, and I suffered loss of all. In all that I ever did, I saw it was in the accursed nature. [c] And then something in me cried: 'Just and true is his judgement!' My mouth was stopped, I dared not make mention of his name, I knew not God. And as I bore the indignation of the Lord, something rejoiced, the serpent's head began to be bruised, and the witnesses which were slain were raised ... [d] And as I did give up all to judgement, the captive came forth out of prison and rejoiced, and my heart was filled with joy. I came to see him whom I had pierced, and my heart as broken, and the blood of the prophets I saw slain, and a great lamentation. Then I saw the cross of Christ, and stood in it, and the enmity slain on it. And the new man was made ... the holy law of God was revealed unto me and written on my heart. (Barbour and Roberts 2004, pp. 173–4)

Ultimately, this experience would lead to (e) the convinced gathering together, (we can think of Howgill's phrase of being 'gathered as in a net' (Burrough 1672, prelim leaf e3) and in the years which followed, (f) calling 'the world' towards a new mode of religious experience: Howgill and Edward Burrough were to lead the mission to London. Quakerism would grow rapidly in England although overseas mission work was unsuccessful except in the American colonies. (Perhaps the fact that Quakers did not feel the need for translators, believing their message would be understood beyond the outward language – Bauman 1983, p. 27 – contributed to this.) The reference to Jeremiah 31:31–34 and the new inward covenant (see p. 30 below) in Howgill's account is clear, as it is to Job 7:4, with Howgill wishing time away.

It is not clear of course how many of the first Friends experienced this or made the claim of being beyond falling. What we have are the accounts of (i) the people who chose to repent, (ii) who went on often to lead the movement. Whilst Quakerism had a number of very able preachers, Richard Bailey makes the argument that Fox was seen to be unique within the movement and that for a time he was 'divinised' by it, with all the other Quakers raised up as apostles. Only after 1670 was Fox reduced to an apostle, the others to a more everyday status (1992).

QUAKERS IN THE WORLD

The raising up of the Quakers as co-agents with God brought them up against the blasphemy laws. We will see this in the case of James Nayler below (pp. 38–41), but it is also implied by the passage from Fox above when he claims to be in a state 'in Christ Jesus'. Moore comments on the 1653 epistle from Fox to 'Margaret Fell and every other friend who is raised to discerning'. Here Fox writes:

According to the Spirit I am the son of God and according to my flesh I am seed of Abraham which is Christ, which seed is not many but one, which seed is Christ and Christ in you . . . According to the Spirit I am the son of God before Abraham was, before Jesus was, the same which doth descend, the same doth ascend. (Moore 2000, p. 76)

However, at times, it seems that some early Friends really felt themselves somewhere else, in a separated space whilst still operating in this world. In his tract *A Trumpet Sounded Forth Out of Zion*, Edward Burrough is clear that there is a separation between how he is known by 'the world' and who he really is. The authorship is attributed to 'one whose name is truly known by the children of the same birth, but unknown to the world, though by it called Edward Burrough' (Burrough 1656, cover). Further into the tract, in a piece addressed to other Quakers, Burrough writes:

To all you who are in the light of eternal life, which doth comprehend the world, who are born from above, of the immortal word which doth live for ever, who are not of the world . . . who are not known to the world (though by it scornfully called Quakers) even you doth the Lord also remember with everlasting kindness, and infinite love, of whose beginning and End there is none, and whose height, depth, measure and limit cannot be found out; for you hath he chosen above all the Families of the Earth, to place his Name among, and to establish his everlasting Covenant. (Burrough 1656, p. 33)

Burrough is suggesting that Quakers are those 'born from above' and 'not of the world'. Such sentiment resonates with the passage from Isaiah 65:15 where it is prophesied that God will 'call his servants by another name'; also with the following passage from Revelation.

Him that overcometh will I make a pillar in the temple of my God, and he shall go no more out: and I will write upon him the name of my God, and the name of the city of my God, which is new Jerusalem, which cometh down out of heaven from my God: and I will write upon him my new name. (Rev 3:12)

It is as if Friends claimed an outward human form but a different spiritualised true self as the children of God. It is about a unity with Christ, beyond the world whilst within it. Some of Fox's dying words were 'I am glad I was here' (Fox 1891, vol. 2, p. 505), suggesting a dualism of place.

Bailey and Michele Tarter have both focused parts of their scholarship on the idea of 'celestial inhabitation', the claim that the bodies of Friends were inhabited by Christ. Thus, Bailey argues, when Fox answers in court that he is the son of God, it is the indwelling Christ speaking through him (Bailey 1992, p. 111). For Tarter, the outpouring of the Spirit onto the flesh (after Joel 2:28–29) led to the quaking in worship. This was an embodied spiritual state and led to a range of physical manifestations: quaking in worship, but also the enacting of signs in public. Crucially, this often amplified the criticism levelled at women Quaker ministers whose phys-icality alongside the very act of preaching at all acted as a double threat to the patriarchal establishment (Tarter 2001, p. 149).

The continual nature of the spiritual experience and its potential uni-versality meant that ultimately everyone could become a Quaker and that the world would be visibly and inwardly changed. The word of God was freely given to all, men, women, and children, through the inward Light of Christ and, naturally, Friends refused to pay church tithes or make any contribution to the repairing of 'mashouses' (or 'steeplehouses') or the upkeep of the 'hireling ministry' when particular outward sacramentality was seen as anachronistic. The church was the body of believers, not any building, and all space had equal sacramental potential, that is the potential to live in the presence. Quakers would regularly interrupt ministers' sermons or use their right to speak after the sermon. Certainly, Quakers focused their energy on criticising those in power, those who knowingly and intentionally, as far as Friends were concerned, held the people back from this new spiritual possibility and requirement. In Edward Burrough's *A Trumpet Sounded Forth Out of Zion* (1656), for example, a critique of twenty-three different individuals and groups, he begins with Cromwell and then works his way through the Judges, Captains, Ministers, Seperated Preachers, magicians, etc. It is also true though that he included a critique of the Seekers, in spite of having been one himself, for merely waiting and not acting. Even former allies were now apostate (see Box 3).

Whilst not the poorest of the nation (it seems Fox had a private income and many Quakers were yeoman farmers (Vann 1969, pp. 47–87)), the early Quakers appeared to have a political sympathy for the poor and a theological affiliation with those led rather than those leading: Quakers too were led; it was simply that Christ and God were to lead this true church, not any bishop or priest. They refused to call days and months by anything other than number so as not to condone the pagan and Roman emphases.

So, Sunday was first day, Monday second, etc.* Quakers refused to partake in the received etiquette of the day – they would not use titles or flattery or the 'you' form of address to social superiors but called everyone 'thee'. They refused to take their hats off to anyone but God. Thomas Ellwood recounts meeting old friends having just been convinced of his Quakerism:

A knot of my old acquaintance [at Oxford], espying me, came to me. One of these was a scholar in his gown, another a surgeon of that city . . . When they were come up to me, they all saluted me, after the usual manner, putting off their hats and bowing, and saying, 'Your humble Servant, Sir', expecting no doubt the same from me. But when they saw me stand still, not moving my cap, nor bowing my knee, in way of congee to them, they were amazed, and looked first one upon another, then upon me, then one upon another again for a while, without a word speaking. At length, the surgeon . . . clapping his hand in a familiar way upon my shoulder and smiling on me said, 'What, Tom, a Quaker!' To which I readily, and cheerfully answered, 'Yes, a Quaker.' And as the words passed out of my mouth I felt joy spring into my heart, for I rejoiced that I had not been drawn out by them into a compliance with them, and that I had the strength and boldness given me to confess myself to be one of those despised people. (Moore 2004, pp. 24–5)

Ellwood's father was less amused than his friends and Fox recounts how enraged people would be at this breaking of etiquette.

Because I could not put my hat off to them, it set them all into a rage. But the Lord showed me that it was an honour below, which he would lay in the dust and stain it, and honour which proud flesh looked for, but sought not the honour which came from God only, that it was an honour invented by men in the Fall, and in the alienation from God, who were offended if it were not given them, and yet would be looked upon as saints, church-members, and great Christians . . . oh the rage and scorn, the heat and fury that arose! Oh the blows, punchings, beatings, and imprisonments that we underwent for not putting our hats off to men! (Nickalls 1952, pp. 36–7)

Here Fox's dualism is again clear in his differentiation between above and below, heaven and earth, and a time past (alienation from God) and a new age of revelation. It is also important that Fox saw this not as an optional protest but as a direct consequence of faith.

Gay Pilgrim has analysed the style of early Friends in terms of the Foucauldian concept of heterotopia, the alternate ordering of everyday reality, i.e. the deliberate subvention of order through unexpected

---

* This led to complications in 1752 when the first month of the year changed, but remained a testimony until the twentieth century in most forms of Quakerism, and continues in part of the Conservative tradition (see p. 227 below). Friends justified this position by reference to Galatians 4:9–10 and Colossians 2:16–17.

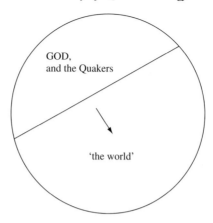

Fig. 1.2 Quakers and God and the world, 1650s

juxtaposition (2004, pp. 208–9). She cites the examples of 'plain dress' and 'plain speech' and the refusal, such as with Ellwood, to conform to the world's manners, but also the use of the courtroom and the prison.

Their court trials serve to illustrate the ways Friends created heterotopic sites. Far from feeling intimidated, marginalized, and properly subordinated (let alone silenced) as the judicial system intended, Friends used this arena as a space in which to evangelize and inspire: as a platform from which they could preach. They treated a courtroom as a 'church', which was incongruous, unexpected *and* confusing . . . A space designed to impose a proper social order was used instead to challenge the prevailing power relations, encourage resistance to the prevailing culture and witness to an alternate ordering. It became a heterotopic site. (Pilgrim 2003, p. 149)

This was not a polite Quakerism, nor was it an ecumenical one. 'The world', that pejorative term to refer to the apostate, those who had fallen from the faith, was for early Friends everyone not Quaker. Quakers were co-agents with God over and against the world, 'Trampling all that is contrary under' (Nickalls 1952, p. 263) (Fig. 1.2).

MISSION

All had fallen but, optimistically, all could be restored through the one true church, the Friends in the Truth or the Children of the Light as they were called (Braithwaite 1912, p. 131) (see Box 4). All could be part of the elect. This was an Arminian view (Moore 2000, p. 100) different from the medieval ideas of the 'sacred canopy' (Berger 1967) in which the top of

---

Box 4 The name of the group

The term 'Quaker' had been used as a term of abuse for a group of Muslim women held at Southwark, London, in 1647 (Braithwaite 1912, p. 57). For Friends, 'Quakers' was initially an insult coined by Justice Bennett at Fox's blasphemy trial in Derby in 1650 but its usage spread, and it was soon adopted by the group (Punshon 1984, p. 71); but we can find tracts from early on written by one of the 'people in scorn called Quakers'. According to Rosemary Moore the early Quaker movement nearly adopted the name 'The Church of the First Born' (after Hebrews 12:23) instead of the Friends of the Truth or the Children of the Light (Moore 2000, p. 132). The Religious Society of Friends did not emerge as the formal name of the group until the early nineteenth century (Lloyd 1950, p. 145).

---

the social hierarchy was closest to heaven, and from Calvin's concept of predestination in which the elect were scattered throughout society.

All needed to be brought to the experience and teaching of the inward Light of Christ. Quakers were engaged in 'the Lamb's War', the spiritual battle for the New Jerusalem. In 1654, over thirty pairs of Ministers and Elders set out south on a mission initially to England and Wales. This reflected Luke 10:1 ('After these things the Lord appointed other seventy also, and sent them two and two before his face into every city and place, whither he himself would come') but Fox put the number sixty in his journal to play down the comparison which could have reignited anti-Quaker sentiment in the 1670s. These pairs of missionaries, labelled 'the valiant sixty' in modern Quaker usage, worked as close partnerships, one to 'elder out the word' (pray that the vocal ministry be rightly guided), the other to minister. Edward Burrough and Francis Howgill went to London, John Camm and John Audland to Bristol. Many of these companions had been Seekers (see Box 3) together before they had joined the Quaker movement and Rosemary Moore argues that it was the depth and breadth of this early Quaker leadership that helped its immediate success in the 1650s (Moore 2004, p. 50). Margaret Fell administered the movement from Swarthmoor Hall; Fox and James Nayler, seen by many as the co-leader of the movement, moved around at will (when not in prison), preaching as led.

In 1657, six Friends set off to convert the Sultan of Constantinople and Mary Fisher had a cordial and successful meeting with him in May or June 1658 (Braithwaite 1912, p. 423). Two of that party, John Luffe and John Perrot, diverted to Rome. John Luffe met Pope Alexander VII. Again, we see an emphasis on the preaching framed by a sense of access to Truth.

'Thou pretendest to sit in Peter's chair,' said Luffe according to this account. 'Now know that Peter had no chair but a boat: Peter was a fisher, thou art a Prince: Peter fasted and prayed, thou farest deliciously and sleepest softly: he was mean in attire, thou art beset with ornaments and gay attire: he fished for men to convert them, thou hookest souls to confound them: he was a friend and disciple to Christ, thou art indeed Antichrist.' (Braithwaite 1912, p. 424)

QUAKERS AND THE SECOND COMING

In an exchange regarding the sacraments, Luffe claimed that every day is a Sabbath where we can serve God. The pope asked Luffe, 'Was nothing then to be done for the remembrance sake of our blessed saviour?' Luffe replied, 'no, no, I have Christ about me and in me, and therefore cannot choose but remember him continually' (Braithwaite 1912, p. 425). Here we see that sense of continual spiritual intimacy with God translated into a theological stance on the outward sacraments. They were unnecessary and might indeed get in the way of people experiencing the inward sacramental state. For Fox, the injunction in 1 Corinthians 11:26 to break the bread until the Lord came again had been superseded by his Coming. Indeed, Fox went on to say that Christians had already been called to a different supper, that of the inward marriage supper of the Lamb described in Revelation 3:20 (Dandelion 2005, p. 27). This second coming was not an external one but an inward one. 'Christ is come and is coming' is a description of an inward spirituality, justified scripturally by reference to Jeremiah 31:31–34:

Behold the days come saith the Lord, that I will make a new covenant with the house of Israel, and with the house of Judah: not according to the covenant that I made with their fathers in the day that I took them by the hand to bring them out of the land of Egypt; which my covenant they brake, although I was a husband unto them, saith the Lord: But this shall be the covenant that I will make with the house of Israel; After those days, saith the Lord, I will put my law in their inward parts, and write in their hearts; and will be their God, and they shall be my people. And they shall teach no more every man his neighbour, and every man his brother, saying, Know the Lord: for they shall all know me, from the least of them unto the greatest of them, saith the Lord, and I will forgive their iniquity, and I will remember their sin no more.

Following Pauline teaching, Friends expanded the 'house of Israel' to include the whole world. This passage emphasises the inward nature of the knowledge and experience of the covenant, and the consequent lack of need to teach outwardly (Grundy 2007). We can see the clear connection with the Jeremiah Scripture in the Howgill convincement narrative above (p. 24).

This idea of the second coming is one of the most useful ways of looking at the history of the Quaker movement (Gwyn 1986). Moore claims that Quakers came from different theological backgrounds and brought a variety of interpretations of the endtimes with them, often differentiating between outward political and inward spiritual covenants, but that by the mid-1650s, 'most typical was the belief that while the Kingdom of God was already beginning to be present in the Quaker movement, a final consummation in the (probably near) future was also to be expected' (Moore 2000, p. 68). This was a *realising* eschatology, an unfolding endtime experienced inwardly. One Quaker, James Milner, had to be corrected in print for his errant prophecy that the day of judgement would be 15 November 1653:

And as for James Milner, though his minde did run out from his condition, and from minding that light of God which is in him, whereby the world takes occasion to speak against the truth, and many friends stumble at it; yet there is a pure seed in him. (*Saul's Errand to Damascus*, 1653, p. 10)

Douglas Gwyn has made explicit the connection between the teachings of George Fox and the Scripture he quoted most, the book of Revelation (1986). A decade later, Timothy Peat clarified the connection between Pauline prophecy and the spiritual claims of early Friends (Dandelion *et al.* 1998). Figure 1.3 outlines the Pauline sense of the relationship between God and humanity from the fall to the second coming. Humanity (Adam and Eve) begin in great intimacy with God but disobey, drawn by temptation. Humanity is then separated from God, and God's guidance is mediated by the law which acts as a child-minder or that which brings the child to school (Dandelion *et al.* 1998, p. 44). Paul characterises a humanity that is in constant struggle with temptation as spiritual children. The human realm, human time, the earth is separated from God's realm, God's time, heaven. The two realms, the mythic and the mundane, intersect through the life, death, and resurrection of Jesus Christ. Paul claims that he is the last of about 500 to have met the risen Christ, almost out of time (1 Cor 15:8), and that that encounter has given him authority to pass on what has been revealed to him. He claims that a time will come when all will meet the risen Christ, when humanity will take on the faith of Jesus Christ, and that God's guidance will be revealed to humanity directly. The age of the law will have passed and instead humanity will have access to 'faith's inner voice' (Dandelion *et al.* 1998, p. 27). The age of the law had passed and the age of the Spirit was now (Rom 8:1–9, 14–17). Humanity will be set

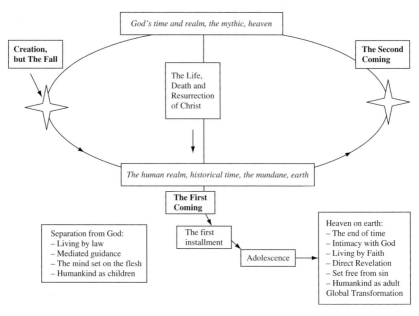

Fig. 1.3 A biblical understanding of time

free from sin and it will be as if they are now adults, living again in intimacy with God but without the possibility of falling. This transformation will not be limited to 500 but will be global (Fig. 1.3).

We can see immediately then how the teachings of early Friends fit the end of this chronology. The only question remaining from Paul's prophecy was 'when?' and the history of Christianity has been about delay, and the subsequent need to wait. In Paul's letters, the expectation that this will happen very soon is then modified to 'quite soon' and then 'whenever' (compare for example the urgency in 1 Thessalonians with the tone of Romans). The church arose as one in waiting and its role has been to help humanity remain faithful, having been given the earnest of what will come (2 Cor 1:21ff) and living in an anticipatory adolescence of the adulthood to follow.

Traditionally it has helped the faithful through outward and separated forms: priests and ministers to teach and administer the outward sacraments of remembrance, communion, and anticipation in set apart buildings on set apart days running to an annual calendar of remembrance and anticipation. Churches vary in how explicit they are about their expectation of the second coming – the Evangelical Alliance are very explicit about an outward second coming for example – but in most outward liturgical forms we can find reference to it. The second coming is the culmination of the Nicene Creed. The Eucharist is a combination of remembrance and anticipation (Dandelion 2005, pp. 24–6).

The Vatican II papers state:

the pilgrim church, in its sacraments and institutions, which belong to this present age, carries the mark of this world which will pass, and she herself takes her place among the creatures which groan and travail yet and await the revelation of the sons of God. [cf. Rom 8:19–22] (Flannery 1975, p. 408)

In 1986, the Church of England published the following on the temporary nature of separated priesthood:

The final chapters of the Revelation to John present a picture of the fulfilment of all things in which the whole company of the redeemed serve God face to face. Part of this picture is that there will be no more temple (Revelation 21:22): God will be immediately present to his people. In other words, there will be no more need for sacraments or priests to mediate God's presence. Thus, whereas those who are redeemed by Christ will be kings and priests forever, the priesthood of the ordained ministry belongs to the realm which is passing away. (*The Priesthood of the Ordained Ministry*, 1986, p. 101)

In other words, the church is explicit about its temporary and pragmatic nature. For the early Friends, that future expectation had been realised. The future had collided with the present and all the temporary and pragmatic outward forms of helping humanity remain faithful in the meantime were over now that the meantime had become the endtime. On a diagram of the Pauline understanding of humanity's relationship with God, early Friends can be placed at the far right, at the time of the second coming, at the culmination as it were of God's plan for the world (Fig. 1.4). They had experienced the risen Christ – Christ has come – and were thus a vanguard for the global transformation which was to follow – Christ is coming (Nickalls 1952, p. 107). All other forms of Christianity were apostate and/or anachronistic and only Quakers represented the true church, i.e. the true body of believers, the saints or new apostles, who would usher in the coming of God's realm, the building of heaven on earth. It was a theology which offered hope amidst post-revolutionary disappointment in the Commonwealth. Quakerism offered a sense of full reformation, the struggle in which so many had been involved since the partial reformation of Henry VIII's break with Rome in 1534. It also appeared to offer the possibility of the bringing of the kingdom when so many of the groups of the 1640s, such as the Levellers and

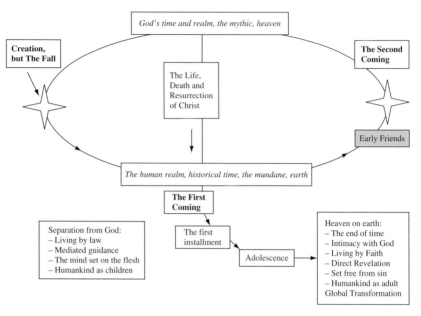

Fig. 1.4 A biblical understanding of time and early Friends

the Diggers, had failed, and when Cromwell had appeared to betray the cause.

Wilcox has précised Fox's demonstration of how the new covenant differed from the old in his *A Clear Distinction Between the Old Covenant, or Old Testament, and the New Covenant, or Testament* (1680) (see Table 1.1).

QUAKER WORSHIP

This continual state of inward intimacy with the risen Christ that has no need of remembrance had profound effects on Quaker liturgy. There was no need of outward sacraments or indeed of any of the outward means other Christian groups had traditionally used to help humanity remain faithful, both remembering the first coming and anticipating the second coming, in between times, i.e. in the meantime. Quakers eschewed set apart places (churches), people (priests), sacraments, times (the Christian calendar and the idea of the Sabbath), and of future states of heaven and hell.

Quakers claimed they did not need this kind of external and 'mean-time' (see p. 33 above) help. Living in the endtimes, their experience

Table 1.1. *The old covenant and the new covenant (Wilcox 1995, pp. 36–7)*

The old covenant	The new covenant
For Jews	For Jews, Gentiles, and all nations
From Sinai	Law of life from heavenly Sion
A 'thing decayed', having 'many outward things'	'Christ hath abolished all outward things'
The priests' lips to preserve people's knowledge	Christ's lips to preserve people's knowledge
Law written on stone	Law written on heart
Sanctuary, tabernacle, temple	Bodies of believers = temple of God – outward temple abolished
High priest lights candles, lamps, in temple	Christ lightens every man's spirit with his heavenly light
Sacrifices, offerings	Christ offered himself once for all and ends outward sacrifices
Aaronic priesthood	Christ = everlasting high priest after the order of Melchizedec
Priests lived in chambers in temple	Christ lives in the chambers of the heart
Feast of Passover	Jews in spirit pass out of spiritual Egypt and feed on Christ the heavenly Passover
Priesthood of one tribe	All believers priests, both male and female
Circumcision in flesh – by priests	Circumcision of spirit – by Christ
Outward death to those resisting high priest or Moses	Eternal death for those resisting Christ the heavenly high priest and prophet
Spirit poured out on House of Israel	Spirit poured out on all flesh
Observations of days, months, feasts, etc.	Observation of days etc. abolished – heavenly feast, day of Christ
Sabbath	Eternal rest and day of Christ
Swearing of oaths	Christ the oath of God abolishes swearing
Moses = leader of outward Jews	Christ = leader and commander of his people, and calls all people
Of natural and outward things	Of inward and spiritual things

was sufficient and moreover showed them that the church had been called to a new age, the age of the gospel or of a new covenant, or of the end of the world and the beginning of heaven on earth. Worship was simple, unadorned, in any place and at any time (though held regularly on Sundays and Wednesdays). It could last any length of time, sometimes up to nine hours but frequently three, and was based in silent waiting. It was a response to God, not to human agency. It was as such untimed and not pre-programmed. Music was acceptable, singing out of a book was not. Anyone present could offer ministry as led. Quaker

---

Box 5 Types of Quaker Meeting

Quaker worship could take place anywhere and at any time. Equally its length could be variable. Accounts claim Meeting of up to nine hours. There were also other types of meeting. Public meetings would be occasions for preaching and debate. Threshing meetings were opportunities for those interested to 'thresh' and discuss the ideas in greater depth, a prelude to joining with others for worship.

---

worship was a second coming or endtime liturgical form (see Box 5 for different types of Meeting).

The history of Christianity is a history of groups predicting the end of the world/the second coming. For these early Friends, the second coming, the endtimes were unfolding. They were living out a realising eschatology. This was not a new Pentecost but the culmination of Pauline prophecy (Dandelion *et al.* 1998), the book of Revelation (Gwyn 1986), and of other endtime prophecy in Scripture. Quakers may have borrowed their silent waiting form of worship from the Seekers but equally Fox cited Revelation 8:1 and the half an hour of silence in heaven after the breaking of the seventh seal to justify the unusual form. As above, the inward communion supper was the marriage supper of the Lamb, not the anachronistic and contested injunction of 1 Corinthians 11:26 to break the bread and take the wine until the Lord comes again. Quakers were involved in the Lamb's War, the spiritual crusade to establish the kingdom of heaven on earth.

WOMEN AND QUAKERISM

Gwyn has noted the attraction of Quakerism to women and that 40–50% of converts were women (1995, p. 111). Tarter has suggested that the physical quaking was emblematic of a feminine and embodied form of worship:

With the advent of Quakerism, a world of possibilities opened to women as a result of Fox's theological vision. Whereas in the seventeenth century they were generally ecclesiastically disempowered (originating with St Paul's injunction that women keep silent in the church), Quakerism invited women not only to worship, but also to quake, prophesy, travel, preach and write in the beginning of the Quaker movement. Women held authoritative roles as 'Spiritual mothers' giving birth and then nursing the Children of the Light with their 'Milk of the Word of God'. (Tarter 2004, p. 89)

Nearly half of the early missionaries were women, and women were critically important in the pamphlet wars (Mack 1989). Women were spiritually equal and Fell used Scripture to justify the preaching of women. Where 'women' was used to refer to the weak, early Quakers argued, it did not necessarily mean female. Alternatively, Fox suggested that the whole of humanity was as a wife to Christ and that Paul's suggestion that women be silent in church referred to the human church, the body of believers in its intimate relationship with Christ (Gwyn 1986, p. 199). The role of women within Quakerism was unprecedented (Gwyn 1995, p. III) and defined the radical nature of the movement in its early years.

SUMMARY

This early expression and formation of Quakerism was filled with a sense of power and possibility. It was radical and outspoken and proved to have widespread appeal. It harnessed apocalyptic expectation with a strong moral line and supported its mission with a depth of very able leadership. The bringing of heaven on earth was felt to be within the grasp of the early Quaker movement.

RESTORATION QUAKERISM, 1666–1689

As the movement grew, so it faced the usual problems. First, it needed to modify its theology in order to meet the criticisms of the anti-Quakers where inconsistencies or embarrassments emerged. As Rosemary Moore states, pinning down a single Quaker theology is not easy. Often pamphlet wars focused on single issues. Second, Quakers were not consistent in the use of terms such as 'Light' and 'seed' (Moore 2000, pp. 103–5): 'Fox's theology was ... obscure' (2000, p. 109). Nevertheless, Moore claims that as early as 1653/54, it is possible to notice a definite change of message (2000, p. 215). We can identify five main areas of modification: (a) Quakers emphasised the historical Jesus more; (b) Quakers adapted their doctrine of perfection; (c) Quakers emphasised collective authority over individual revelation; (d) Quakers established a committee to police the publication of Quaker theology; (e) Quaker claims about the immediate second coming diminished.

Based on an inward spirituality of the second coming of Christ, Friends had little need to emphasise the historical Jesus and this was a theme of much of the critique of the early movement. John Bunyan was one of the critics who took Friends to task over this (Moore 2000, p. 105).

The second modification was on the topic of the controversial doctrine of perfection. How was the movement to sustain its claim when individual Quakers might be found drunk in the street or involved in a sexual scandal. The answer was to introduce the idea of different Friends being given different 'measures of the Light', and that what was important was that all should 'live up to their measure' (Moore 2000, p. 102): Nayler, as early as 1653, wrote in his *Saul's Errand to Damascus*: 'And none can witness redemption, further than Christ is thus revealed in them, to set them free from sin: which Christ I witness to be revealed in me in measure' (Barbour and Roberts 2004, p. 258).

The third problem early on for Friends was the claim of direct revelation and what happens when one person's version of God's will differs from another's. Indeed, how at all could anyone discern God's will apart from imaginations. This issue was brought particularly to the fore by the actions of James Nayler in 1656.

THE NAYLER INCIDENT

Nayler (1618–60) was a Yorkshire Quaker, who had left his family in order to follow God.

I was at the plough, meditating on the things of God, and suddenly I heard a voice saying unto me, 'Get thee out from thy kindred, and from thy father's house'. And I had a promise given with it, where upon I did exceedingly rejoice that I had heard the voice of that God which I had professed from a child, but had never known him . . . And when I came at home I gave up my estate, cast out my money; but not being obedient in going forth, the wrath of God was upon me, so that I was made a wonder to all, and none thought I would have lived. But after I was made willing, I began to make some preparation, as apparel and other necessaries, not knowing whither I should go. But shortly afterwards going a gate-ward with a friend from my own house, having on an old suit, without any money, having neither taken leave of wife or children, not thinking then of any journey, I was commanded to go into the west, not knowing whither I should go, nor what I was to do there. But when I had been there a little while, I had given me what I was to declare. And ever since I have remained not knowing today what I was to do tomorrow . . . [The promise was] that God would be with me, which promise I find made good every day. (Nayler 1716, pp. 12–13)

He became in time the perceived co-leader of the Quaker movement and was particularly popular in London and the south. There is the story that Howgill and Burrough, entrusted with the care of the mission to London, wrote to Margaret Fell asking for an additional minister to be sent, but adding *not to send George Fox*. It seems George Fox was not well received in the capital. Perhaps because of this, perhaps because of his general popularity, it seems that a rivalry developed between James Nayler and George Fox. In August 1656, Nayler had refused to remove his hat when Fox was praying. As Damrosch suggests, this implied an insult either to Fox, or to God (Damrosch 1996, p. 141). Some were concerned that Nayler was subject to the wishes of his immediate followers but the implication was that Nayler should be more subject to Fox. However, as Moore points out, Nayler alone amongst the Yorkshire Seekers had always treated Fox as an equal (Moore 2000, p. 19). Later, Nayler felt that Fox was giving credence to lies about him. When Nayler spoke against Fox in public, Fox was furious at the public breaking of ranks (Damrosch 1996, p. 142). Hubberthorne tried to mediate and a meeting was arranged to effect a reconciliation. A most curious account was recorded by Richard Hubberthorne in a letter to Margaret Fell.

Afterwards George passed to him again in prison, where he and some others with him was sitting in a place where he lies which is much lower than the rest of the chamber, and George spoke much to him. James wept and professed a great love and again offered George an apple and said 'If I have found favour in thy sight, receive it.' But he denied it and said, 'If thou can say thou art moved of the Lord to give me it.' James said, 'Would thou have me to lie?' Then James, having George by the hand, he asked him if he might kiss him. George, standing above the low place would have drawn James out to him, but he would not come out; but George standing still could not bow down to him at his asking of him in that thing which if he had come out he could have suffered him to have done it. Then George gave him his hand to kiss but he would not, and then George said to him, 'It is my foot.' So with some few more words we passed away. (Damrosch 1996, p. 143)

This is not an easy account to understand and its symbolism can be interpreted variously. But we can see that the desire to reconcile is easily shaken by the fact that neither protagonist concedes to the other. Subsequently, Fox claimed he was moved by God to slight Nayler (Nickalls 1952, p. 269). The battle for authority, both in terms of religious truth and within the Quaker movement, continued and was brought to a head on 24 October 1656.

That day, Nayler rode into Bristol on a horse, accompanied by seven other Friends including Dorcas Erbury and Marth Simmonds, sister of Giles Calvert, the London Quaker printer (Peters 2005, p. 57), some also on horseback, singing 'Holy, Holy, Holy' as they came through the rain. It was not at all unusual for Quakers to enact signs. Bailey comments on the proliferation of different signs enacted by Friends in the 1650s (1992, p. 195). Bristol was a key Quaker stronghold and a major city. However, this enactment of Christ's entry into Jerusalem, or of Christ's second coming, previously carried out at Wells and Glastonbury (Damrosch 1996, p. 147), was met with hostility from the authorities and indifference from Bristol Quakers, uneager to fuel local opposition to them. Nayler was arrested and tried for blasphemy for believing he was Christ.

Letters found on Nayler did not help his case. One from Hannah Stranger identified Nayler as Jesus and one from her husband claimed 'Thy name is to be no more James but Jesus' (Damrosch 1996, p. 152). In court, Nayler answered the question 'Art thou the only Son of God?' with 'I am the Son of God but I have many bretheren', a view in accord with the 1653 epistle from Fox mentioned above (p. 25). Equally, Nayler was accused of claiming to raise Dorcas Erbury from the dead (although Fox himself accounted 150 miracles, a record later suppressed).

Parliament examined Nayler, and as it was his second blasphemy trial there was the possibility of execution. Central was the question as to whether Nayler was used by the Lord or claimed that power for himself. The death penalty was avoided by a vote of 96 to 82 (Damrosch 1996, p. 213). Instead he was branded, had his tongue bored, and was lashed. Finally he was symbolically placed backwards on a horse and led out of Bristol. The punishment was so severe that it had to be given in two halves to preserve Nayler's life. Robert Rich kissed his wounds and licked his branded forehead and three of his women supporters gathered around him (after John 19:25) (Reay 1985, p. 55). Paradoxically, Spencer suggests that Nayler was seeking martyrdom as the ultimate form of celestial inhabitation (see Box 1) and would have been initially disappointed in his survival (Spencer 2001).

Fox wrote to Parliament that they must do with him as they saw fit. This may sound unsupportive but it may equally have been an attempt to show allegiance to the state should they have decided to punish all Friends. This would have been uncharacteristic of Quakerism at this stage but the trial of James Nayler, thought by many to be the leader of the movement, was a major scandal for Quakerism, a perfect moment for their critics, and one that Quakers needed to work through swiftly. 'Nayler was a leading Quaker, some said the leading Quaker, so it was an ideal opportunity to demonstrate the effectiveness of savage punishment as a deterrent. "Cut off this fellow, and you will destroy the sect"' (Reay 1985, p. 54). Quakers were highly popular and therefore deemed especially dangerous: 'These vipers are crept into the bowels of your Commonwealth, and the government too', explained one; 'They grow numerous, and swarm all the nation over;

every county, every parish' (Reay 1985, p. 54). They preached perfection, minimised the historic Christ, gave revelation authority over Scripture, and rejected ideas about heaven and hell. Some felt Quakers could play Protestantism into the hands of the Catholics. They were rude and they were politically suspect (Reay 1985, pp. 57–61). Certainly they were misunderstood. For example, Fox needed to tell Ranters keen to join the Quaker group that they were mistaken as to its nature and that Quakers had a different view of perfection (see p. 23 above).

There was also popular hostility (Reay 1985, pp. 65–71). Quakers were accused of being Catholics in disguise, of incest, buggery, witchcraft, and child sacrifice. They were stoned, mobbed, urinated on, and spat at. Most people in England in that period travelled less than 10 miles from their home in their lifetime so these preachers coming with their strange accents from elsewhere played into the xenophobia of the time. The trembling and shaking of the Quakers only made them appear more unusual. As Tarter explains, the physical aspects of particularly women's ministry brought a strong reaction.

Women Friends, in particular, were viciously punished for their 'transgressive' Quaker behavior. They were incarcerated, pelted, stoned, kicked, spat upon, verbally harassed, and locked behind a 'scold's bridle,' a twenty-pound headcage used to punish any seventeenth-century Englishwoman for 'having too much tongue.' In the first two decades of Quakerism, literally thousands of these quaking women's bodies were put under the control of the British state, who then systematically abused, tortured, and reinscribed their marks of power on these radical, subversive living texts of Christianity. (Tarter 2001, p. 152)

Nayler was imprisoned, ostracised by his fellow Quakers, but released in 1659 under a general amnesty. He met Fox once again after his release but any real reconciliation between the two men was made impossible by the death of Nayler in 1660 following an attack as he made his way from London to Yorkshire. Bailey notes that Fox performed another miracle of healing in London after Nayler's release, possibly to emphasise that this was a spiritual gift given more to Fox than to Nayler. Nayler wrote some beautiful reflections on his spiritual journey but in general Fox opposed the publication of works by Nayler and his restoration to the status of leading early Quaker is quite recent.

OTHER MODIFICATIONS OF EARLY QUAKER THEOLOGY

As well as losing such a capable and beloved leader to prison, the 'Nayler incident' also brought into sharp relief the problem of the authenticity of direct revelation. Those Quakers embarrassed by Nayler's actions or needing to distance themselves from them needed to assert that he had acted out of his own will or at least a lack of discrimination or discernment of the leadings of others. In November 1656, the Balby Elders, including William Dewsbury and Richard Farnworth, issued an epistle which included provision for the reproval of those 'disorderly walking'. It also advised: 'Ministers to speak the word of the Lord from the mouth of the Lord', without adding or diminishing. If anything is spoken out of the Light so that the 'seed of God' comes to be burdened, it is to be dealt with in private and not in the public meetings, 'except where there be a special moving to do so' (*Faith and Practice: The Book of Discipline of New York Yearly Meeting*, 1998, p. 57). Personal infallibility was now to be complemented by corporate discernment.

The fourth area of modification of Quaker theology was that of claims judged in time to be awkward or unsustainable. Bailey (1992), Tarter (1993), and Reynolds (2004) each claim that early Quaker writing was censored by a second generation of more reserved Quakers. Moore claims there was less blasphemy after 1652, perhaps owing to the influence of Thomas Fell, and Trevett argues there was less prophecy after 1672 owing to the Second Day's Morning Meeting (2001) (see pp. 48–9 below). This meant less publication of women's material as women writers were more prophetic (Wilcox 1995, p. 240). In 1662, a Quaker had spilled blood on the altar in St Paul's Cathedral. In 1700, when a Chester Friend ministered in the street he was jailed but also received a rebuke from his Monthly Meeting (Reay 1985, p. 112).

The fifth area of Quaker theological modification concerned claims to do with the second coming. Whilst Fox and Margaret Fell maintained an eschatological emphasis to their preaching and writing until they died in 1691 and 1702 respectively, this framing of the Quaker experience was to be generally dropped after 1666. It had already waned in the mid-1650s, but was resurrected by the political uncertainties of 1659 following the death of Oliver Cromwell and the ineffectual rule of his son Richard. Dorothy White, the most prolific woman Quaker pamphleteer, wrote to Parliament:

Friends, you that are of the Parliament, hear the word of the Lord as it comes to me concerning you . . . how your downfall is near, and this is the word of the Lord God of Hosts unto you all that are now sitting in Parliament, the Lord will overturn you by his Powerful Arm, for the decree of God and his purpose is . . . to throw down and break up Parliaments . . . God himself will rule, and bear rule in the hearts of men, and such as know God . . . shall rule for God . . . for God will throw down and overturn, root up and consume both root and branch of all your parliaments, until he hath brought in the Royl heir, the Prince of Peace, the Everlasting King of Righteousness and he will reign in the destruction of his enemies. (White 1659)

In 1666, the plague, the Great Fire of London, and the destruction of some of the best of the Navy's ships by the Dutch at Medway seemed as if they might be signs of the endtimes. But still the world did not change in the way that readers of Revelation would have hoped for. By the time Robert Barclay came to write his *Apology for the True Christian Divinity* in 1676 he made no mention of eschatology (see pp. 53–6 below).

QUAKERISM RE-PRESENTED

Rather, the 1660s saw a more pragmatic and cautious presentation of the Quaker experience to the world, or, as John Punshon has suggested, a more mature one. Margaret Fell met with Charles II early in his reign and wrote to him of Friends' peaceability (Kunze 1994, p. 16).

This wee declare, That it is our principle [,] life & practice to live peaceably with all men, And not to act any thing against the King nor the peace of the Nation, by any plots, contrivances, insurrections, or carnall weapons to hurt or destroy either him or the Nation thereby, but to be obedient unto all just and lawfull Commands. (Glines 2003, p. 281)

Left to Charles' own devices, Quakers might have been afforded freedom of worship. But the Court advisers wanted a return to a strong Anglican church and the outlawing of all the heretical sects which had ascended during Cromwell's rule. Quakers numbered perhaps 66,000 in 1660 in Britain and Ireland and just under 0.76% of the population of Britain and Ireland (Rowntree 1859, p. 73). One in ten of the population of Bristol was possibly Quaker at this time. In 1661, thirty-five Fifth Monarchists staged an armed rising in the City of London. This was a group, named after reference in the book of Daniel to the fifth monarchy at the end of time, keen to usher in the second coming and prepared to use force if necessary. They held out for four days before most of the leaders were hanged (Braithwaite 1919, p. 13) but Braithwaite claims that 4200 Quakers were held in preventative detention (Braithwaite 1919, p. 9). Rude, and claiming to be the true church, this group looked too dangerous to leave at large. In 1662, a Quaker Act was passed, outlawing Quaker worship, and the Conventicle Acts of 1664 and 1670 reinforced this ruling. Quakers were to struggle for their rights for the next twenty years or more, prior to the Act of Toleration of 1689. They could be imprisoned for a wide range of offences (Ayoub 2005), notably for attending Meetings at all or for non-payment of tithes and rates. Work by Simon Dixon and Gareth Shaw shows that different laws were used in different areas. Recusancy was used as an offence more in east Yorkshire than in London, for example. When new laws were introduced, such as the Quaker Act or Conventicle Acts, these would often be used as primary measures against nonconformists for the few years following. Between times, tithe and rate offences were used as the fallback offence (Dixon and Shaw 2005; Horle 1988, p. 284).

Barry Reay suggests that 'for most, political defeat reinforced faith in the need for a longer term spiritual regeneration of humankind before the millennium could be realised' (1985, p. 107). In 1661, following the Fifth Monarchist uprising, twelve Quakers, including Fox, put their signatures to a statement rehearsing the points Margaret Fell had made in her 1660 epistle as to the spiritual, not carnal, nature of the Quaker warfare (Kunze 1994, p. 131). Sue Bell (personal communication) has suggested that there was a military wing to Quakerism, led by Nayler, and that some Friends were involved in the Kaber Rigg Plot against the King of 1663. Barry Reay has also pointed out that Quakerism was not pacifist in its entirety in the 1650s. Burrough even suggested in May 1660 that Friends held a testimony against outward warring and fighting on the basis of knowing more than they had before (Reay 1985, p. 107). However, Fox had declined a captaincy in the army in 1650, and whilst some Friends had military backgrounds, there seems little ground to suggest that the 1660 and 1661 declarations were not reflecting the mainstream Quaker position. Even if they were pragmatic and political gestures designed to help ensure survival, they have proven over time to reflect an enduring witness amongst Friends, first against the taking up of arms, and after the start of the twentieth century for 'peace'. Individual Quakers have joined the armed forces in most major conflicts but few have questioned the corporate holding of the testimony (see pp. 139–40 below).

ORGANISATION AND CENTRALISATION

Imprisonment and sometimes banishment were to become major features of the Restoration period. Braithwaite claims that over 15,000 Friends were held in jail over the whole Restoration period and that over 400 died there (Braithwaite 1919, p. 115). Critically, the death toll included early leaders such as James Parnell, the teenage Quaker minister, Mary Dyer, who was hanged in Boston, Richard Hubberthorne, and the skilled preacher and pamphleteer Edward Burrough. Fox spent many of these years in prison and Fell was imprisoned for four years for failing to swear an oath (Kunze 1994, p. 171). Fox fell into periods of depression from time to time, but, emerging from Scarborough Jail in 1666, close to death, he immediately rode to London to support Farnworth's directive, *A Testimony from the Brethren* (1666). Building on the sentiment of the Balby Epistle (see p. 42 above), this document in particular gave authority to the Quaker church over the inspired individual. It claimed the church had the right and responsibility to judge individual inspiration and to deal with those who ignored its authority. It was another manifestation of the sharp moral line Quakers had held since their inception, as well as a further attempt to quell individual dissent. Its strong tone may reflect the character of Farnworth but also a degree of corporate anxiety.

The *Testimony from the Brethren* proved controversial, especially amongst those who were disinclined to centralised control. It seemed to some Quakers that, having campaigned against a church structure, Friends were reinventing it. Fox may have felt he had faced opposition with Nayler in 1656. Certainly he had fallen out with a Nottinghamshire convert named Rice-Jones in 1651, accusing Jones' group of being 'proud Quakers' and of being some of the best wrestlers and footballers in the land (Braithwaite 1912, p. 46). In 1662, the Irish Quaker John Perrot had returned from his imprisonment in the Vatican. Whilst there, he had written many moving and beautifully crafted letters to Friends in Britain and Ireland, and he returned as a loved and influential Friend (Carroll 1970, p. 48). John Perrot then claimed new revelation. In particular he questioned the practice of holding Meeting for Worship at fixed times. Surely, he argued, a group led by the Spirit should meet when moved to. He also questioned the practice of hat honour. This was the way in which Friends never removed their hats (again levelling everyone down rather than up, before God), except in prayer when the person praying would kneel and the rest of the Meeting would stand and take off their hats. Why did Friends remove their hats, Perrot asked? Why not their shoes, equally scriptural? Fox and his allies moved quickly to quell this 'new Light', claiming Friends had already been given their Truth (Gwyn 2000, p. 344). Perrot initially won some support but Fox's view prevailed and Perrot became disaffected with Friends by the time of his death in Barbados in 1665. *A Testimony from the Brethren* can be seen as explicitly anti-Perrot (Braithwaite 1919, p. 247). For example, the second point reads:

We do declare and testify, that the spirit of those that are joined to it, who stand not in unity with the ministry and body of Friends, who are stedfast and constant to the Lord and his unchangeable Truth, (which we have received and are witnesses and ambassadors of,) have not any true spiritual right, nor gospel authority to be judges in the Church, and of the ministry of the gospel of Christ, so as to condemn them and their ministry; neither ought their judgement to be any more regarded by Friends, than the judgement of other opposers, which are without: for of right the elders and members of the church, which keep their habitation in the Truth, ought to judge matters and things which differ. (*A Testimony from the Brethren*, 1666, p. 320)

We can see the Balby Epistle of 1656 and *A Testimony from the Brethren* of 1666 as key documents to try and protect a particular vision of Quakerism in the face of tensions from within and outwith the movement caused by the Nayler and Perrot controversies. A 1670 list of advice from Fox reads as follows:

Friends keepe the ancient principles of truth:
1. Att a word, in all your callings and deallinges, without oppression (*keep your word and do not make undue profit*).
2. to the sound language, Thou, to everie one.
3. your testimony against the worldes fashions.
4. Against the old mashouses, and their repairinge.
5. your testimony against the priestes, their tythes and maintenance.
6. against the world joyning in marriage, and the priestes, and stand upp, for godes joining.
7. against swearinge, and the worldes manners, and fashions.
8. and against all lousenes, pleasures and profaneness, whatsoever.
9. and against all the worldes wayes, worshipps, and religions, and to stand up for gode.
10. And for that everie one, that hath done wrong, to any one, that they do restore.
11. And that all differences be made upp, speedily.
12. And that all bad things bee judged speedily, that they do not flie abroad, to Corrupte peoples minds.
13. And that all Reportes bee stopped to the defaming of any one.
G. F. (Transcribed by Angus Winchester from the Cumbria Record Office (Barrow), BDFC/F, Swarthmoor Monthly Meeting Minute Book, 1668–74, p. 97)

Whilst the first nine reflect public testimony amongst these Friends and signal what would become a complete behavioural code in the following century, it is noteworthy that the last four are all about the maintenance of public unity and the management of internal disputes.

As it was, 'The Spirit of the Hat' was to re-emerge in the opposition by John Wilkinson and John Storey of Preston Patrick Meeting (see

Fig. 1.1) to the new proposals for a national structure. In 1671, Preston Patrick Friends separated (possibly with some degree of mutual enmity with Margaret Fell). These Friends were also opposed to the settling of women's Meetings for Business, the idea of an organisation of representative business meetings comprised of women parallel to that of the men. Women's Meetings had been around from the 1650s but by the 1670s they had become more powerful, increasingly handling discernment over marriage, and the advice from Fox was that they should become universal. High Wycombe was also to split over women's Meetings. Whilst the spiritual equality of women had been a keystone of early Quaker thinking, it did not extend to political equality. Fox thought that separated Meetings would help overcome prejudice, but the separation of the sexes also played into secular hierarchies. It would be seventy-five years before women's Meetings were established in all Monthly Meetings and women did not have their own Yearly Meeting until 1784.

Braithwaite, Ingle, Moore, and Reay tend to suggest that Quakerism lost its eschatological edge in the 1660s and adopted a pragmatic approach essential for survival. Reay argues that 'Quaker self-censorship did the State's job for it in the 1670s and 1680s' (1985, p. 111). Wilcox claims that the diminishment of eschatological emphasis resulted in a diminishment of women's role in the early Quaker movement (Wilcox 1995, p. 239). Once a transformation of the world seemed less imminent, more traditional views resurfaced for the meantime.

Friends' first venture into property ownership was the acquisition of land for burials. In the 1670s, in spite of continuing persecution in Britain, the first Meeting Houses were built. Brigflatts at Sedbergh, in an area which through its magistrates offered a measure of protection to Friends, saw a Meeting House built in 1675 with tons of slate on its roof – a clear signal that Friends were not ephemeral (Plate 4). Also, too, a sign perhaps that the world was not transforming in the way that at least some Friends had once thought.

The internal architecture mirrored the ecclesiology, and by the time Friends were building Meeting Houses these included a 'facing bench' for the Elders and a 'Ministers' gallery' just above them. Men and women sat in different parts of the Meeting House and multiple ministry was restrained. Monitors were appointed to awaken the sleeping (Reay 1985, p. 122).

As well as local 'Monthly' and 'Quarterly' Meetings of local Friends, national committees such as the Box Meeting, Two Weeks Meeting, the

Plate 4 Brigflatts Friends Meeting House (photograph taken c.1952)

executive 'Meeting for Sufferings', and 'Yearly Meeting' were established. After the Great Fire destroyed the Bull and Mouth, which had acted as Quaker headquarters, Devonshire House was acquired in the 1660s, a building which would serve as the central offices of British Quakerism until the move to the present 'Friends House' in 1926. Ellis Hookes was employed as the first secretary to the movement, a position which would develop into that of 'Recording Clerk'.

In 1668, Fox instructed all Meetings to keep proper minute books, an instruction which led not only to the initiation of the practice in some areas but also alas the discarding of older ones in others. In Bristol the new books started midway through an item of business. In 1671, the Second Day's

---

Box 6 Gospel order

This is the name given to the ecclesiastical system laid down by Farnworth, Fox, and Fell in the 1660s. It has been seen by historians and sociologists as pragmatic and shrewd, contributing to the survival of the group. Theologically, it was claimed that this was the gospel order, i.e. the divinely ordained structure for the chosen people to work within.

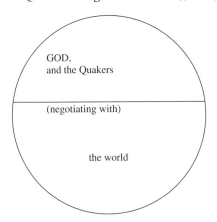

Fig. 1.5 Quakers and God and the world, 1660s

Morning Meeting was established. Meeting on a Monday, hence its name, it acted as a publications or censorship committee, deciding which publications could be published in the name of Friends (Trevett 2001). In terms of relations with 'the world', returning to our earlier diagram (see Fig. 1.2), we can see it modified in terms of this pragmatism or alternative expression of Quakerism (Fig. 1.5).

THE HOLY EXPERIMENT

In Britain Quakers worked with those of other allegiances to attempt to secure a toleration that would only be granted in 1689, and struggled within the confines of censorship reintroduced after the free press of the 1650s. Reay relates how Second Day's Morning Meeting refused to publish a tract against the Baptists in 1674 because 'as the Case now stands between the Bapts & Friends They would not willingly have other Controversyes brought in to make more worke' (Reay 1985, p. 111). However, in the colonies, Quakers would move beyond such pragmatism to epitomise religious toleration where they had the power to grant it. In these settings, notably in Rhode Island and Pennsylvania, Quakers did not so much work with 'the world' as become architects of how the world might work. William Penn took on several tracts of land from the Crown and named them after his father in creating his 'Holy Experiment'. William Penn (1644–1718) was well educated and from a privileged background. He was a convert to Quakerism in the

Plate 5 William Penn's treaty with the Indians (etching after the painting by Benjamin West)

1660s and not part of the founding movement. He is best known for his trial with William Meade in 1670 which secured the right of jury to decide a verdict without or against the direction of judge, and for the settlement he effected in the new world. In both Rhode Island and Pennsylvania, Quakers would secure peace with the Native Americans (Plate 5).

Histories of Quakerism written by Quakers suggest that the thousands of Quakers who went to America did not do so because of the persecution in Britain; but rather, something about the new world must have had an appeal. For Quakers in Wales, the appeal was so widespread that Quakerism virtually disappeared from that country until the Nantucket whalers stimulated a revival by establishing a Meeting in Milford Haven in 1792 (Allen 2003, p. 64). New England Yearly Meeting was the first in the world, beginning in 1661, and Quakerism became established there in the 1670s, in spite of the earlier hanging of Mary Dyer and her companions (Plate 6). The early ally to the young George Fox, Elizabeth Hooten, was whipped out of Boston three times in the 1660s. A royal directive helped bring toleration but it was slow to become universal. Elsewhere, throughout the colonies, Quaker

Plate 6 Mary Dyer statue, Boston, Massachusetts (photograph c.1970)

missionaries were active from the 1650s or 1660s. Penn's experiment began in 1681.

Penn promised settlers land and liberty of conscience and religious practice in return for a religiously based moral settlement. For example, the lottery and drunkenness were outlawed, as were swearing, duelling, cock-fighting, and stage-plays (Sharpless 1911, p. 476). Soon Quakers were to be outnumbered by Presbyterians and German Pietists although they retained control of the Pennsylvania Assembly beyond Penn's death in 1714 until 1756. Then, required again to raise taxes to help the Crown fight the French and Indian War, and undergoing internal spiritual renewal, most Quakers in the Assembly resigned (Marietta 1984, pp. 146–68). This voluntary withdrawal contrasted hugely with the continuing campaigns in Britain for Quakers to be able to have the same rights as Anglicans. Thus, in terms of the socio-political dynamic, Quakerism was always different on the two sides of the Atlantic. In terms of spirituality and of course kinship, Quakerism remained a single transatlantic community until the Great Separation of 1827 divided Quakerism in North America (chapter 2).

Quakers in North America had the choice to participate in or withdraw from political life and they chose to 'swim upstream'. In 1758, Philadelphia Yearly Meeting advised any Friend against holding any civil office which might involve compromise with Quaker principles and, urged on by the likes of John Woolman (see Box 8), Anthony Benezet, and Benjamin Lay, adopted the position that slaveholding was wrong. In 1780, slaveholding in general became a disownable offence in that Yearly Meeting. During the War of Independence, Quakers generally maintained an agreed position to help neither army. A small number decided to fight for independence and were disowned. They called themselves the Free Quakers and asked for their membership to be reinstated under the Quaker tradition in Pennsylvania of freedom of conscience (Kashatus 1990, p. 136). This appeal was unsuccessful, and to this day the Free Quaker Meeting House, in use until 1836, stands in the centre of Philadelphia. Their discipline forbade disownment.

SUMMARY

In a time of persecution and continued growth, the 1660s and 1670s were a time in which Quakerism needed to reformulate some of its earlier claims and organise for a longer and more sustainable future. It nevertheless continued to be radical, innovative, and active in the world. William Penn's Holy Experiment was a daring attempt to create a utopian form of social and religious order, and American Quakerism would be forever influenced by it.

Most of the first generation of leaders had died by the 1690s, including Fox himself in 1691. Some of the second generation of leaders, such as Barclay in 1690, also died at this time (see Box 7). The passing of these early leaders led to the publication of journals and collected works which became standard texts for the third generation.

Box 7 George Keith (1638–1716)

George Keith, like Penn and Barclay, was a second-generation leader who had converted to Quakerism in the 1660s following a university education. Like Barclay, he was Scottish. He joined with Fox and Penn and Barclay in visits to Germany and came to New Jersey as a surveyor. He was part of a small group of the Quaker elite who met with the philosophers Anne Conway and Van Helmont at Ragley Hall in the 1660s. In the early 1690s, he became more critical of Friends, and in particular of their emphasis on the inward Light at the expense of the outward historic Christ and the Scriptures. In 1688 Keith published a catechism, the views of which he was to attack three years later. Both London and Philadelphia Yearly Meeting attempted to ease his doctrinal concerns by rehearsing their positions and tried to suggest that he should not take individual shortcomings as representative of Friends as a body (Sharpless 1911, p. 450). In 1692 Philadelphia Yearly Meeting publicly distanced themselves from Keith's approach (1911, p. 452). He set up separate Meetings and appealed to London Yearly Meeting in 1693. London Yearly Meeting acted as Philadelphia had, claiming Keith was no longer in 'holy fellowship of the Church of Christ' (1911, p. 454). On Keith's return to America, he found that many of his followers had left his Meeting, either returning to Friends or more usually joining the Baptists. Keith joined the Anglican Church and worked for the United Society for the Propagation of the Gospel, sent to America in 1702, to bring Quakers to the Established Church. He ended his life as vicar to the church in Epworth, Sussex, and is buried there.

QUIETISM, 1690–1820s

Other than the formalisation and centralisation of the church government, the interpretation of 'gospel order' (see Box 6), the most significant element in the shift towards a consolidated sectarian spirituality, came with the work of Robert Barclay (1648–90). Barclay was a Scottish Quaker, a second-generation convert, who became a Friend in 1666. Like Penn, he was from a privileged and educated background and he had studied at the Scots College in Paris, where he had learnt Hebrew and Greek. He began writing theological defences of Quakerism in 1670 and his *Anarchy of the Ranters* (1676) was an important defence of gospel order. In the same year, he published his *Apology for the True Christian Divinity* in Latin (Second Day's Morning Meeting appointed somebody to check the Latin!). It appeared in English in 1678. As early as 1677, it was being distributed in Germany by Fox, Penn, Barclay, and Keith on their travels to convert Pietists to Quakerism (Martin, L. 2003, p. 42).

After Barclay's early death in 1690 at the age of forty-two, following a fever, his complete works were published by William Penn in a single volume and this book was to become a household text for Friends. Fox's journal, edited and amended by Thomas Ellwood, appeared in 1694 (see Box 2).

Quaker worship was no longer persecuted with the Act of Toleration in 1689 and this inaugurated a new period of Quakerism, characterised by consolidation. It was guided in part by George Whitehead, one of the few of the valiant sixty (see p. 29 above) still alive. Margaret Fell, who had married George Fox in 1669, was to live until 1702, William Penn until 1714, but most of the first two generations of leaders were to be replaced by a Quakerism which felt less in need of leaders and prophets. Acts of witness which would not have been questioned in the 1650s were now matters of discipline (see p. 42 above).

British Quakers still ran foul of the authorities over church tithes, would not be able to be Members of Parliament until 1832, and were not afforded access to the universities and professions until 1870; but in 1722, Quakers were given permission not to have to swear an oath in all but the criminal courts, the Hardwicke Act of 1753 legalised the Quaker manner of marriage and gave special rights to Friends, otherwise afforded only to Jews, and in 1762 the Militia Act absolved Friends from needing to serve in militias (Punshon 1984, p. 108).

THE INFLUENCE OF ROBERT BARCLAY

Barclay's *Apology* was the first widely read systematic theology of Friends, and only Elizabeth Bathurst, in the seventeenth century, and Joseph John Gurney, in the nineteenth century, would come close to producing anything similar. It comprised fifteen propositions and was essentially a scholarly argument for the theological validity of Quakerism. In particular it refuted Calvinist doctrines of predestination and scriptural authority, and argued for universal salvation and the authority of direct revelation. Pyper (1998) and Keiser (2001) have recently discussed the degree of Cartesian dualism in Barclay's thought, a debate echoing that over celestial inhabitation in the writings of Fox. Certainly Barclay emphasised the inward nature of revelation and spiritualised Christ in the same way as earlier Friends did. Christ is within but Friends are not equal to Christ (2002, p. 121). There was a clear distancing from the confusion caused by the words of Fox and Nayler claiming to be the son of God. Strategically, too, he also left room to emphasise the historical Jesus. Indeed, Frieday (2003, p. 19) has argued that Barclay was far more concerned with the restoration of New Testament Christianity than with a newer dispensation (see p. 30 above).

Interestingly, Barclay maintained the doctrine of perfection (see p. 23 above). Whilst stating that he had not reached this state himself, he claimed that perfection is possible: 'there may be a state attainable in this life, in which to do righteousness may become so natural to the regenerate soul, that in the stability of this condition they can not sin' (2002, p. 207). Barclay used 1 John 3:9 to affirm this truth. There were two caveats. The first was that this perfection may still 'daily admit of a growth' (2002, p. 206). In other words, whilst Barclay believed in perfection without sin, it would always leave room for further growth. Barclay was not claiming the perfection of divinity for the saints. And second, in this sense, he affirmed the idea of 'individual measure' introduced in the early 1650s to circumvent the problem of the sinning Quaker. Thus humanity cannot 'will up' perfection but God gives each the proportion of perfection they require (2002, p. 207).

Barclay also maintained the concepts of inward revelation and of convincement offering regenerated life. It is an inward experience of atonement and communion available to everyone. Like earlier Friends, Barclay stated that this convincement experience is not available on request: 'this Light and Seed of God in man he cannot move and stir up when he pleaseth; but it moves, blows, and strives with man, as the Lord seeth meet' (2002, pp. 127–8).

Unlike Fox, Barclay detailed the 'day of visitation'.

First, then, by this time and day of visitation which, we say, God gives unto all, during which they may be saved, we do not understand the whole time of every man's life; though to some it may be extended even to the very hour of death; as we see in the example of the thief converted on the cross; but such a season at least as sufficiently exonerateth God of every man's condemnation, which to some may be sooner, and to others later, according as the Lord in his wisdom sees fit. (2002, p. 119)

Thus 'the day', metaphorical or elastic, not literal, is sufficient but is not an endless invitation. Crucially for the individual, there is the possibility of missing the day.

So that many men outlive this day, after which there may be no possibility of salvation to them, and God justly suffers them to be hardened, as a just punishment of their unbelief, and even raises them up as instrument of wrath, and makes them a scourge one against another. (p. 119)

Barclay thus accounts for the death of the unregenerate. The first Friends had said little about heaven and hell, focusing more on the soon-coming kingdom. Gwyn has talked about a spirituality of anxiety in relation to

Calvinist predestination (1995, pp. 80–1). Were people part of the elect or not? Obviously salvation was a primary concern in this age but the anxiety was fruitless (Matt 5:34) given that it was predestined. For these Quakers reading Barclay, however, and in particular for the daughters and sons of those who had experienced convincement, here was a doctrine bound to induce an anxious cautious waiting: 'I saw closely in that Day by that eye the Almighty had opened ... that unless I came to be acquainted with the same Power that had Wrought a Change and Alteration in my dear Parents ... I should be miserable and undone forever' (Deborah Bell, 1715, quoted in Vann 1969, p. 173).

The first generations of Friends had often left their families to be Quaker ministers. Nayler was instructed by God to do so and in 1696 John Love headed a tract *An Epistle to all Young Convinced Friends, whom the Lord hath reached by His mighty power, and separated from the World, and turned their Hearts, so as to forsake Father, and Mother, Wife, and Children, for his Name sake.* Vann has claimed that 'the conversion experiences of the first generation of Friends had usually taken place not in emulation but in defiance of parents' (1969, p. 174). Nicholas Gates 'became as an alien to my father's house ... and was rejected by my father, and many times threatened with being cast off; but the Lord was exceedingly good to me in my trials ... though I say I loved my father tenderly ... the Lord was more to me than my earthly father' (Vann 1969, p. 174). As the eighteenth century dawned, the Quaker household became more the focus of energy and attention, the primary unit of Quaker affiliation (Vann 1969; Damiano 1988, p. 185). The children of Quakers were necessarily to be brought up in the true church even whilst they had not yet made a voluntary confession of faith. In a world beset by continuing apostasy and spiritual corruption, the home and the Meeting House became the twin cloisters of spiritual renewal and purity. It was from here that Quakers would engage in the world's affairs, 'in the world but not of it' (cf. Rom 12:2). They never set up convents or monasteries or separated communities but they created what has been called a 'familied monasticism' (Abbott *et al.* 2003, p. 99).

Tousley has analysed the convincement narratives of the later seventeenth century in relation to those of the 1650s. She concludes that 'while the two generations have a similar explicit theology of revelation and knowing, the experience of second-generation Friends left more room for doubt and their narrative theology suggests greater reliance on other sources of knowledge' (2003, p. 78). Damiano argues that eighteenth-century Friends were still part of a realising eschatology in that they still lived under the direct guidance of Christ (1988, p. 96), but this seems an insufficient basis for claiming that the endtimes were still unfolding. Further, Tousley describes how the second-generation converts marginalised the eschatological vision or omitted it altogether from their accounts. Their spiritual epistemology seemed less secure and they no longer placed their personal salvation at the heart of a global eschatological picture. In turn this led for some Friends to a separation of justification and sanctification, a minimisation of the historic cross, and an ethical perfectionism in the place of sanctification through grace (Tousley 2003, p. 83). Critically, Barclay's *Apology* does not end with a proposition concerning eschatology but with 'salutations and recreations', i.e. how to live in the meantime.

Seeing the chief end of all religion is to redeem men from the spirit and vain conversation of this world, and to lead into inward communion with God, before whom if we fear always, we are accounted happy, therefore all the vain customs and habits thereof, both in word and deed, are to be rejected and forsaken by those who come to this fear; such as taking off the hat to a man, the bowing and cringings of the body, and such other salutations of that kind, with all the foolish and superstitious formalities attending them, all which man has invented in his degenerate state to feed his pride in the vain pomp and glory of this world, as also the unprofitable plays, frivolous recreations, sportings and gamings which are invented to pass away the precious time, and divert the mind from the witness of God in the heart, and from the living sense of his fear, and from that evangelical spirit wherewith Christians ought to be leavened, and which leads into sobriety, gravity, and godly fear, in which as we abide, the blessing of the Lord is felt to attend us in those actions, which we are necessarily engaged, in order to the taking care for the sustenance of the outward man. (Barclay 2002, p. 430)

Gone is the fearless sense of being a vanguard people on the cusp of the end of the world and the New Jerusalem. Instead, fear and sobriety are the meantime emphases Barclay insists on at the end of his *Apology*. The spatial dichotomy of inward and outward is as clear as it was for the first-generation Friends but the emphasis here on 'godly fear' sits more easily with the Quietist period, which followed Barclay's life, than with the Quakerism he first came to. This is a clear measure, given that Second Day's Morning Meeting approved this text for publication, of how far Quakerism had changed in twenty-five years following Fox's ascent

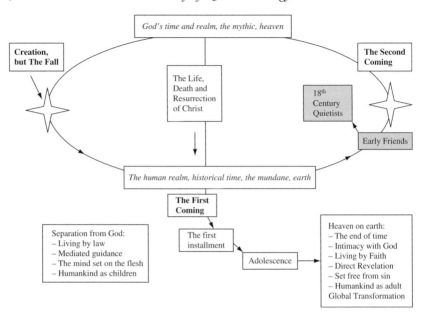

Fig. 1.6 A biblical understanding of time and eighteenth-century Friends

of Pendle Hill and the convincements at Firbank Fell and Swarthmoor Hall.

Barclay's defence of the Quaker eschewal of outward communion rests on an alternative interpretation of 1 Corinthians 11:26, and the meaning of the phrase 'break the bread until the Lord comes again', rather than on the more radical line taken by Fox, that Quakers had been called to a different supper, the marriage supper of the Lamb (after Rev 3:20). Barclay is not disputing the reality of the meantime, just how to wait. Barclay, and the Friends influenced by him, were firmly pressing the snooze button of the alarm clock of the second coming as if to say, 'not now, not yet'. In terms of our earlier diagram (see Fig. 1.4), this shift is represented in Figure 1.6.

QUIETISM AND DILIGENCE

Following 'restoration Quakerism' (Reay 1985, pp. 103–22), the eighteenth century represents a third period of Quaker theology. Alongside the more watchful attitude to soteriology implicit in Barclay, and the changes in knowing identified by Tousley, Rufus Jones has claimed that this period of Quaker thought and practice was underpinned by the influences of continental Quietism and the teachings of Molinos, Fénelon, and Guyon (1921, pp. 32–103). It is the influence of this theory that has led to this period of Quakerism now being routinely described as Quietist.

Key to Quietism is the idea that the path to God is based in retreat from the world and the self. There is a supernatural plane and a natural one. The natural one is corrupt and corrupting and the faithful in their aspiration towards the supernatural need to guard themselves against the worldly, both outwith and within their own selves. Guyon claimed, 'the soul must die to everything which it loves for self-sake, even to its desires for states of grace, gifts of the Spirit, supernatural communications, and salvation itself' (Jones 1921, p. 49). 'Sanctification is the attainment of the state of holy indifference, of absolute non desire' (p. 49).

Thus even the Quaker self was to be mistrusted as it was beset by human emotions and motives. Key was the need to follow the Light of Christ within rather than the human drives and preferences, 'natural willings and runnings'. Sarah Lynes Grubb wrote in 1780:

I am often afraid lest by indulging my own ideal of what is good, and not labouring after total resignation of mind … I should frustrate the divine intention, which may be to humble and reduce self more than flesh and blood would point out. (Jones 1921, p. 65)

Absolute passivity was seen as the highest form of prayer (p. 51). Jones quotes the epistles of London Yearly Meeting. The 1745 epistle tells Friends to:

wait diligently on the Lord … that you may witness His Holy Spirit to influence and direct you in all your words and actions: and as you attend with a single eye to its holy and unerring directions, you will be preserved from looking outward and having your expectations from abroad. (1921, p. 102)

Diligence was crucial and the dualisms between the self and God and the self and the world were explicit. The 1748 epistle included: 'wait in awful silence for the manifestations of the divine Life … not having your eye to man, but fixing your expectation on the Lord alone' (p. 102). This emphasis on getting the meantime right and on faithful waiting was made explicit in the 1789 epistle from London Yearly Meeting, part of which ran:

Wait in humble reverence for spiritual ability to worship acceptably the Lord of heaven and earth. Wait humbly and diligently in the spirit of your minds for the (inward) coming of Him who told His disciples, 'Without me ye can do nothing'; that ye may happily experience the influence of His Spirit to enlighten and

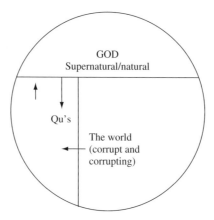

Fig. 1.7 Quietist Quakers and God and the world

quicken the soul to a true sight and sense of its condition; that feeling the spirit of supplication ye may approach the throne of grace. (p. 102)

Thus Quakers moved from a position of being co-agents with God released from the possibility of sin to a group of people, literally world- and God-fearing (see Fig. 1.7), potentially preoccupied with their propensity to sin. Both early and Quietist Friends believed in original sin but early Friends had a greater sense of sanctification which took them into a new spiritual plane, lifted out of the natural plane. The Quietists felt trapped there, a 'gathered remnant' needing to be diligent at all times. The Irish Friend Richard Shackleton wrote to his daughter:

Mayst thou, dear child, be preserved in simplicity and nothingness of self; in humility and lowliness of mind, seeking diligently after, and waiting steadily for, the inward experience of that which is *unmixedly good*. This is the way to be helped along from day to day, through one difficulty and proving after another, to the end of our wearisome pilgrimage. (p. 65)

Again, we have the emphasis on diligence and the dualism between the 'unmixedly good' and the 'difficulty and proving' of the pre-convincement life.

As with the early Friends, all was still to be guided and revealed directly. It was simply that Quietist Friends felt they had to be particularly careful in their discernment as to what was truly from God. Good examples of this care can be found in the stories of marriage plans described by Kathryn Damiano. Catherine Phillips waited twenty-three years before being sure that her intended was truly God's choice and not just her own. She even considered other men but finally, in 1766, she recounted, 'I had an intimation in my mind, which seemed to point to revival of our intimacy.' She married aged forty-six (Damiano 1988, pp. 183–4). When John Conran met Louisa Strongman:

I felt in silence, a strong draft of love more than natural, and a secret intimation impressed my mind that she would be my wife; this I hid in my heart, and it was nearly two years before I felt at liberty to disclose it to any one, waiting as I apprehend the Lord's time to communicate it . . . and when I felt the way open to proceed in it at that time, it was nearly six years after this before we were married. (Damiano 1988, p. 184)

Again, note the phrase 'more than natural' to signal the spiritual authenticity of the experience. It is clear that Quietist Friends were concerned with the discernment of the 'what?' and the 'when?', a practice parallel to the discipline of discerning when to minister in Meeting.

Being unfaithful could result in ministry which should not have been given or ministry never spoken which should have been. William Williams from North Carolina was laid low for several days in 1800 for failing to pray when bidden to by God at a Meeting in Tennessee.

At one of these little meetings the power of the Lord on me was so great that I could hardly sit still; and again I felt the word of command to fall down on my knees and supplicate the Most High. But I let in the reasoner again, and reasoned until meeting broke; and then, O! the horror I felt. And for many days it appeared that all goodness was withdrawn from me. O! then, how did I desire to feel one moment's presence of my Master, but could not. Then did I often retire to lonely places, and try to call on the name of the Lord my God, but could not find a word to utter before Him. Then did I again covenant, that if He would be pleased to appear again to my distressed soul, let Him require what He would, I would obey His command. But it was some time before He was pleased to show me his face again, so that my will for the present was fully brought down, and self laid low in the dust, when I was made willing, through His strength, to do His will, and what he might be pleased to require of me. And when the Lord of Glory knew I was fully humbled, He again appeared with the incomes of His precious love to my poor soul, and overshadowed me with His everlasting arm of strength, in such a manner that the whole man was made to bow before Him in awful solemn silence . . . It was an awful solemn time, and many sincere hearted friends were much affected, and broken into tears . . . O! the joy and sweet consolation I felt . . . feeling His love to fill my heart, but felt not the word of command for some time: – but as I was sitting in meeting with my mind much gathered and stayed on the Lord, I felt His power to overshadow me in a remarkable manner, and a Scripture text was brought to my remembrance, which I believed I was required to relate, with a few words of exhortation. (Jones 1921, pp. 90–1)

Reason was seen as the enemy of obedience and humility as its ally. The inward impulse had to be discerned but also acted on faithfully. Friends felt their lives ordered. In forty-six years of travelling in the ministry, Thomas Shillitoe claimed he felt led to face dangerous situations on numerous occasions, knowing God would not permit him to be harmed. At a more mundane level, he also once felt led to change his hotel room in Geneva three times (Jones 1921, pp. 94–100). Everything was to be guided and in everything Friends were to remain faithful. Twenty-two Meetings in a row in Dublin in 1770 passed without a word being spoken. Ministry was given in a distinct nasal tone to differentiate the divine message from the human vessel.

PECULIARITY, WORSHIP, AND MINISTRY

Barclay's *Apology* has Titus 2:11–14 on the front cover.

For the Grace of God that bringeth salvation hath appeared to all men, teaching us that denying ungodliness and worldly lusts, we should live soberly, righteously, and godly in this present world, looking for that blessed hope and glorious appearing of the great God and our Saviour Jesus Christ. Who gave himself to us, that he might redeem himself from all iniquity, and purify unto himself a peculiar people, zealous of good works.

There is here a meantime emphasis on anticipation but it is the last phrase which I want to highlight here: Quakers saw themselves as that peculiar people, purified unto Christ. Peculiarity was a positive term, found in Scripture (e.g. Exod 19:5, Deut 14:1–2) and today the practices of these Friends are still referred to as 'the peculiarities'. In the nineteenth century, as we shall see below, the value and nature of the 'hedge' these peculiarities set up between Friends and the world became highly contested (chapter 2). However, in the eighteenth century, they were, I suggest, a crucial means of helping this true church remain faithful.

Given that Quakers ceased to operate as a 'second coming church' and joined most of the rest of Christianity in the 'meantime', it would then have been totally legitimate to have altered the liturgical form so embedded in ideas of the beginning of the end. The inward marriage supper of the Lamb (Rev 3:20), the silence of worship mirroring the half hour of silence in heaven following the breaking of the seventh seal (Rev 8:1), the view of the rest of church practice as anachronistic, were all based in the sense of being beyond meantime, of the future rushing towards the present. By the end of the seventeenth century Friends did not hold this view. The loss of immediacy and sense of an unfolding second coming could have been used to justify the use of a Christian calendar, more outward liturgical forms, traditional Christian ways of helping humanity remain faithful.

However the foundational experience of the direct and intimate guidance of Christ remained, and with it the whole of the Quaker liturgical form, albeit in a new socio-theological context. Those with the gift of ministry were 'recorded' by their Monthly Meetings after 1722, a status held for life. In most Meeting Houses, these Ministers would sit above the Elders on a two-tier 'facing bench' on one side of a square of benches (Plate 7). However in general, as with membership lists ('the Rules of Settlement', which in 1737 recorded who belonged to which Meeting in relation to Quaker poor relief), this was a regulation of what had already been in place. These lists did not mark out spiritual achievement but simply the geography of those who had already committed and their children. Little in terms of the outward form of Quaker worship changed, except it shortened by about half an hour (a pattern repeated in each century) to two and a half hours. Quakers did not

Plate 7 Gracechurch Street Meeting, London, c.1770. Oil painting. The central figure ministering has been identified as Isaac Sharples

use the mechanics of the Quaker rite as a way specifically to help them remain faithful; what they used instead was the practice of travelling in the ministry and the peculiarities.

Travelling in the ministry was as old as Fox moving around England in the days before Quakerism. In the eighteenth century, with Monthly Meetings now sharing the authority of ensuring the survival and nurture of Quakerism, Ministers were given minutes of release or certificates for the service affirming their sense of call to travel amongst Friends. These could be very specific. Sylvia Stevens relates how Mary Kirby had a minute to travel amongst Friends in Ireland but then felt led to change her plans.

Our Friend Mary Kirby being return'd from her Religious Visit to friends in the North part of this Nation, gave an acct of her Visit to the following Import – that tho' when she first left us she apprehended her Concern lay chiefly for Ireland, yet as she passed along something seem'd to lay in Her way; but waiting to know the Lords mind herein; being desireous to walk in the way of duty, she found it her place to Visit the families of friends pritty generally in Westmorland in wch. service she was favour'd with the Company of several solid weighty Elders. (8 September 1765, as in Stevens 2004, pp. 80–1)

These Ministers would often feel led to minister at Meeting or at specially 'called' Meetings and would also sometimes give public talks, although their activity was often directed to the nurture of the church rather than to mission. Vann reports that there were few convincements in the first half of the eighteenth century and in some Meetings none in thirty years (1969, p. 205).

PUBLIC FAITHFULNESS

Paradoxically for a group so dedicated to the higher spiritual authority of the inward over the outward, it was the outward and visible expression of Quakerism which acted in the same way as the meantime practices of other churches. In other words, instead of altering the liturgical form, Friends helped each other remain faithful by visibly and audibly separating themselves from the world. Endogamy, plain dress, plain speech, the avoidance of the arts, literature and anything which was fictional or might excite the emotions, a separated and only basic education for Quaker children, and the testimony against the world's ways (for example resistance to gravestones and 'times and seasons' (see pp. 26–7 above) and war), all acted as a collective mutually reinforced reminder of what the group was trying to achieve. It did not alter its collective apostolic succession but found ways to affirm it within the new theological and experiential framework. The group saw itself as led by revelation and remained convinced that this was the highest form of spiritual authority.

Alongside this came respectability, a shift which eased the inclusion of Quakers in the Act of Toleration. In the 1802 *Extracts*, there is advice on Civil Government dating from Yearly Meeting, 1689.

Advised to walk wisely and circumspectly towards all men, in the peaceable spirit of Christ Jesus, giving no offence or occasions to those in outward government, nor way to any controversies, heats, and distractions of this world, about the kingdoms of it; but to pray for the good of all, and submit all to that divine power and wisdom, which rules over the kingdoms of men. (*Extracts*, 1802, p. 15)

The highest authority was still God but outward government was to be respected too. Number 6 of the Advices to Ministers and Elders of the same year read: 'Men and women are cautioned against travelling as companions in the work of ministry: to avoid all occasions of offence' (*Extracts*, 1802, p. 150). Outward respectability before the world had become important for its own sake, it seems. The Queries were used for corporate reflection and response to Quarterly and Yearly Meeting. Numbers 7, 8, and 9 of the men's queries for 1802 read as follows:

VII. Do friends bear a faithful and Christian testimony against receiving and paying tithes, priests' demands, and those called church rates?
VIII. Are friends faithful in our testimony against bearing arms, and being in any manner concerned in the militia, in privateers, letters of marque, or armed vessels, or dealing in prize-goods?
IX. Are friends clear of defrauding the king of his customs, duties, and excise, and of using or dealing in goods suspected to be run? (*Extracts*, 1802, p. 143)

Here, we can see a blending of traditional Quaker testimony on issues of integrity with a fresher concern for the monarch's excise.

The dangers to the Quaker were worldliness and the self. There was a preoccupation with who was a Quaker, where you were a Quaker, and how you were to be as a Quaker. The first Friends were obvious through their dress and speech but even so Business Meetings were only open to 'the fit': Friends should 'send from their respective Meetings, such persons as they know to be faithful to Truth, and fittest to do service to the Lord in the monthly and Quarterly Meetings' (Vann 1969, p. 110). One Quietist family refused to teach their children the Lord's Prayer for it was too much like learning by rote (Isichei 1970, p. 24). Bible learning, for the Quietists, was 'a carnal wisdom, a head knowledge, outward learning' (Isichei 1970, p. 24). It was this reliance on the inward that would later allow Evangelical Friends to question the idea of the inward Light as being potentially based on feeling, an idea which horrified the Quietists as much as it did the Evangelicals (see p. 93 below). Amos 6:1, 4–7 was used to warn of being 'at ease in Zion' and there were frequent warnings about overtrading and the danger of wealth (Braithwaite 1919, p. 512). For instance, Solomon Eccles was a music teacher when he joined Friends in the 1660s. He felt compelled to sell his violins but then felt a further impulse that he buy them back and set fire to them: when the crowd tried to prevent him, he smashed them with his feet (Greenwood 1978, pp. 13–14). For Roger Hebden, a Quaker draper, it meant burning all his ribbons (Braithwaite 1919, p. 515).

(see p. 93 below)

MAINTAINING FAITHFULNESS

The aspects of the religious life that had once been the consequences of spiritual experience, such as plain dress and plain speech, became part of a code of behaviour and consumption which was used to try to defend the spiritual. What had been consequences of the faith became rules of the faith. Two cousins from Munster in Ireland, Joseph Pike and Samuel Randall, were appointed to visit Friends in their homes in the 1690s. Persecuted less than in Britain, Quakers in Ireland were concerned to safeguard the spiritual life in the face of worldly freedoms and material success, and strict discipline was adopted earlier than in Britain (Braithwaite 1919, p. 502). Pike was a zealous advocate, and the two men decided to start with their own homes. Pike recounts:

As to our own clothing, we had but little to alter, having both of us been pretty plain in our garb, yet some things we did change to greater simplicity. But my dear cousin, being naturally of a very exact and nice fancy, had things in more curious order as regards household furniture than I had: and therefore as a testimony against such superfluities and that spirit which led into it, he altered or exchanged, as I did, several articles that were too fine ... Our fine veneered and garnished cases of drawers, tables, stands, cabinets, escritoires, & c., we put away, or exchanged for decent plain ones of solid wood, without superfluous garnishing or ornamental work; our wainscots or woodwork we had painted of one plain colour; our large mouldings or finishings of panelling, & c., our swelling chimney-pieces, curiously twisted banisters, we took down and replaced with useful plain woodwork, & c.; our curtains, with valences, drapery and fringes that we thought too fine, we put away or cut off; our large looking-glasses with decorated frames we sold, or made them into smaller ones; and our closets that were laid out with many little curious or nice things were done away. (Braithwaite 1919, p. 507)

'Plain' is the key word here. Peter Collins suggests that Quakers 'plained' their lives and their Meeting Houses and that 'plaining' acted as the creation of a symbolic order *vis-à-vis* the apostate church they defined themselves against (1996). Plaining points towards the inward spirituality even whilst its emphasis is the outward reduction of superfluity. Collins suggests that theologically it points to the hidden, to God, only to be revealed once the outward is removed (Collins 1996, p. 285). Fox had issued this advice on dress in 1688:

Away with your skimming-dish hats, and your unnecessary buttons on the tops of your sleeves, shoulders, backs and behind on your coats and cloaks. And away with your long slit yokes on the skirts of your waistcoat; and short sleeves, and pinching your shoulders so as you cannot make use of your arms, and your short black aprons and some having none. And away with your visors, whereby you are not distinguished. From bad women, and bare necks, and needless flying scarves like rollers on your back. (Braithwaite 1912, p. 511)

Superfluity is constrasted with necessity. London Yearly Meeting minuted in 1709 that all should be 'examples to their children, in wisdom, moderation, and plainness in language and habit' (*Extracts*, 1802, p. 131).

Fashion became a preoccupation for Quakers, with women's fashions a particular concern of men. David Hall wrote in 1758:

Of all the giddy Modes, antick and fantastick Inventions, that ever old Satan or his Agents, with respect to external Dress, have hitherto vampt up, since the Fall of Adam; was there ever any Thing contriv'd so much for the Ruin of Female Modesty, and the Incitement to Sensuality and Corruption, as these immodest, indecent, odious, extravagant Hoops. (Vann 1969, p. 194)

As the latter part of the quotation suggests, this says more about the man's sense of threat to integrity than that of the wearer. In November 1714, even wigs were regulated: 'if any Friend wants hair, they should acquaint the men's meeting they belong to, and have approbation and consent, before they get any' (Vann 1969, p. 192). The reference to men's Meeting means that it is likely wigs for men are being talked about.

Perhaps sensing where this increasing attention to detail may lead, Margaret Fell, as early as 1700, described the Quaker dress code as a 'silly poor gospel':

Christ Jesus saith, that we must take no thought what wee shall eat, or what wee shall drink, or what we shall put on: but bids us consider, the Lillies how they grow in more Royalty than Solomon [Matt 6:28–31]: But contrary to this wee must look at no Collours, nor make any thing that is changeable Collours as the hills are, nor sell them, nor wear them. But wee must bee all in one Dress, and one Collour; This is a silly poor Gospell, It is more fitt for us, To be which Leads us, and Guides us into Righteousness, and to live Righteously and Justly and hollyly in this profane evill world: This is the Cloathing that God putts upon us, and likes, and will bless. (Glines 2003, p. 471)

POLICING FAITHFULNESS

Fell's view of a 'silly poor gospel' notwithstanding, the regulation of this movement led by the Spirit had always been necessary and had become more visible as the movement grew. We can think of the Balby Epistle in late 1656 after the Nayler incident and the laying down of the Business Meeting structure in the 1670s (see pp. 44–9 above).

As Vann has pointed out, the eighteenth century saw advice become codified and enforced. As the century wore on, the list of rules increased, particularly in the mid-part of the century when Friends on both sides of the Atlantic began to feel that their diligence was lacking (see p. 73 below).

The 1738 list of extracts and advices was published as the first British 'book of discipline' in 1783. This was all part of a much longer-running shift of energy away from converting the world to Quakerism towards a presentation of Quaker spiritual purity to the world and of maintaining the faith. The index of the similar 1802 edition is telling: it is a compendium of testimony, a guide to the way in which Friends aspired to approach life. Chapters are listed alphabetically and the elements of general advice to particular discipline sit side by side. As well as advice on plainness and simplicity, including strongly worded opposition to mourning habits and gravestones, there are the more publicly political traditions of opposing all outward wars, gaming, and tithes, and the need to affirm in court rather than swear an oath.

Because of the Quietist mindset of the transatlantic Quaker community, these first books of discipline were books of practice and the faith that underpinned it. There was little explicit doctrine here other than that associated with the testimony of practice. The whole book was a reflection of Quaker testimony rooted in the spiritual experience of the group. However, as Margaret Fell had suggested, sociologically, consequence had become form. From being apostles to change the world, Quakers became a discrete people. The Light remained the Light of Christ but acted within reason and conscience (Barclay 2002, pp. 125–6).

A major question facing Friends was how to treat those who transgressed. Yearly Meeting in 1706 talked of exclusion offences (Vann 1969, p. 110) but, even earlier, Friends had been at times keen to distance themselves publicly from those 'running out from the truth' or denying their Quakerism, and thus their part in the true church. Quaker identity became constructed around performance ethics. Disownment was about the maintenance of spiritual purity within the group to avoid contamination from worldly ways and the presentation of this purity to the outside world to obviate criticism and as a model of the gathered community.

Marietta's 1984 study of discipline and 'reformation' within Philadelphia Yearly Meeting is highly instructive. Table 1.2 charts the offences of Quakers who violated the discipline between 1682 and 1776 across four Quarterly and nineteen Monthly Meetings in Pennsylvania, which comprised most of Philadelphia Yearly Meeting.

Table 1.2. *Offences, 1682–1776, across most of Philadelphia Yearly Meeting;*
N = 12,998 (Marietta 1984, pp. 6–7)

Offence	Number	Percentage of total	Percentage disowned
Marriage delinquency	4925	37.4	45.8
Sectarian delinquency			
Drunkenness	1034	7.8	60.9
Military activity	504	3.8	71.0
Inattendance	497	3.8	70.8
Disciplinary[1]	408	3.2	77.1
Loose conduct	359	2.7	54.3
Profanity	231	1.8	68.9
Attending irregular marriage	217	1.6	27.4
Quarrelling	214	1.6	41.1
Entertainments	178	1.4	39.9
Neglecting family responsibilities	142	1.1	49.6
Use of law[2]	129	1.0	31.7
Gambling	107	0.8	48.1
Disapproved company	81	0.6	75.0
Business ethics	64	0.5	70.3
Schism	54	0.4	28.8
'Gospel order'[3]	38	0.3	56.8
Oaths	35	0.3	60.0
Voluntary withdrawal	35	0.3	94.3
Courting and fraternising	23	0.2	54.5
Public activity[4]	22	0.2	50.0
Lying	21	0.2	76.2
Disobeying parents	21	0.2	81.0
Dispensing liquor	21	0.2	23.8
Theology	15	0.1	20.0
Dress and speech	11	0.1	68.8
Printing	7	0.0	71.4
Sabbath breaking	5	0.0	60.0
Miscellaneous	42	0.4	31.7

Table 1.2. (*cont.*)

Offence	Number	Percentage of total	Percentage disowned
Sexual delinquency			
Fornication with fiancé(e)	1311	9.9	39.6
Fornication	727	5.5	70.6
Incest	174	1.3	75.7
Adultery	46	0.3	87.0
Delinquency with victims			
Debt	613	4.6	51.4
Assault	391	3.0	41.3
Slander	124	0.9	35.2
Slaveholding	123	0.9	22.0
Fraud	118	0.9	58.1
Theft	61	0.5	60.0
Violating laws	17	0.1	17.6
Destroying property	11	0.0	36.4
Fleeing master	9	0.0	76.2
Counterfeiting	7	0.0	57.1
Smuggling	6	0.0	50.0

Notes:
[1] Disciplinary violations were occasions when the offender showed contempt for the Society's authority over his conduct.
[2] This violation is the prosecution at law of one Friend by another, without having exhausted the arbitration procedure of the Society.
[3] 'Gospel order' was Quaker arbitration. Violators ignored it in various ways. One of them was to seek redress at law and this error is separately tabulated here.
[4] Prohibited public activity was the holding of public offices that entailed activity that violated Quaker ethics.

The most common form of offence was breaking the rule of endogamy and/or of not marrying under 'the care of the Meeting'. In Marietta's table, this accounts for 37.4% of all offences and nearly half of all disownments. If a Friend wanted to marry a non-Friend this would need to take place before a priest because of the rule on marrying only other Quakers. Equally, a Friend wishing to marry another Friend but failing to secure the permission of the parents, and therefore the Meeting, might also 'run out from the Truth' and marry before a priest.

Sexual delinquency was more difficult to detect. Marietta claims that Meetings would act on rumours when more explicit evidence, such as being seen, or parenthood, was not available (1984, p. 11). Getting married whilst secretly pregnant could bring a double dose of disapprobation once the truth was out (Marietta 1984, p. 13). 'Fornication with Fiancee' was an offence under Quaker law even whilst it was accepted behaviour in 'the world'. Similarly, British Quakers forbade marriage between first and second cousins whilst the state tolerated it. (This prohibition accounts in part for the incest figure in Table 1.2.) After 1753, Philadelphia Yearly Meeting forbade marriage to the spouse of a dead sibling or to the sibling of a dead spouse. Those who committed fornication while betrothed were twice as likely to be readmitted as those who were not. There was also the moral point that such transgression at least appeared monogamous (Marietta 1984, p. 14). Marietta claims that this was not an attempt to increase numbers, as the membership of children was discouraged after the 1750s and proselytisation was not a dominant activity. Rather, he claims, it was a way of reducing the number of bastard Quakers who would need the assistance of the public Treasury. Adultery was one of the most disownable offences at 87% of all cases (Marietta 1984, p. 19). Men were twice as likely to commit this offence as women.

What Marietta refers to as sectarian delinquency involves those activities, excluding marriage, which only Friends found wrong, such as non-attendance at Meeting, and those forbidden by law generally, such as drunkenness, gambling, etc. They are included in this category because Friends paid particular attention to them even as the state became more tolerant. Drunkenness was seen as a particular problem because typically that offence would lead to another: Marietta gives a figure of 50.1% of drunkenness offences being compounded by a subsequent one (1984, p. 19). Also, it was often a very conspicuous category of delinquency. Non-attendance was also usually a compound offence and rarely the sole transgression (Marietta 1984, p. 21). Perhaps their other offences, such as irregular marriage, kept the Friends away. Not surprisingly, we see that 77.1% of those who disregarded the authority of the Religious Society were disowned. Marietta claims the category of 'loose behaviour' was similar to the Roman Catholic idea of 'near occasions of sin', e.g. flirtations without fornication, liaisons without adultery: 'In sum, the Society of Friends had not just a code of behaviour, but a style as well, and one could be ignored just for ignoring the style' (1984, p. 22). Delinquency involving victims accounts for only 11.2% of offences for this period. It is noteworthy that debt itself was not treated as delinquent, but careless or wilful debt was. Debt, again, was often a compound offence, linked mostly with drunkenness and non-attendance.

When a Friend transgressed the discipline (and thus gospel order, the God-given ecclesiology) and was reported, the Meeting appointed several Friends to visit the delinquent, inform him or her of the allegations, and ascertain his or her disposition. Was the Friend disposed to admit guilt and condemn the breach or refuse to condemn it and face disownment (Marietta 1984, p. 5)? To condemn the breach involved preparing a confession and appearing before the Monthly Meeting. The Friend would also need to attend his or her own Worship Meeting and have the paper read out (Marietta 1984, p. 7). The confession or the notice of disownment would also be posted outside the Meeting House to inform the world's people of the confession, or of the disownment where the Friend had refused to admit wrong. If the offence had taken place in a particular location, the paper would be read out there. If it was widely known, the paper would be widely circulated, as in the case of Edward Shippen in 1706, who had been a very public political figure and whose offence of marrying his third wife before a priest was well known (Marietta 1984, p. 9). This was all about the presentation of purity, the continued public cloistering of the peculiar people, but also about the nature of the true church. The case of Grace Hawks provides a telling example of how far Friends would go to distance themselves from any perception of spiritual delinquency. Vann claims:

Grace Hawks of Chesham 'from a child had been accustomed to go with her mother to Meetings'. But she 'ran out from Truth' in marrying a man of 'the world'. She was ordered on 1 August 1687 to write a paper condemning her action, because '(although Friends that knew her, seeing her to be a proud vain Lass, did never value her as a friend, yet) by reason of her so going to Meetings, the World's people there do in some measure account her a Quaker'. (Vann 1969, pp. 135–6)

In this case, the Meeting is claiming that the woman is not a Quaker but is proceeding against her because the world may think she is. In other words, the Meeting is ordering a non-Quaker to conform to the discipline of the group because some may think she belongs to the group. Disownment was, thus, about denying the Quakerism of the delinquent.

'Right ordering', i.e. due process, was crucial. One Quarterly Meeting reinstated a member because the Monthly Meeting had failed to show him his disownment paper before publishing it (Marietta 1984, p. 8). Self-condemnation without a confession would still lead to disownment. Equally, lack of humility or sincerity even within correct process would not convince the Monthly Meeting to waver from the default position of disownment (p. 8). Women and men were disowned to an equal degree (p. 30). However, some Monthly and Quarterly Meetings tended to be more severe than others (p. 27) so the normative style of Quakerism, or the seriousness with which it maintained its discipline, varied. Also, some of the more severe Quarters, such as Chester County in Pennsylvania, would later pioneer the Quaker reformation of the latter part of the eighteenth century.

Disownment was not necessarily final, although convincing the Meeting to readmit an offender was not always easy. Disownment did not mean not being able to attend Meeting, which was, after all, public. It meant the ex-Friend could not call themselves a Quaker, attend Meeting for Worship for Church Affairs (i.e. Business Meeting), and could not have recourse to Meeting funds. It is worth remembering that the formal 'lists of settlement', or membership lists, were all to do with managing poor law relief. This financial aspect is part of the reason why even today a Friend cannot normally be a member in two places. In the case of marrying another Friend before a priest, the family and the Meeting might not disown or might readmit after a time. Where the Friend had married a non-Friend but could show that both were living as Quakers and attending worship, and were contrite about their original offence, then the Meeting might readmit. However, Moses West, in his widely circulated *A Treatise on Marriage*, had the following to say about the contamination by the non-Quaker, one of the world's people, at worship.

Non-Quaker spouses brought to Meeting by the 'violators of endogamy' created 'an inlet to much degeneracy, and mournfully affected the minds of all those who labour under a living Concern for the Good of all, and the Prosperity of Truth Upon Earth'. (Marietta 1984, p. 65)

Where an offence created a victim, as was the case with bankruptcy for example, the Meeting required the demands of the victim to be met before considering readmission. This might take many years but once the demands were satisfied, both of the victim and of the Meeting, the Friend could be readmitted. Marietta claims that no offence was without the possibility of readmission (1984, p. 10).

THE REFORMATION OF QUAKERISM

The reformation Marietta charts happened simultaneously on both sides of the Atlantic, transmitted across the transatlantic Quaker culture (Tolles 1948) mainly through the system of travelling ministers. For example, John Churchman of Chester County (1705–75), who would become one of the leading pioneers of the reformation in Pennsylvania, felt his call to this ministry whilst travelling in the ministry in London (Marietta 1984, p. 34). Churchman was a thorough Quietist, waiting always on inward guidance and encouraging the autonomous unmediated spiritual life. He was Pietistic and wary of enthusiasm. Churchman took a scrupulous line with those he felt to be falling short of the discipline, refusing to eat in their homes for example, and on his mission to England sat silent through many Meetings instead of giving the expected vocal ministry because he felt the Meeting lacking in spiritual depth. He found a relaxed Quakerism overfond of extravagance and pride, and susceptible to exogamy, drunkenness, deism (see p. 83 below), and the payment of tithes. These were the unconvinced, the Quakers in waiting, but ones who had perhaps relaxed their anxiety about outliving their day of visitation. Churchman was opposed to birthright membership (Marietta 1984, p. 35).

Structural reform accompanied spiritual renewal. Churchman and his companions, John Pemberton and William Brown, suggested to London Yearly Meeting in 1753 that Ministers and Elders meet immediately prior to Yearly Meeting and that a Women's Yearly Meeting be set up to complete the symmetry of the corporate expression of gospel order. The former new Meeting began in 1755, the latter in 1784.

One of Churchman's English collaborators was Samuel Fothergill and he accompanied Churchman back to Philadelphia in 1754. He was to stay two years and unlike Churchman was an ardent and eloquent preacher. Fothergill famously told Pennsylvania Quakers:

Their fathers came into the country in its infancy, and bought large tracts of land for a trifle; their sons found large estates come into their possession, and a profession of religion which was partly national, which descended like the patrimony from their fathers, and cost as little. They settled in ease and affluence, and whilst they made the barren wilderness as a fruitful field, suffered the plantation of God to be as a field uncultivated, and a desert. Thus, decay of discipline and other weakening things prevailed, to the eclipsing of Zion's beauty . . . A people who had thus beat their swords into plowshares, and the bent of their spirits to this world, could not instruct their offspring in those statutes they had themselves forgotten. As every like begets its like, a generation was likely to succeed, formed upon other maxims, if the Everlasting Father had not mercifully extended a visitation, to supply the deficiency of their natural parents. (Marietta 1984, pp. 40–1)

By 1755, there was a clear and visible group of reforming Ministers on both sides of the Atlantic. The cause in Pennsylvania was aided by the conversion to reform of Israel Pemberton Jr, Clerk of the Yearly Meeting and a person of great energy and standing. Reforms rolled out from the 1755 Yearly Meeting onwards.

Marietta claims that the zeal of the reforming movement mirrored the degree to which the 'world' began to see Quakers not as benign but as eccentric or awkward. In numerical minority within Pennsylvania, a consequence of universal religious toleration, Quakers were to leave the Assembly *en masse* after 1756 to avoid compromise, institute renewed

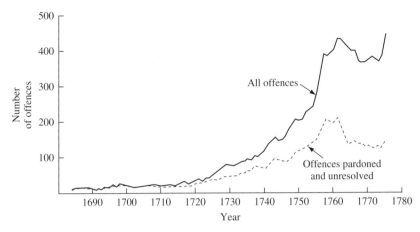

Fig. 1.8 Three-year moving average of total offences per year and offences pardoned
and unresolved (after Marietta 1984, p. 48)

testimony against war, and begin to campaign corporately against slavery. As the eighteenth century wore on, the number of offences grew in line with tightening of the discipline. In Britain membership fell, but to the architects of reformation and to the Quietist sectarian mindset, this was only further proof of purity and the fact that the corrupting world would cause some to fall away from the true church. Rather than be a cause for concern, falling numbers affirmed the spiritual integrity of the cloistered group. In Britain, the advice of 1717 on removing gravestones where Friends had fallen into that vain custom had to be repeated in 1766 (*Queries and Advices*, 1802). In America, numbers rose but the number of offences also grew (Fig. 1.8). In 1760, London Yearly Meeting agreed to the systematic visitation of all Monthly Meetings by Elders to report on the health of the Meetings.

QUAKERS AND SLAVERY

Marietta notes that the economic value of slaveholding held up its abolition within Quaker circles. Additionally, many of the early abolitionists were tainted by the 'heresy' of George Keith and his Christian Quakers (see Box 7) who had advocated abolition, or by their own disorderliness (1984, p. 112). Benjamin Lay, the anti-slavery campaigner active in the 1730s and disowned in 1738, was seen as less than sane for his personal preferences of

---

Box 8 John Woolman (1720–1772)

John Woolman was a New Jersey Friend best remembered for his campaign against slaveholding within the Religious Society and his devotion to discerning the will of God in his daily life. In 1756, at the height of the Quaker reformation (see p. 73 above), he gave up his retail business to focus on his spiritual life. The following gives an example of his mystical experiences:

> THIRTEENTH fifth month, 1757. – Being in good health, and abroad with Friends visiting families, I lodged at a Friend's house in Burlington. Going to bed about the time usual with me, I awoke in the night, and my meditations, as I lay, were on the goodness and mercy of the Lord, in a sense whereof my heart was contrite. After this I went to sleep again; in a short time I awoke; it was yet dark, and no appearance of day or moonshine, and as I opened mine eyes I saw a light in my chamber, at the apparent distance of five feet, about nine inches in diameter, of a clear, easy brightness, and near its centre the most radiant. As I lay still looking upon it without any surprise, words were spoken to my inward ear, which filled my whole inward man. They were not the effect of thought, nor any conclusion in relation to the appearance, but as the language of the Holy One spoken in my mind. The words were, CERTAIN EVIDENCE OF DIVINE TRUTH. They were again repeated exactly in the same manner, and then the light disappeared. (Moulton 1989, p. 57)

His journal remains a classic spiritual autobiography, but his essays are also noteworthy. Most notable are *Some Considerations on the Keeping of Negroes* (1754), which was influential amongst Philadelphia Friends, and *A Plea for the Poor* (published in 1793) (Heller 2003, p. xiv). He was concerned on a whole range of justice issues. Whilst travelling in the ministry, he remained active in the organisational life of his local Meeting. He died of smallpox in England.

---

living in a cave, refusing to drink tea or wear the wool of any animal or eat meat, and for advocating abolition. Lay wrote:

I know no worse or greater stumbling blocks the devil has to lay in the way of honest inquirers than our ministers and elders keeping slaves; and by straining and perverting Holy Scriptures, preach more to hell than ever they will bring to heaven by their feigned humility and hypocrisy. (Marietta 1984, p. 113)

Twenty years later, John Woolman (1720–72), who wore undyed homespun clothes, and who refused to take sugar or use silver tableware because of their connections with slavery, and who travelled long distances on foot at times (see Box 8), was given a better reception. Women Friends dyed and redyed their bedspreads with walnut leaves rather than use indigo, a product of the slave trade. Attitudes shifted in two decades (Marietta

1984, p. 113). In 1754, Philadelphia Yearly Meeting published Woolman's *Some Considerations on the Keeping of Negroes* and included extracts in its Yearly Meeting epistle. Abolitionists such as Anthony Benezet were by this stage in positions of authority and responsibility. In 1758, the same Yearly Meeting proscribed the buying or selling of slaves, although this carefully failed to discipline existing ownership. It was 1776 when Philadelphia Yearly Meeting finally made slaveowning a disownable offence.

This progress mirrors in some regards the parallel withdrawal of Philadelphia Friends from the wider 'world'. The increased sectarianism after 1756 accommodated and affirmed this non-wordly repositioning on slaveowning (Marietta 1984, pp. 121–7).

SUMMARY

This period of Quakerism is not popular, either with the Quakers who worked against its continuing influence or amongst later scholars and historians. It remains under-researched and misunderstood. People see the rules and the disownments and a view of the self difficult to comprehend in today's psychologised world and fail to see the rich and deep spirituality of the journals, of the life underpinning the testimony (see Boxes 10 and 11 for accounts of how these Friends combined their testimony with industry and scientific enquiry). These Quakers too continued to campaign for reform and justice (note the opening of the innovative mental health hospital 'The Retreat' in York in 1793), particularly against slavery but also in the more mundane such as fixed-price trading which eventually became normative. Quietism represents the longest single period of Quaker theology to date, an enduring and distinctive interpretation of Quaker faith and practice.

It is easy to see how the world-rejecting Quietism could lead to alternative theologies separated from or antagonistic to Scripture such as deism or rationalistic perspectives on Scripture, or to a reaction based on a more world-affirming spirituality such as Evangelical Christianity. Theologically, Methodism lay between Quietistic pietism and the expressive Christianity of evangelicalism. As Churchman sat in Meetings silently as part of the campaign for reform, John Wesley attended the Methodist revival, attracting many Quakers to the movement. In Warrington, England, there was a group called the 'Quaker Methodists' (Punshon 1984, p. 150), but, as Punshon suggests, Quakers in Britain were not ready to become a mass movement again after the early days of the 1650s (p. 150) (see Box 9 for other examples of small-scale schism that took place in this period).

Box 9 Separations of the Quietist period

The 'Shaking Quakers', later Shakers, or more formally the United Society of Believers in Christ's Second Appearing, are a group who began as a breakaway from the Quaker Meeting in Bolton, England, in 1747. Led initially by the Wardleys, and later by 'Mother' Anne Lee (1736–84), the group moved to America in 1774 and became communitarian and celibate, establishing communities as far west as Kentucky. Their worship was ecstatic. They are also well known for their seed business, cooking, music, and furniture. A small group of Shakers continue to live in Maine.

Nicholites or 'new Quakers' were a separation initiated between 1766 and 1770 local to the Carolinas where Joseph Nichols gathered together Friends determined to take a stronger line on the issue of slaveholding. Wearing undyed clothing, as John Woolman did, these Friends were from all walks of life, from ex-slaves to ex-masters. They disapproved of riding except for long distances. Nichols died in 1770 and the group officially organised in 1774 but gradually reaffiliated with Philadelphia Yearly Meeting (Carroll 1962).

The Society of Free Quakers were those Friends disowned from taking up arms in the American War of Independence in the 1770s. They lamented their enforced separation and adopted a discipline which proscribed disownment. Their Meeting House in Philadelphia was used until 1836 and still stands today (Kashatus 1990).

Jemima Wilkinson (1752–1819), universal public Friend, was a Rhode Island Quaker disowned in 1776 for her association with the New Light Baptists, non-attendance, and failure to use the plain language. Two months later she felt herself to have died and been reborn as Christ come again. Her ministry as the Publick Universal Friend began. She converted her family first, then travelled widely preaching. Crowds came to hear her, given the variety of rumours that spread about her. The most famous legend about her was that she could walk on water. A test was set up. Opponents claimed she had a platform just beneath the surface to stand on; others claimed it had been taken away by the opponents before the time of the test. At the appointed time, Wilkinson asked her supporters if they doubted her ability to walk on water. They said they did not, and with that Wilkinson felt no further need to prove her divinity and turned back from the water's edge. Wilkinson settled a community in New York State and the Universal Friend's Society continued until 1863 (Wisbey 1964).

David Willson (1778–1866) led his group, the Children of Peace, out of New York Yearly Meeting in 1812. Having failed to gain readmittance to the Society, they remained a distinct group until 1889. They settled a village called Hope, built a magnificent temple at Sharon, Ontario, and adopted various Old Testament rituals. At one time they were renowned for the best silver band in the province. They were firmly pacifist and millennialist, expecting a messiah who would abolish British colonial rule in Canada (Schrauwers 1993).

Box 10 Quakers and industry

Denied access to the universities and the professions, Quaker work in the world was focused on commerce. The Quaker position in favour of fixed-price trading was influential but also gained them a reputation for honesty. Quaker businesses sometimes acted as banks too and two of the major British banks, Barclays and Lloyds (the latter now part of HSBC), had Quaker origins. Many food and clothing companies also had Quaker roots, such as Huntley and Palmer, Reckitt and Coleman, Macy's, Strawbridge and Clothier, and Clarks Shoes. The British chocolate companies of Cadburys, Frys, and Rowntrees are perhaps the most famous of these. Cocoa was originally a temperance drink but the development of chocolate made each of these companies a huge enterprise, sometimes in competition with each other. James Walvin (1997) tells the story of inter-Quaker industrial espionage! The Darby family of Coalbrookdale were at the forefront of the iron industry and manufacturing innovation across three generations and are said to have introduced the shift system of factory working. They are also an example of how Quaker families with similar business interests might intermarry. Quakers were also prominent in the development of the railway system in Britain and the Pease family at Darlington was so prominent in the commercial life of the town that the local football club is still nicknamed 'the Quakers'. In the twentieth century, the number of Quaker industrialists has fallen sharply. Scott Bader introduced the idea of a 'commonwealth' at his factory, whereby all those working there had a share of the decision-making and the profits, but in general Quakers have moved away from such direct involvement with industrial capitalism.

Box 11 Quakers and science

Whilst some of the earliest Friends claimed they saw creation anew as part of their convincement experience, later Quakers came to look for God within creation or justify scientific enquiry for its own sake. Geoffrey Morries' forthcoming doctoral thesis charts this in careful detail. Geoffrey Cantor has refuted the idea that Friends were vastly over-represented, given the population as a whole, as Fellows of the Royal Society prior to the mid-nineteenth century (2003, p. 223). However Quakers were, by the eighteenth century, embracing science and its practical applications. Quaker botanists, such as Peter Collinson and John Bartram, were at the forefront of their field, and John Dalton's work on atomic theory remained influential for centuries. Arthur Eddington was at the forefront of astrophysics in the twentieth century. Numerous Quaker scientists have been awarded Nobel prizes and today science is generally seen as a legitimate activity which can complement the religious search.

CHAPTER 2

The beginnings of Quaker diversity

The nineteenth century saw the fragmentation of Quakerism as a single transatlantic community (Tolles 1948). Where familial and geographical ties became distant, so did the sectarian impulse to cohere around a single identity separated from the world. On both sides of the Atlantic, Quakerism suffered defection and schism, as it had since its first years, but this time on a much larger scale. In Britain, over 400 would leave over the Beaconite controversy after 1836. By the middle of the century, in some areas of North America there would be as many as three Yearly Meetings each claiming to be the inheritors of the Quaker tradition. Quakerism ceased to be a coherent whole and for most Quakers their own self-perception ceased to be that of being the one true church. In other words, Quakers fragmented in the quest for a greater internal purity and integrity of interpretation. At the same time, they came to see that their own path, however hard they had fought to preserve it, was only one amongst many. In this way, Quakers came to see themselves as *part* of the true church in most of its branches by the 1820s rather than the *one true* church itself. This was timely, given the multiplicity of Quakers the enquirer could choose from by the end of the century. Even whilst each branch would claim to be the true Quakerism, they could at least offset the obvious criticism that each could not also represent one true church. In this way, as Isichei (1967, p. 162) suggests of British Friends in the Victorian era, Quakers 'denominationalised'.

Sects are defined sociologically in terms of voluntary association which makes high demands on its participants. Membership of denominations can be nominal and they are more permissive and more relaxed. The Quakers moved from operating a sect with very high internal demands on members – a separated language and a world-rejecting stance (Wallis 1984) – to one which was world-affirming. In other words, 'the world' shrank and ceased to include other Christians who were now seen as co-religionists rather than the apostate (see Fig. 2.3 below). This ecumenism can be found in Barclay's *Apology* but became pronounced and explicit in the nineteenth century as the urban elites of Quakerism started to mix with social counterparts of other churches and were influenced by evangelical revival. As Berger has suggested (1967, p. 141), it was also a way of pooling resources, for example in the campaign against slavery or in the work of Bible societies and adult literacy. It is important to remember that the Quietist influence in Britain had led to a severe drop in membership. For the Quietists, this was a mark of purity, a sign that they were indeed the gathered remnant as few could follow the narrow path. For the evangelicals, it was seen as a sure road to extinction. Thus, as evangelical influence grew, Quakerism was to open its doors to the world and relax its sectarian attitudes, a move which proved highly successful numerically: in Britain for example, numbers rose from about 13,000 members in 1860 to 20,000 in 1900.

Barry Reay (1985) suggests that Quakers lost their pure sectarian stance as early as the Restoration in 1660, and Richard Vann (1969) has charted the move from movement to organisation in the period 1655–1725. Niebuhr (1975) claims Friends denominationalised in the second generation but Isichei's thesis is more compelling.

The introduction of 'birthright membership' was a key factor in the institutionalisation of the movement in Vann's opinion (1969). It was a marker of a denomination in that membership was automatic rather than by voluntary confession. Theologically and sociologically nineteenth-century Friends were playing out the tensions of a transition from Quietist sect to evangelical denomination on both sides of the Atlantic.

Schism is rarely pleasant. Either those leaving are so disaffected that they set up something entirely new, as in the case of David Willson and the Children of Peace in Ontario in 1812 (see Box 9), or the protagonists reach a point of such personal antipathy that the issues take on a greater priority than the gospel injunction to love. Where Quakers broke ranks with Quakers, each claiming to be the true Quakers (and each claiming the minute book and Meeting House as their right), the animosity could be huge, and there are records of personal injury in the scuffles over property and legitimacy. Kinship ties and links to the wider Quaker family had become tenuous enough to accommodate and enable dissidence and open quarrel, and the group had become established enough within wider society that it seemed it could afford to air its conflicts freely. In this sense, schism was a luxury born of stability and self-assurance. Fox's advice in the seventeenth century had been clear: do not let rumour fly abroad, especially to the defaming of anyone (see p. 46 above). This was advice given to secure unity in the face of hostility. For such large-scale schism to take place implies a security or even arrogance in the face of societal acceptance. This was partly the reason the breaks were bigger in America. Not only were kinship ties less close and the geography of Quakerism ever expanding as the frontier moved and Quakers migrated, but Quakers in the colonies had often been running government at a time when their British counterparts had been petitioning for toleration. To reiterate (see p. 74 above), in 1756 most of the Quakers in the Pennsylvania Assembly chose to leave over the raising of yet more taxes for the Crown to fight the French. It was their choice. In Britain, Quakers would not be full citizens, able to go to the universities and join the professions without the spiritual compromise of assenting to the authority of the Church of England, until 1870. This socio-political disparity played itself out in the nature and range of disaffection and schism in the nineteenth century. If Quakers in Britain were to divide as completely as happened in America, it would have not been likely until after 1870, but then familial ties and the geographic proximity of this group of Quakers, bounded on a small island, acted as further deterrents. Finally, falling out with the state over conscription in 1916 sealed a more coherent unity. In North America in contrast, one schism led to another. First, counter-balancing influences were lost which led to the new traditions spiralling into further tensions. Second, once you had fought to the end over the nature of true Quakerism a first time, it was easier to do it a second, and in some cases, such as Ohio, a third or fourth. Third, numbers of Friends were far greater in North America, as the chart by Jennie Levin and Rebecca Berridge shows (see Fig. 3.8).

In Britain, numbers of Quakers increased through the 1670s (Lacock 2001, p. 99), but then fell though the Quietist period and reached an all-time low of 13,755 in 1864 (Stroud and Dandelion 2004, p. 122). This trend caused consternation amongst evangelicals and gave rise to a prize essay competition to air both symptoms of the malaise and its cure. John Stephenson Rowntree's winning entry included the following numerical analysis:

In 1856 the number of the Friends in England and Wales ('members') appears to have been 14,530. Adding 7,000 for non-members, and 4,000 for all, either in membership or profession, in Ireland, &c., we shall have a total, short of 26,000 persons in the United Kingdom, representing the entire numerical strength of the Society of Friends at the present time; equivalent to about one person in eleven hundred of the general population, as contrasted with one in one hundred and thirty in 1680. (1859, p. 76)

Evangelicalism espouses experiential faith in Christ guided by scripturally based doctrines, and is committed to mission rooted in love to convert those who have not yet found that path. As British Quakerism became evangelical in the nineteenth century, falling numbers seemed to contradict the logical consequences of the new missionary theology. Rowntree quoted marriage statistics as proof of decline. From 203 registered Quaker marriages in the early years (1640–59), a peak of 2820 was reached in the period 1670–79. There was steady decline throughout the eighteenth century and early nineteenth century, so that by the middle of the nineteenth century the total was a mere one tenth of its seventeenth-century peak (Rowntree 1859, p. 80).

The Quietists and their 'hedge' against the world were blamed, and the hedge, as we shall see (p. 113 below), was dismantled. In North America, numbers rose as the frontier moved westward and were never at a potentially fatal level. Thus, again, it was more possible for those in America to contemplate division. To do so in Britain, even after 1870, might have felt suicidal.

Aside from sociological reasons supporting the possibility of schism in North America and the difficulty of doing so in Britain, the theological stakes remained high for those involved, and should not be marginalised. It was not just Quaker identity that was at stake but the path to salvation, the means to remain faithful to God's will. Theological purity was crucial and arguments over doctrine replaced the disownment processes, over behaviour, that had characterised the Quietist period. The cases of Isaac Crewdson (see pp. 92–5 below) and David Duncan (pp. 117–18 below) were both symptomatic of this kind of debate. In time, doctrine would be replaced again by form and behaviour within British Quakerism, as it transformed itself in the twentieth century into a branch of Liberal Quakerism with an emphasis on experience over doctrine (chapter 3).

THE GREAT SEPARATION

DEISM AND RATIONALISM

The start of the nineteenth century brought with it two tendencies perceived as heretical by the majority of the Friends at the time, deism and rationalism. A third influence, evangelicalism, was also to take Quakerism in new directions but became part of Quakerism in a less contested fashion.

Deism was the idea that God had acted as a kind of divine clockmaker, who upon completing the creation had then let it run on its own (Cross and Livingstone 1997, p. 465). In other words, humanity had a responsibility to act as if it were now God as there was no higher power intervening.

This circumvented the philosophical problem of how a loving God could allow suffering in the world. It also allowed a more optimistic view of humanity and of society than the God- and world-fearing attitudes of the Quietists.

The second and related tendency was to approach faith from a rationalist perspective, putting reason above faith, or rational authority above scriptural. For both Quietists, who were fearful of human reason, and evangelicals, who were concerned for the authority of Scripture, this was a troubling theology. Two notable disownments at the turn of the nineteenth century (Abraham Shackleton in Ireland and Hannah Barnard of New York Yearly Meeting) were as a result of the questioning of scriptural authority. The 'New Lights', as Barnard and her followers were called, challenged the legitimacy and accuracy of Scripture when it contradicted their own 'sense' of what God was like. For example, Shackleton and Barnard claimed the Bible could not be inerrant as the God of the New Testament would never support such warlike sentiments as found in the Old Testament. This was rationalism mixed with an inward intuitive epistemology and equated to a form of deism.

The Rhode Island Quaker minister Job Scott befriended the Shackletons prior to his death in Ireland in 1793. Scott was not a deist but a Quietist who advocated the inward experience of God over any outward authorities and placed personal experience as central to authentic spiritual experience, after Jacob Boehme, William Law (Jones 1921, p. 290), and indeed George Fox. In this, he could find some sympathy for the inherent anti-evangelicalism of Shackleton's position. Scott wrote, 'Nothing but a true and living birth of God in the soul, of the divine and incorruptible seed, a real and substantial union of the divinity and humanity in one holy offspring, has ever brought salvation' (Jones 1921, p. 290).

Deist, rationalist, and extreme Quietist ideas flew in the face of growing evangelical influence. This influence came from wider society but proved increasingly persuasive. In 1805, Henry Tuke, who had already published *The Faith of the People Called Quakers in our Lord and Saviour Jesus Christ* in 1801, published his *Principles of Religion, as professed by the Society of Christians, usually called Quakers*. The latter volume went into twelve editions and Rufus Jones claimed that by the middle of the century 'there was hardly a single Quaker home which did not own a copy, and it became one of the greatest evangelical influences' (1921, p. 287). It is a book of theology firmly focused on the first coming of Christ and the propitiatory sacrifice. Scott refuted ideas of imputed righteousness and claimed that only the felt transforming experience of Christ being born within was authentic. In 1806 Philadelphia and Baltimore Yearly Meetings decided that to question the divinity of Jesus or the inerrancy of Scripture was a disownable offence. In Ireland in 1798, the same kind of formalism which had hastened the Quietist discipline there (see p. 66 above) asserted itself in favour of scriptural authority. In the next years a number of influential Irish Friends, taking up a position similar to Shackleton's, would leave and/or be disowned and this 'intellectual awakening' and its consequences weakened the Society there (Jones 1921, p. 298).

ELIAS HICKS

The suspicion of deism and rationalism was to haunt Quakerism throughout the century and would promote schism and charges of apostasy, although ultimately large parts of both Liberal and Evangelical Quakerism adopted a modernist rationalist approach (see Box 24). When Elias Hicks (1748–1828) of Jericho, New York, was identified by his critics as a theological trouble-maker, he was often branded with deism and rationalism, both inaccurate claims. Nevertheless, Hicks and his followers were to become the nemesis of the growing group of Evangelical Friends and the focus of their anxieties and concerns. In 1827, the point was reached where there was little love to be lost between the two camps and Yearly Meeting after Yearly Meeting began to divide.

Walt Whitman said of Hicks: 'The basic foundation of Elias was undoubtedly genuine religious fervour. He was like an old Hebrew prophet. He had the spirit of one and in his later years he look'd like one' (Kaplan 1982, p. 1242). He believed, after Scott, in 'a type of religion which began and ended in inward processes' (Jones 1921, p. 442), not external authority. He preached against deism, and was not a rationalist, 'modern', or a 'liberal' and not a logical thinker. He was against railways, schools, and Thanksgiving as a national holiday. However, in following Scott, the Light became almost equated with personal experience: it is wholly inward and assists reason. Human will has little part to play except in deciding whether or not to accept the Light (1921, p. 447). In this, Hicks is a typical Quietist: 'We must present ourselves as creatures who have no right to act anyway but to sit *as blanks* before God Almighty, with nothing included in our minds to hinder him from speaking' (1921, p. 448). Unlike earlier Friends, this emphasis on the inward led Hicks to such a critique of the outward that he did not admit the Bible as authoritative. Scripture led to superstition rather than authentic faith. The inward is wholly sufficient, a position that was bound to lead to increasing controversy with those

finding evangelicalism attractive. The historical Jesus was similarly marginalised as being outward but operated rather as an inward exemplar. Jesus
then was not Saviour but model. For Hicks, the Christ was the eternal
principle in the soul, and Jesus became the Christ through perfect obedience (Hamm 2003, p. 40). Most radical of Hicks' views was his rejection of
the fall and original sin and in turn of the atonement (Jones 1921, p. 453).
Righteousness came through obedience to the inward principle.

> This mode of redemption generally held by professing Christians as being effected
> by the death or outward dying of Christ Jesus upon the outward wooden cross . . .
> I consider a vulgar error, that came in with the apostasy from primitive
> Christianity. (Hicks, as in Jones 1921, p. 454)

Outward redemption would only release Jews from their outward rites and
mark the new dispensation. As such, inward redemption was the authentic
mode of salvation. True redemption comes from the death of the
corrupt will, an emphasis Hicks shared with the earliest Friends. But unlike
earliest Friends, Hicks believed that all God required was complete repentance and surrender and he took the idea of original sin out of the picture of
salvation.

Hicks was active in the itinerant ministry and drew attention to his views
in this way. As early as 1808, the French convert and Evangelical Friend
Stephen Grellet claimed that Hicks lessened the authority of the Holy
Scriptures. As early as 1793, two English Friends had claimed that Hicks
would one day 'be a troubler in Israel' (1921, p. 441). Jones argues however
that Hicks' views were not radically different from those of earlier Friends
but were stated more forcefully and unswervingly and, most significantly,
clashed so strongly with the prevailing transition from Quietism to evangelicalism (1921, pp. 457–8). In 1805 Philadelphia Yearly Meeting had
attempted to unite American Yearly Meetings within a uniform discipline,
an idea frequently revived in the following years as divisions became more
apparent.

SEPARATION IN PHILADELPHIA

In 1819, disapproval of Hicks became public. Hicks had left a men's
Meeting to adjourn to the women's Business Meeting, only for it to disband
in his absence. In 1822 there was more formal opposition. A number of
Philadelphia Elders requested a private interview with Hicks, having heard
reports of his unsoundness, but refused to proceed with the meeting
when Hicks turned up with friends and supporters. They signed a

document charging Hicks with 'holding and promulgating doctrines different from and repugnant to those held by our religious Society' (Jones 1921, p. 461). It was a form of disownment even though Hicks was from New York Yearly Meeting. On a procedural point, they initiated a theological divide and the existence of a public document encouraged the taking of sides. Hicks described the Orthodox Friends as resembling his 'no-horned cattle': they carried no outward weapon but 'had a hard bunch of bone on their heads which they cover with a soft bush of hair' (Ingle 1986, p. 17).

In 1823 Philadelphia Yearly Meeting narrowly avoided crisis by postponing a decision as to whether or not to accept an anti-Hicksite confession of faith authorised by Meeting for Sufferings (the executive body). 'Hicksites' thus found themselves aligned against the conservative Elders as well as against the evangelical elite of Sufferings. It was not Hicks himself who was centre stage in the 1827 separation but Thomas Shillitoe (1754–1836), a British Friend travelling in the ministry, with Jonathan Evans on one side, and John Comly, Assistant Yearly Meeting Clerk, on the other. Comly came to see that separation was inevitable but also might salvage the Society from total self-destruction. All three were Quietistic in their temperament, 'led' in their actions. Comly wrote:

My mind was opened to see that this contest would result in a separation of two conflicting parts of the Society, as the only means of saving the whole from a total wreck and the way and manner of this separation was clearly unfolded to my mental vision: that on the part of Friends it must be effected in the peaceable spirit of the non-resisting Lamb – first by ceasing from the spirit of contention and strife, and then uniting together in the support of the order and discipline of the Society of Friends, separate and apart from those who had introduced the difficulties, and who claimed to be the orthodox part of the Society. (Comly, as in Jones 1921, p. 465)

The issue had become the adoption of theological standards by the 'Orthodox' party as opposed to pure reliance on the inward advocated by the Hicksites. Ministry was traded on the issues. Shillitoe had written in his journal of a Meeting in Canada in late 1826:

Early in the meeting, I rose on my feet and delivered that which I believe was the word of God to the people. After I sat down, an acknowledged minister, who stood high with a party in the meeting, arose declaring that our supposing Adam's transgression had in any way affected his posterity was an absurd thing, and to suppose the coming of Christ in the flesh was to redeem mankind from sin, was equally absurd. Never before having heard such a manifest public avowal of anti-Christian principles, which were so evidently making their way in the minds of

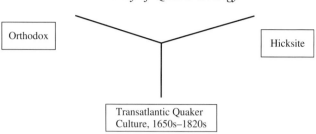

Fig. 2.1 The Great Separation

many of our society in this half-year's meeting, I was brought into a trying situation; but feeling I must not suffer the meeting to close without endeavouring, as help should be offered me, to maintain the ground I had taken in the opening of the meeting . . . I stood upon my feet and informed the meeting, notwithstanding what had last been communicated, was in direct contradiction to what I offered in the meeting, and altogether at variance with the well-known doctrines of the Society of which I was a member, yet I durst not recall a word of anything I had offered. In propagating these anti-Christian principles, a party spirit had so spread in the minds of some of the members of this meeting, and such opposition was manifested to the conducting the discipline in the true spirit of it, that the meeting sat from eleven in the a.m. until near six in the evening before it closed. (Dorland 1968, p. 143)

Comly had openly advocated separation in the time leading up to the 1827 Yearly Meeting. Indeed separation was suggested in the opening session of the Yearly Meeting after the Meeting could not find unity on the selection of a new Clerk, each party having its preferred candidate. In the end, the existing Clerk, the Orthodox Samuel Bettle, carried on, as no new decision had been made, with the Hicksite John Comly at his side. Separation was only sealed in the closing session of the Yearly Meeting when one Friend announced that a separated organisation (Hicksite) had already met at Green Street the previous evenings of April 19, 20, and 21, and had drawn up a document to send to all the constituent meetings (Fig. 2.1).

THE ISSUES BETWEEN HICKSITES AND THE ORTHODOX PARTY

The Green Street document read in part:

It is under a solemn and deliberate view of this painful state of our affairs, that we feel bound to express to you, under a settled conviction of mind, that the period has fully come in which we ought to look toward making a quiet retreat from this scene of confusion, and we therefore recommend to you deeply to weigh the momentous subject, and to adopt such a course as truth, under solid and solemn deliberation, may point to, in furtherance of this object, that our society may again enjoy the free exercise of its rights and privileges. (Jones 1921, p. 468)

The Hicksite party alluded here to constraint by the authority of the Elders. They continued:

And we think proper to remind you, that we have no gospel to preach; nor any other foundation to lay than that already laid, and proclaimed by our forefathers, even 'Christ within, the hope of glory' – 'the power of God and the wisdom of God.' Neither have we any other system of discipline to propose, than that which we already possess, believing that, whilst we sincerely endeavour to live and walk consistently with our holy profession, and to administer it in the spirit of forbearance and love, it will be found sufficient for the government of the church. (Jones 1921, pp. 468–9)

Again, the Hicksites drew a comparison between themselves and what they saw as the 'gospel' of the Orthodox party and its new modes of discipline.

And whilst we cherish a reasonable hope to see our Zion, under the divine blessing, loosen herself 'from the bands of her neck,' and put on her strength, and Jerusalem her 'beautiful garments,' and our annual and other assemblies again crowned with that quietude and peace which become our Christian profession; we feel an ardent desire that in all our proceedings tending to this end, our conduct toward our brothers may, on every occasion, be marked with love and forbearance: that when reviled, we bless; when defamed, we entreat; and when persecuted, that we suffer it. (Jones 1921, p. 469)

The reference to Isaiah 52:1–2 continues the theme of purity in opposition to the unclean and unchristian contamination of the Yearly Meeting. The final section is all about being seen to be the true inheritors of the true Christian (Quaker) inheritance, and an epistle from a Hicksite General Meeting in June 1827 talked of 'the blessings of a gospel ministry unshackled by human authority' and 'the preservation of our religious liberty' (1921, p. 469).

These were the issues for the Hicksite party. For the Orthodox, they saw the Hicksites as propagating a dangerous laxity about theology, one which could terminally corrupt or fragment the Society. The Orthodox produced a thirty-two-page Declaration following the separation. Part of it read:

The Society of Friends have always fully believed in the authenticity and divine authority of the Holy Scriptures, and acknowledge them to be the only fit outward test of doctrine, having been dictated by the Holy Spirit of God, which cannot err ... We believe it to be a religious duty thus to stand forth in the defense of the gospel of Christ, against the Spirit and principles of libertinism and infidelity. (Ingle 1986, p. 26)

The separation split families, and property became an issue everywhere as each side claimed to be the true Quakers and thus owners of the Meeting House and of the minute books, symbols of the true lineage. Both sides called themselves the Quakers and each side disowned the other. The Hicksites disowned the Orthodox for improper discipline, 'for deviating from the good order of the Society', and for setting up and/or attending 'separate meetings contrary to discipline' (Dorland 1968, p. 151); the Orthodox disowned the Hicksites for irregular theology. The idea of heresy and apostasy, previously reserved for those outside the one true church, was now applied to the deviant insiders, the zeal amplified by the intimacy of the problem.

Jones gives the numbers of Friends each side claimed. The Hicksites claimed that 18,485 of 26,258 stayed 'within' the Yearly Meeting (Jones 1921, p. 471) whereas the Orthodox party questioned the proportions in five of the eleven Quarterly Meetings. The majority of Ministers and Elders were Orthodox, as were the vast majority of Meeting for Sufferings. In line with the Hicksite grievance, the majority of those who carried and enforced the discipline were of the other party.

THE SPREAD OF THE SEPARATION

The Separation spread, partly because other Yearly Meetings needed to decide which of the two Philadelphia Yearly Meetings to recognise, partly under the catalytic influence of Thomas Shillitoe. The attendance of Hicksites, deemed no longer to be Friends by the Orthodox, at New York and Ohio Yearly Meetings also precipitated division. At New York Yearly Meeting in May 1828, Shillitoe rose immediately at the opening of Yearly Meeting to say that he felt it laid upon him to protest against the Meeting proceeding when so many 'who have no claim or right to sit in this Yearly Meeting' were present (Jones 1921, p. 475). Hicks disagreed. Disagreement broke out about whether or not the Yearly Meeting should proceed and the Clerk, Samuel Parsons, sensing separation, prepared a minute of adjournment. Shillitoe reports that the Hicksites tried to prevent Parsons reading the minute:

'Don't let him read it' – 'Pull him down'; – others calling out, 'He is no Clerk of the Yearly Meeting, – we have a Clerk of our own; – the representatives have met and we have chosen a new Clerk.' . . . E. Hicks then called upon their new-chosen Clerk to come forward, which he did over the backs of the forms, and heads and shoulders of Friends . . . on his reaching the front of the Clerk's table, E. Hicks put out his hand to assist him in gaining admittance to the table, but by some means, he failed, on which some of the Hicksite party turned their newly-chosen Clerk heels first into the Clerk's seat. Attempts were now made to wrest the minute the Clerk had made out of his hands, which they were not able to effect, nor prevent his reading of it; but to preclude what he thus read being heard over the meeting, they struck their sticks against the wall of the house, they stamped on the floor with their feet and umbrellas, they hooted and hissed, and some were heard to swear: the windows being down, the tumult was so great, people outside of the house compared it to thunder at a distance. The minute of adjournment being read, Friends left the house and went towards the basement-storey, but care had previously been taken by the Hicksite party to keep Friends out of this part of the house by locking the doors against them; one of their party threatened Friends with consequences if they attempted an entrance, on which a Friend present proposed our adjourning to the medical college in Duane Street, which accordingly took place. From the solemn manner in which Friends moved slowly along the streets, many strewing their tears on the way, from having left behind them some near relatives and some intimate friends, together with the painful feelings occasioned by the scene of uproar and violence they had so recently escaped, inquiry was made by people, 'Was a burial coming?' On reaching the college, and after taking our seats, a time of silence ensued; praises were vocally offered up to the Great Shepherd of Israel for this signal deliverance of his people when the waters of the Red Sea were made to stand on heaps. (Jones 1921, pp. 476–7)

The bias and flourish are clear and yet the pain and violence of the situation undeniable. The distress for some was purely in the process.

What a gloomy day we live in! Darkness seems to cover the earth and gross darkness the people. Happy are they who have got beyond it all, out of the reach and noise and strife of the times. I have known the Society for nearly sixty years, and I never knew anything to equal it. Where, or in what storm will end, there is One only who knows. (Dorland 1968, p. 148)

As in Philadelphia, Hicksites in New York Yearly Meeting were in the majority.

At Ohio Yearly Meeting, Hicks and Shillitoe were again both present. On the first day Hicks and his supporters spoke at length and found themselves excluded the next. However, they were so numerous that the doorkeepers could not keep them out. Again an argument broke out about who was to Clerk the Meeting and again the Hicksites suggested their own nominee. However, they could not persuade Jonathan Taylor, the sitting Clerk, to leave. According to Shillitoe, they staged a panic by claiming the house was falling down (one Friend fell out of an upper window in the commotion) and gained access to the table, although the table itself was smashed and Taylor suffered a broken rib. Finally the Orthodox party, of about equal size to the Hicksite one, left for another Meeting House (Jones

1921, pp. 478–80). A small division took place in Indiana and Baltimore with the Hicksites in a majority, but New England, North Carolina, and Virginia all remained Orthodox without schism, as did London and Dublin. In 1829, representatives of the American Orthodox Yearly Meetings met and adopted *A Testimony*, clearly aligning this branch with Protestant evangelicalism (1921, pp. 482–83).

SOCIOLOGICAL ISSUES

Robert Doherty explored the sociological factors in the schism. He claimed that the Orthodox were clearly wealthier than the Hicksites (1967, p. 44), were involved in occupations bringing status and wealth (p. 46), and were more likely to live in urban settings. Even whilst liberal leadership of the Hicksite cause may have been at odds with the conservative Hicksites, Hicks was able to maintain their support through the use of rural imagery and his own farming background (1967, p. 86). The division could also be interpreted as resulting from tension between sectarian and denomination-alising tendencies: between the desire to remain closed, cohesive, and pure, on the one hand; or more open, and part of wider Christianity, on the other. Who was 'the world'? The Orthodox party were far more sympathetic to other Christian groups: for them, the world had shrunk somewhat and it was this group who would ultimately relax the discipline. As with the Nayler controversy, one of the consequences was the attraction of the unwanted. Unitarians were attracted by what they had seen and heard of the Hicksites, and the relaxed Hicksite attitude to doctrine allowed them into the Yearly Meetings. In time, the Hicksites would suffer further small schisms from congregationalist groups of Progressives who emphasised political radicalism and freedom from all discipline, taking the Hicksite impulse to a logical if unforeseen conclusion (see Box 18). Another consequence was the depletion and duplication of energy and resources. Additionally, as above, once split, it was easier to split again. Having been prepared to divide for truth once, and having had apostates so close by, it became easy to perceive yet others in the same way.

ORTHODOX DIVISIONS

BRITISH ULTRA-EVANGELICALISM

Mingins shows how the spectre of Hicks united British Friends in their opposition – they were clearly more in sympathy with the Orthodox party

(2004). Yearly Meetings traditionally exchanged 'epistles', letters of greeting adopted by Yearly Meetings in session for 'Friends everywhere'. Once Quakerism had divided into two, each Yearly Meeting had to decide to whom to send its epistles, and from whom to receive them. For those who had been part of a division, this was obvious. For those outside the immediate separation, they had to choose. London Yearly Meeting officially ceased contact with the Hicksites until 1908 (Kennedy 2001, p. 24).

However, as Mingins has also shown, the anti-Hicks coalition in Britain was itself made up of at least four tendencies:

1 the Quietist traditionalists;
2 the evangelicals who wished to balance scriptural authority with the authority of the inward Light, a position which became known as Wilburite, after the New England minister John Wilbur;
3 the evangelicals who gave a higher authority to Scripture but who felt the inward Light could help Friends read the Scriptures (Hamm 1988, p. 21), a position characterised by the British evangelical Joseph John Gurney and the Gurneyite wing named after his influence in America;
4 the 'ultra-evangelicals' (Mingins 2004, p. xiv) who believed the inward Light to be delusional, a position characterised by Isaac Crewdson in his publication *A Beacon to the Society of Friends* in 1835 and taken up by his followers called the Beaconites or Crewdsonites.

Crewdson, like many British Friends, was alarmed at the spectre of Hicksism and deism and used quotations from Hicks' sermons to argue against the use of the inward Light as an adequate or even acceptable basis for religion. The idea that the inward Light is 'a delusive notion' (Jones 1921, p. 491) was his main point. In this he took a solely scriptural emphasis and ultimately took up an anti-mystical position which was too extreme for most British Friends of the time. He similarly attacked other Quaker phrases which were not scriptural such as 'creaturely activity', 'sinking down', 'turning inward' (1921, p. 491). Only the Gospel could save – 'the unscriptural notion of the light within . . . [is] another gospel' (p. 492).

Hardshaw East Monthly Meeting, the area around Manchester, was divided over Crewdson's publication and Lancashire Quarterly Meeting (the larger body to which the Monthly Meeting belonged) appointed a committee to investigate the disunity. However, sensing the depth of disquiet and the Crewdsonite reaction to those who made up the local committee, Yearly Meeting appointed a committee to try and restore harmony, a task it tackled over the following eighteen months. The Yearly Meeting Committee was more balanced in its theological spectrum and included Joseph John Gurney. Gurney felt himself to be in a difficult position. He was a fervent evangelical and Crewdson had been influenced by him, yet he also felt Crewdson had gone too far in his theological analysis. This committee issued a statement outlining the main areas of disagreement with Crewdson's position. Contrary to Crewdson's Scripture-centric view, the committee emphasised the workings of the Holy Spirit as a source of both revelation and authority, as well as the essential and experiential nature of silent worship. It was ironic that Crewdson criticised the silent method of worship, as one in which feelings and imagination could usurp true faith, when the Quietists went to such great lengths to quell human distractions. Crewdson resisted this attempt to modify his views and the Yearly Meeting Committee recommended that he cease to speak at Meeting for Worship as a Minister, and that he should not attend any further meetings for Ministers and Elders (Mingins 2004, p. 96). Crewdson refused to comply and his followers were further excited by the evangelical content of the 1836 Yearly Meeting epistle (see p. 99 below). In September 1836, Monthly Meeting decided to enforce the Yearly Meeting Committee recommendation that Crewdson not speak as a Minister, in other words that his 'recording' (see p. 63 above) be suspended. In late 1836, Crewdson and fifty-one of his followers resigned their membership. Among the fifty-two who resigned at Manchester, there were only twenty-two surnames (Isichei 1970, p. 46). Kinship ties to Kendal meant that a similar proportion of the Meeting resigned there. Many of those who left in Kendal, and some who did in London, were instrumental in setting up Plymouth Brethren congregations (Mingins 2004, p. 217). In Manchester, Crewdson formed a group called the Evangelical Friends, published *The Inquirer*, and built a chapel on Grosvenor Street, close to the city centre, to seat 600. In December 1837, they adopted a new church polity. Having studied the Bible carefully, they agreed there should be two offices, Elder and Deacon. 'They rejected the ministry of women as unscriptural and birthright membership as non-evangelical' (Isichei 1970, p. 48). They also drafted a statement of faith. Silent worship was abandoned in place of a service. Isichei records this visitor's account:

When the Meeting House in Grosvenor Street was opened for public worship, though not a dissident Friend, I attended at one of the earliest services. The room was by no means well-filled. It was plain and unassuming with a low platform and rostrum, but no pulpit. There were seats on the platform and in the room, and from the rostrum one of the leaders conducted the service, which was rather tame and frigid. There was hymn singing, Bible reading, prayer, and an address; altogether, in form, just such a service as the Rev. James Griffin would be conducting in Rusholme Road hard by, without the prestige of recognised status, or a historical name from Cromwellian times. It is no wonder that the cause languished and eventually 'scattered'. (Isichei 1970, p. 49)

As well as breaking with the traditional form of Quaker worship, the Crewdsonites also began to question the nature of baptism and communion. Many chose outward water baptism and records of these were printed in *The Inquirer* (Isichei 1970, p. 49). Kendal Friends tried to raise the issue at Yearly Meeting and it was a topic that was to resurface informally from time to time within British Quakerism over the next thirty years. In America, David Updegraff would take the matter further in the 1880s (see p. 114 below). In 1837, the Crewdsonites met at the same time as London Yearly Meeting and issued their own epistle. However Isaac Crewdson died in 1844 and in the same year the chapel was sold to the Baptists, only seven years after it had opened. It has been suggested that the *Beacon* was merely twenty years ahead of its time and that 'any Quaker evangelical could look into his own heart and see a Beaconite' (Isichei 1970, p. 52). In 1861, one Friend suggested at London Yearly Meeting that the term 'inward Light' be dropped as it was unscriptural (Isichei 1970, p. 7). Certainly some twentieth-century Quaker evangelicals would reach a position very similar to that of Isaac Crewdson (see p. 184 below).

JOSEPH JOHN GURNEY

Hamm suggests that the Orthodox party's unity lay mainly in its opposition to Hicksism and its dedication to the disownment of Hicksites, a process that lasted for many years as young Friends, still on the Orthodox lists, would be disowned on coming into adulthood for attending their parents' (Hicksite) Meetings (Hamm 1988, p. 19). Below that Orthodox unity lay division between those who held a primary allegiance to Quaker tradition and those who were devoted 'to the larger principles of Christianity' (Hamm 1988, p. 20). These two positions were epitomised by John Wilbur and Joseph John Gurney and they became the leading protagonists in a second wave of schism that rent Orthodox Yearly Meetings. As Edwina Newman states,

> Gurney saw it as his mission to bring the Society into the 'true and universal church of Christ', while Wilbur held firmly to the belief that it was God's will that Quakers should be a 'peculiar people' and that their testimonies would be lost if they should mingle 'with those from whom they came out'. (Newman 2005, p. 242)

Joseph John Gurney (1788–1847) was part of the banking dynasty which would ultimately become Barclays Bank (Plate 8). His family lived at Earlham Hall near Norwich and life appeared from all accounts quite

Plate 8 Gurney family photograph, c.1842 (from a sepia albumen print, probably from a daguerrotype). Joseph John Gurney and his third wife, Eliza, are in the back row. Elizabeth Fry sits in the centre front row; one of Elizabeth's daughters (probably Katherine) to her right. To her left are Joseph John's daughter Anna and his son John Henry; Josiah Forster is to the left of Katherine (Forster was a weighty evangelical friend who in time would mentor Joseph Bevan Braithwaite)

worldly. Those who resisted the discipline were called the 'gay Quakers' (as opposed to plain). Gurney's sister, Betsy, better known as Elizabeth Fry, is famed for having gone to Meeting in purple boots with scarlet laces, only to be convinced of a greater truth by visiting minister, William Savery (see Box 12). Dance and music had replaced Quietistic annihilation and withdrawal at Earlham Hall. Louisa Gurney related in her diary:

Yesterday we had a most delightful dance . . . I was in ecstasies after supper with dancing Malbrook. Two things raise my soul to devotion – nature and music. As I went down the dance yesterday, I gave up my soul to the enchanting Malbrook. I thought of heaven and of God. I really tasted heaven for a minute. (Jones 1921, p. 494)

Gurney was tutored at Oxford and took over the family firm in 1809, aged only twenty-one. His theological training and urban connections may have made Anglicanism an attractive possibility but he remained dedicated

---

Box 12 Elizabeth Fry (1780–1845)

Part of the wealthy and influential Gurney family, Elizabeth Gurney grew up at Earlham Hall near Norwich, England. The Gurney family was worldly and pushing against Quietistic formalism. One Sunday, Elizabeth went to Meeting in purple boots with scarlet laces under her Quaker grey. However, the influence of travelling minister William Savery converted her to a more sober and self-effacing lifestyle. Her own ministry was to prove hugely influential. Married to Joseph Fry, she moved to London and became concerned about women prisoners and especially those due for deportation. Through her own endeavour, and ultimately through the establishment of Ladies Committees, she helped thousands prepare for their journeys, providing them with quilting kits so they would have produce to sell when they reached Australia. Her work was part of the ongoing Quaker concern for penal reform. She had six children and was encouraged, often by admonishment, towards greater discipline by the Elders when some of them married non-Friends. Her husband was disowned when his banking business failed (Skidmore 2005, p. 8).

---

to the Quaker method of worship and the direct guidance of the Spirit. His commitment was further confirmed by an experience he had soon after his father's death. He had already been inspired by his first visit to Yearly Meeting ('despite of my youth and lapelled coat, I was appointed representative' (Jones 1921 p. 497)), and by the ministry of Ann Jones (who was later to be one of the English Friends who opposed Hicks in America). Then:

Soon after my return home I was engaged to a dinner party at the house of one of our first country gentlemen. Three weeks before the time was I engaged, and three weeks was my young mind in agitation from the apprehension, of which I could not dispossess myself, that I must enter his drawing room with my hat on. From this sacrifice, strange and unaccountable as it may appear, I could not escape. In a Friend's attire, and with my hat on, I entered the drawing room at the dreaded moment, shook hands with the mistress of the house, went back into the hall, deposited my hat, spent a rather comfortable evening, and returned home in some degree of peace. I had afterwards the same thing to do at the Bishop's; the result was, that I found myself the decided Quaker, was perfectly understood to have assumed that character, and to dinner parties, except in the family circle, was asked no more. (1921, p. 497)

Gurney felt the call to ministry aged twenty-nine and became a powerful and beloved preacher. In 1824 he published the first systematic theology of Quakerism since Barclay and Bathurst, entitled *Observations on the Religious Peculiarities of the Society of Friends* (1979), and he was prolific in the decade that followed. He would become in time the most read Quaker inside and outside of the Society, and one of the most persuasive.

If the Orthodox party had moved Quakerism from a peculiar sect to a peculiar branch of evangelicalism (Hamm 1988, p. 23), Gurney was prepared to mould Quakerism around a more mainstream Protestant evangelical theology even at the expense of losing the primacy of direct revelation and corporate mysticism. He felt earlier Friends had been wrong in some ways. The atonement was central to Gurney and the inward Light was for him the means to better read Scripture (Hamm 1988, p. 21). Gurney reinterpreted many of the ways earlier Friends had used Scripture. For example, 2 Peter 1:19, about the day star rising in the heart, had been used previously to refer to the inward Light. Gurney used it to refer to written Scripture (Jones 1921, p. 503). Unlike early Friends, he separated justification (acceptability to God) and sanctification (sinlessness) experiences and put forward a systematic and rational, hence modernist, interpretation of Quakerism. Like Barclay, he did not see the second coming as imminent, but it is even more distant in Gurney's theology. The gift of the Holy Spirit was given to the justified, who could then later achieve sanctification on a Wesleyan model – as a second blessing rather than as all part of a single experience as it had been for early Friends. The full inheritance was in the future, rather than unfolding. Later, Gurneyites would differ on how the kingdom of heaven was to be achieved (see pp. 108–9 below). In some ways Gurney wound back the clock of the early Quaker culmination of 'God's plan for the world' (see p. 32 above) and claimed the possibility of an individual Pentecost rather than a collective day of judgement. Like Barclay on the Lord's Supper, Gurney disputed the meaning of the 1 Corinthians 11:26 passage and came to a very similar position on it (Dandelion 2005, p. 56).

Gurney used the instructive passage from 1 Corinthians 11:23–26 to break the bread until the Lord comes again (and added the next three verses, up to 29) as an instruction, not to institute a ceremony but to avoid the abuse of it, as the Corinthians had been doing (Gurney 1979, p. 155). Equally, he suggested that the correct emphasis of the phrase 'Do this in remembrance of me' should be on the word '*me*'. That is, Jesus was trying to ensure the remembrance of him as opposed to remembrance of anything else (p. 156). Finally, Gurney turned his attention to the 'Till he come' of the 1 Corinthians 11:26 passage. He did not claim that the second coming was unfolding, but did claim, from Revelation 3:20, that the true supper was available, and that it was an inward one (p. 165). In other words, Gurney used Jeremiah 31:31–34 and Revelation 3:20 to uphold a sense of an inward intimacy with Christ, as early Friends had (see p. 30 above), but one held in the meantime, not the soon-coming endtime. He wrote in an ecumenical spirit, asking Friends not to judge those who continue these practices as God accepts the sincere heart and 'is pleased to bless a variety of means to a variety of conditions' (p. 168).

At the 1836 Yearly Meeting, the epistle included a clear statement on the authority of Scripture. It ended with the statement that 'whatsoever any man says or does which is contrary to the Scriptures, though under profession of the immediate guidance of the Spirit, must be reckoned and accounted a mere delusion' (Jones 1921, p. 510). Gurney had taken a leading part in the discussion leading up to its adoption and Jones claims that from this time forward he became the champion of Evangelical Quakerism (p. 510).

GURNEYITE AND WILBURITE SEPARATIONS

The most determined resistance to Gurney's ministry came from John Wilbur (1774–1856) of Hopkinton, Rhode Island. Wilbur took the opposite view to Gurney on the inward Light and declared it to be not only sufficient but primary in its authority. Human preparation and learning, and worldliness in general, hindered the operation of the Light. An over-emphasis on scriptural authority was seen to be a worldly snare, confining humanity to the natural rather than supernatural plane, the kind of apostasy the earliest Friends had reacted against. Bible study and Bible distribution were seen as equally wrongheaded. In Britain, Quietists and Wilburite Friends watched with alarm as Gurney and his supporters gradually instituted reforms such as the introduction of systematic Bible instruction at Ackworth Quaker school (Newman 2005, p. 242). Gurney's personal wealth and background only confirmed the anxiety about worldliness, or some kind of crypto-Anglicanism, creeping into the Religious Society. Wilbur believed in simultaneous justification and sanctification and emphasised that this was an inward and painful process 'wrought in the heart' (Hamm 1988, p. 30). Wilbur travelled in Britain and Ireland between 1831 and 1833, and in 1832 published *Letters to a Friend on some of the Primitive Doctrines of Christianity*. These six letters reveal a mix of evangelical and quietistic theologies. Wilbur was Orthodox and believed strongly in the propitiatory sacrifice of Christ, but believed that to place too much emphasis on the outward was as big a mistake as Hicks had made placing all emphasis on the inward. Wilbur defended the 'hedge' and the peculiarities as a way of protecting the inward. He disagreed with Gurney that earlier Friends had been wrong.

Wilbur was not alone in his concerns about Gurney. Shillitoe and others who had supported the Orthodox party were concerned at Gurney's ministry. Shillitoe on his deathbed claimed Gurney had placed a 'linsey woolsey garment' (an expression also used by early Friends to refer to an external system of theology) over the Society. At Yearly Meeting in 1837, Ann Jones was similarly cautious about Gurneys' ministry. Gurney had requested a certificate of release for ministry in America from the Yearly Meeting of Ministers and Elders. Whilst the certificate was granted, the Meeting did not find unity. Sarah Lynes Grubb said that:

> she had hoped she might have been allowed to remain silent, but since coming into that meeting she felt that she durst not be otherwise than faithful to her Divine Master in this matter ... that as she sought to know the will of God in deep intercession of soul, 'Restraint, restraint, restraint' had been the impression upon her mind ... 'The Spirit suffereth it not now', 'The Spirit suffereth it not now.' (Jones 1921, p. 516)

Ann Jones affirmed this position. The deliberation took all morning and five hours of the afternoon. The concern was Gurney's worldliness. Full unity was not reached but the certificate was granted, a move which was to have dramatic consequences for Quakerism.

Whilst those present were asked not to share the disunity of the Meeting, a full account of it was sent to America ahead of Gurney's arrival. At the same time, John Wilbur was ready to warn Friends of the dangers of Gurney's position. Gurney's visit to America was to have a dramatic effect on Orthodox Quakerism and, in the theological struggle with Wilbur, was to begin a second series of separations. Gurney was a powerful and hugely popular preacher. Two thousand are reported to have packed into Arch Street Meeting House in Philadelphia upon his arrival, and he proceeded to travel throughout American Quakerism over a three-year period. Opposition was strongest in Philadelphia, Ohio, and New England, John Wilbur's base. Wilbur was convinced that Gurney was guilty of 'profession without possession', of an outward carnal theology which omitted inward surrender and obedience. It was too much head and not enough heart. Wilbur also travelled widely, warning and counselling Friends against innovation, and maintained an extensive correspondence with sympathetic Friends in Britain.

The leadership, and indeed the majority of New England Yearly Meeting, was in sympathy with Gurney and decided to discipline Wilbur. His own Monthly Meeting had no case against him and ultimately Yearly and Quarterly Meeting committees acted to by-pass the Monthly Meeting's loyalty to Wilbur, branding it 'insubordinate', dissolving it and transferring his membership to a neighbouring Monthly Meeting who disowned Wilbur in 1843. Wilbur appealed but

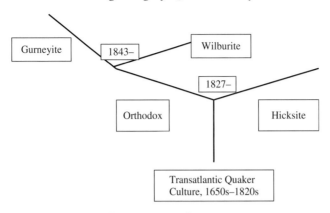

Fig. 2.2 The Gurneyite/Wilburite separations

Yearly Meeting 1844 upheld the decision. Division in Rhode Island Quarterly Meeting had also taken place, and following an attempt to decide which of two Rhode Island Quarterly Meetings was the legitimate one, the Yearly Meeting divided, with two groups, each claiming to be New England Yearly Meeting, meeting in parallel. At one point, representatives demanded the use of the room for New England Yearly Meeting to be told that New England Yearly Meeting was already in session (Jones 1921, pp. 522–4). In 1845 there were two New England Yearly Meetings, both claiming to be the legitimate successor of the previous body (Fig. 2.2). A court case decided in favour of the larger Gurneyite body and London Yearly Meeting corresponded with that body alone. Philadelphia Yearly Meeting, which was generally Wilburite in its sympathies, was less quick to decide whose epistle was the rightful one. Over a nine-year period, Philadelphia refused to take a final decision on this matter and refused to send delegates to gatherings of Orthodox Yearly Meetings in 1849 and 1851 because only the larger (Gurneyite) New England body had been invited.

In Ohio, the Wilburite and Gurneyite parties were of equal strength. In 1845, epistles from both New England Yearly Meetings were read, in 1846 neither. In 1854, Eliza P. Gurney, the widow of Joseph John Gurney who had died in 1847, attended Ohio Yearly Meeting, as did Thomas B. Gould, a leading Wilburite from New England, both with certificates. This brought the issue of allegiance to a head and again the procedural catalyst for schism was the appointment of the Clerk. The Wilburite Benjamin Hoyle had served as Clerk since 1845 because the Representatives had never been able to unite on a new name. In 1854, the Gurneyite Friends claimed they had found a new Clerk in Jonathan Binns but other Representatives claimed that unity had not been found. The Yearly Meeting divided into Hoyle and Binns parties, the Wilburite group being the larger on this occasion.

Philadelphia was now faced with a further question of epistolary legitimacy and only just avoided its own schism by finally deciding in 1857 to cease communication with other Yearly Meetings. (In 1860, Philadelphia General Meeting left Philadelphia Yearly Meeting in a bid to align themselves explicitly with Wilburite Friends. They rejoined the Yearly Meeting in 1950.)

GURNEYITE QUAKERISM AND HOLINESS REVIVALISM

Thomas Hamm argues that Gurney's Quakerism was normative for non-Wilburite Orthodox Friends by 1860 (1988, p. 22). Gurney was a very able minister but Hamm suggests he was as much a symptom as a cause, that he gave expression to a nascent Quaker evangelicalism, itself fed by evangelicalism in wider American culture. Hamm argues that Quaker reading increasingly included evangelical journals and books, and that reform activity, for example on temperance (see Box 13) or anti-slavery, amplified interdenominational influence (1988, p. 24). Some Hicksites (see e.g. West, 2001) and some Orthodox were opposed to such worldly co-operation but most embraced it. Bible distribution and study was an obvious influence from outside. Hamm reports that in Spiceland Quarterly Meeting, Indiana, in 1838, 237 out of 287 member families were without a Bible but that within the year the situation had been remedied (1988, p. 25). First Day Schools (i.e. Sunday Schools) were set up, a move mirrored by the Hicksites. Hamm suggests the major shift towards the world happened in the field of politics, where Friends now threw themselves in with zeal and without any spiritual anxiety (1988, p. 26). In part this mirrored reforms in Britain allowing

---

Box 13 Temperance

Early Quakers warned against the excesses of alcohol and drunkenness but it was the nineteenth-century Friends who, together with their evangelical counterparts in other churches, took up the cause of temperance. By the late nineteenth century Quaker homes were expected to be alcohol free. In the USA, many Quakers supported national prohibition, but by the 1930s most temperance committees had become part of wider social justice bodies (Newton 2003, p. 279). In Britain, the Friends Temperance Union, founded in 1852, broadened its remit in the late twentieth century to include work on other drugs. The stance of the group changed from opposition to education.

Quakers to become Members of Parliament after 1832. What would cause a further divide amongst American Friends, given the new levels of ecumenical citizenship enjoyed by these Quakers, was the attitude to breaking the law.

NINETEENTH-CENTURY ORTHODOX FRIENDS AND SLAVERY

In the winter of 1842–43, an eighth of Indiana Yearly Meeting separated after its Meeting for Sufferings removed from its number eight abolitionists. It was claimed that their activities against slavery endangered the purity of the Society by associating with those who did not wait to be led by the Holy Spirit. The Anti-Slavery Friends, as they called themselves, were Gurneyite in their desire to work with whomsoever to abolish slavery, but Wilburite in their theological sympathies. They were critical of the worldly wealth and lack of political fervour of the 'larger body'. Divisions were over methods and alliances. The Indiana Yearly Meeting of Anti-Slavery Friends advocated civil disobedience, including the smuggling of slaves to Canada via the 'underground railroad' whereas the larger Indiana group would not break the law. However, working with the world isolated them from the Wilburites, whilst separating put them at odds with the Gurneyites (Hamm 1988, p. 33). British Friends tried to end the rift and refused to recognise them: the separation lasted about fifteen years.

When the American Civil War came, Friends had generally come to embrace anti-slavery after years of campaigning by the likes of Benjamin Lundy, William Lloyd Garrison, and John Greenleaf Whittier, helped by visiting British Friends such as Joseph Sturge. A wide network of Friends operated the 'underground railroad' during the 1840s and 1850s. Thomas Garrett alone assisted 2700 slaves (Jones 1921, p. 577). Levi Coffin of Wayne County, Indiana, dubbed 'President of the Railroad', recalled how he would need to be ready at any hour on any day for the gentle rap at the door of the 'locomotive' (1921, p. 581). Shelter and food would be offered and directions onward to the next 'station'.

Many were torn about whether to fight for the anti-slavery cause and it was said of Indiana Friends that they were the best recruiters of all the denominations (Hamm 1988, p. 68). Following Lincoln's proclamation of 1862 that all slaves be freed, Quakers became very active in helping those without a living. Freedmen Associations were set up, and help was given with garden plots on land confiscated from slaveholders and offered to the freed by the Government. In time up to 150 schools and colleges for freed slaves were under Quaker auspices. The most famous, Southland College, was set up in 1864 by Indiana Yearly Meeting as an orphanage and boarding school for African American victims of the Civil War. Southland Monthly Meeting, part of Indiana Yearly Meeting from 1873, was the only Meeting at that time with a predominantly African American membership.

RENEWAL AND REVIVAL

Late in the summer of 1875 a Methodist minister decided to indulge his professional curiosity by attending the annual gathering of Indiana Yearly Meeting Friends in Richmond. Unlike his military brother fourteen years before, the Methodist minister felt completely at home. The devotional meeting opened with the singing of a familiar hymn. Then the presiding preacher called for testimonies. Within ninety minutes nearly 300 people had spoken. Then an altar call was issued, and soon seekers after conversion and sanctification crowded around several mourners' benches. To the Methodist visitor, it all had a familiar feeling. 'It resembled one of our best *love feasts* at a *National Camp Meeting* [more] than anything else to which I could liken it', he told the leading interdenominational holiness journal. The scenes in Richmond were not unusual for Gurneyite Friends in 1875. They had set an unprecedented course. (Hamm 1988, p. 74)

By the late 1860s, two distinct approaches emerged within the Gurneyite branch of the Orthodox party. These were the renewal/modernist wing and the revival/holiness wing.

Renewal Friends wished to retain Quaker distinctiveness but fashion it in a modern way, discarding anachronisms such as plain dress and other peculiarities, that limited engagement with a world these Friends wanted to be more a part of (Fig. 2.3). They were keenly involved in social and political activism and joined with other Christians to undertake it. Abolition,

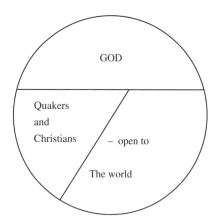

Fig. 2.3 Renewal Quakers and God and the world

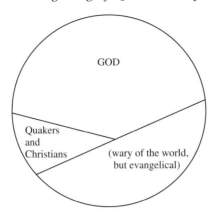

Fig. 2.4 Revival Quakers and God and the world

prior to the war, and temperance were key concerns. These Friends tried to nurture a more vital approach to Meeting for Worship which in places had become dominated by the ministry, or lack of it, of elderly Friends. They encouraged younger Friends to speak of their experience and in particular emphasised the conversion experience. In the 1860s, they instituted general meetings to help educate the newer members and to experiment with mixes of worship and teaching and Bible study. Hamm states that between 1850 and 1870 most Gurneyite Yearly Meetings adopted statements of faith (1988, p. 49). Gurney's theology was largely normative – Scripture-centric but allied to the direct revelation of unprogrammed worship. Education became acceptable and Friends not only attended colleges but also founded them. In 1856 Haverford Boarding School became a College, and Earlham followed suit a few years later (Hamm 1988, p. 40). A new leadership, mainly of educated interrelated birthright Friends who had attended Quaker schools (Hamm 1988, p. 42), drove this programme.

Revival Quakerism was driven from outside the Society and yet paradoxically resulted in a more world-rejecting stance, wary of contamination beyond the Christian fold (Fig. 2.4). It was anti-ballroom, anti-theatre, anti-gambling: 'one blasted football as unworthy of the attention of the sanctified: another proclaimed that union cards were the mark of the beast' (Hamm 1988, p. 164).

THE THEOLOGY OF REVIVAL HOLINESS

Revival Quakerism emphasised religious experience over Quaker distinctives and found inspiration in the interdenominational Holiness movement. Revival meetings, according to Hamm, included the following attributes:

1 services focusing on a small group of preachers;
2 an emphasis on instantaneous experience, whether it be conversion or sanctification;
3 the employment of altar call and mourners' benches;
4 the use of hymns and congregational singing;
5 the toleration and even encouragement of extreme emotionalism (Hamm, 1988, p. 75).

The Holiness influence emphasised the possibility of rebirth resulting in perfection.

Whilst David B. Updegraff (1830–94) was a 'birthright Friend', it was in 1860 that he claimed a conversion experience: 'I was converted through and through, *and I knew it*. I was free as a bird. Justified by faith, I had peace with God' (Bill 1983, p. 16). After this experience, Updegraff began his ministry (Hamm 1988, p. 78) and nine years later, he felt himself sanctified:

But I could not, would not draw back. Every 'vile afection' was nailed to the cross … It came to be easy to trust Him, and I had no sooner reckoned myself 'dead unto sin and live unto God' than 'the Holy Ghost fell upon me just as I supposed He did at the beginning. Instantly I felt the melting and refining power of God permeate my whole being'. Conflict was a thing of the past. I had entered into 'rest.' I was nothing and nobody, and was glad it was settled that way. It was a luxury to get rid of ambitions. The glory of the Lord shone round about me, and for a little season, I was 'lost in wonder, love and praise.' I was deeply conscious of the presence of God within me, and of His sanctifying work. Nothing seemed so sweet as His will, His law written in the heart after the chaff had been burned out. (Clark and Smith 1895, p. 29)

The experience mirrors that of the early Friends. We can compare it with Fox's sensation of entering through the flaming sword (see p. 22 above) and the reference to the Jeremiah 31 quotation is familiar. Only the chronological pattern is different. Here, justification and sanctification have become separated by years. For early Friends, the two usually occurred in tandem. This experience mirrored the theology of Gurney but was a reclamation of the clothing of life by the Holy Spirit.

For the Revivalists, the plain life was both anachronistic and also worldly, given that non-Quakers, such as the Hicksites appeared to be to the Revivalists, also maintained such customs. Silent waiting was unnecessary for the sanctified as they had the Holy Ghost with them continually. This mirrors John Luffe's response to Pope Alexander in 1659 that he had to do nothing to remember the Saviour as he had Christ in and about him and could not but choose to remember him continually (see p. 30 above). It appears a paradox that the Holiness Friends categorised silent waiting in the same way as Luffe characterised outward communion, but there was a shift in what was being waited for. Luffe, already sanctified, would have been waiting for ministry and guidance in the silence. Holiness Friends, given their Gurneyite view on Scripture, would have felt little need to wait for the inward Light as in Gurney's paradigm; this only aided the reading of Scripture (see p. 98 above). Holiness Friends also criticised those who were silent in worship as a sign of spiritual decline: 'It is a sin for people not to praise the Lord' (Hamm 1988, p. 85). Inward-facing Meetings who did not emphasise conversion were seen to be lacking in Christian love. Expression, as part of strategy for conversion, became recommended. From the 1870s, the general meetings of Gurneyite Friends became, in many cases, revival meetings (Hamm 1988, p. 89). As Hamm states, 'the outward cross replaced the inward one' (Hamm 1988, p. 86).

Allegiance was now to true Christianity rather than primarily to Quakerism. None of the peculiarities, not even the testimony against war, were now necessary to spiritual integrity. Even the distinctive form of Quaker marriage became optional as Revival Friends started to marry other Christians beyond Quakerism. Elders found their authority diminished as the Revival ministers became more central. Holiness preachers were the Revivalists' natural allies and Updegraff claimed Wesley was Fox's natural successor. Indeed as Spencer shows, Wesleyan Holiness theology is explicitly and implicitly indebted to Barclay (Spencer 2004a, Appendix C). As Evangelicals often said of the Quietists, they had simply got it wrong, although it is fairer to state that all that really changed, form aside, was the emphasis. Revivalist Friends saw their theology closely linked to the experience of early Friends: it emphasised the experiential, the missionary, unstructured worship with instantaneous experience, the travelling ministry, and perfection. As Carole Spencer has shown, this list could pretty much be applied to the Quietists except for the evangelism (Table 2.1). Unlike more 'mainstream' Gurneyites, they were less wary of mystical experience and more wary of education and its fruits, such as higher criticism. These Friends were not modernist in the way Gurney and the Renewal Friends can be seen to be.

THE SECOND COMING

In terms of the second coming, Revivalist Friends were pre-millennialist. In other words, they believed the world was so depraved that Christ would

Table 2.1. *The eight key characteristics of Quaker Holiness across time (Spencer 2004a, p. 165). Bold print indicates characteristics shared in common with early Friends*

Radical Holiness 1646–66	Formative period 1667–89	Quietism 1690–1820	Orthodoxy 1827–58	Hicksism 1827–1900	Gurneyism 1858–1920	Revival Holiness 1870–1940	Evangelical Holiness 1940–	Modernism 1900–
Scripture	**Scripture**	**Scripture**	**Scripture**	Experience	**Scripture**	**Scripture**	**Scripture**	Experience
Eschatology	Realised eschatology	Realised eschatology				Pre-millennial eschatology		
Conversion	**Conversion**	Sanctification	Community	Community	**Conversion**	**Conversion**	**Conversion**	Community
Charisma	**Charisma**	Leading of Spirit	Leading of Spirit	Leading of Spirit	Leading of Spirit	Charisma	Leading of Spirit	
Evangelism	**Evangelism**	Ministry	Ministry	Ministry	**Evangelism**	**Evangelism**	**Evangelism**	
Suffering	**Suffering**	Quaker testimonies	Quaker testimonies	Quaker testimonies	Quaker testimonies	Christian testimonies	Christian testimonies	Universal testimonies
Mysticism	**Mysticism**	Silent worship	Silent worship	Silent worship	Silent worship	Mysticism		Silent worship
Perfection	**Perfection**	**Perfection**	Obedience	Obedience	Obedience	**Perfection**		

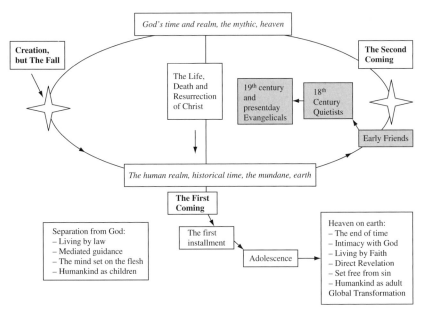

Fig. 2.5 A biblical understanding of time and nineteenth-century Friends

need to come again *ahead* of the thousand-year rule of the saints. Reform, as such, was a waste of time, and the focus should be on conversion. This was especially true given that some of the reform movements were full of heretics such as deists, Unitarians, and Hicksites. The testimony against war was inappropriate, as war would end with the second coming anyway. The 'inward Light' was questioned as difficult to imagine in the unsaved, and because it was not scriptural.

The Renewal Friends tended to be post-millennialist. That is, they believed that their social reform, and the consequent thousand-year rule of the saints, would precede the second coming. What is critically important about both these positions is that they are anticipatory of a second coming sometime in the future (Fig. 2.5). These Friends did nothing to revitalise the eschatological vision of early Friends. Rather they maintained a solidly meantime position (see p. 31 above).

By the 1870s, the Revival was accepted by about 70% of Gurneyite Friends, whilst Philadelphia (better described as Wilburite) was one of the few Yearly Meetings to remain untouched. Hamm argues that the challenge for the Revivalists was that sanctification did not keep up with conversion (1988, p. 129). The Revival had in part been a reaction to formulaic, or silent and empty, unprogrammed worship and the lack of vital leadership within Quakerism. Thousands of converts brought in from the Revival Meetings, without a corresponding rise in those who felt sanctified, resulted in a vacuum of nurture and leadership. At the same time, the critique of the inward Light undermined the very worship method these converts were then expected to adopt. In 1878 for example, Ohio Yearly Meeting declared the doctrine of the inward Light unsound and dangerous. Only repentance and faith in the shed blood of Jesus Christ could bring salvation (Hamm 1988, p. 123).

THE PASTORAL SYSTEM AND CONSERVATIVE SCHISM, 1870S–1880S

Hamm reports that between 1881 and 1889 Indiana Yearly Meeting, a group of 18,000 Friends, had 9000 applications for membership (1988, p. 125). In many Meetings there were no birthright or 'seasoned' Friends, and new-comers could be met by long periods of silence. The fact that induction and nurture was everyone's responsibility meant also that it was no one's in particular. Ministry, when it did come, was not necessarily cogent. During the 1880s, the response was to set up pastoral committees.

The Revivalists, however, favoured the single pastor, someone who had responded to their 'call'. The duties laid on the pastor, however, and the preparation seen to be required to fulfil the vocation, meant that it soon became a full-time office, and one which needed to be funded. What was critical to the Revivalists was that there was a regular teaching ministry, but this emphasis in turn further undermined unprogrammed worship. There is no necessity for a Meeting with a pastor to be programmed but that was the ultimate consequence of the introduction of one-person pastorates. The question then arose about authority and the free ministry and the focus of the worship. Did the authority rest in the preaching, the rest of the programming, or the silence which was sometimes maintained within the new form? The first attempts at a pastoral system began as early as 1875 but it took off in the 1880s. By 1900, pastors had been accepted by every Gurneyite Yearly Meeting except Baltimore (Hamm 1988, p. 127).

Those in favour of pastors looked to the earliest Friends and 'the valiant sixty', and claimed they were a proto-pastorate.

Every church must be provided with a living gospel ministry, someone whose business it is to care for the flock; to visit the sick – to look after the newly awakened, and lead them to the feet of the Saviour; to encourage the new converts, pray with, and for them, and to teach them the way of salvation more perfectly; to visit the membership of the church at their homes, socially and religiously; share with them their joys and sorrows; enter into sympathy with them in their trials and difficulties; see that none stray from the fold and become prodigals; reprove those who sin, and win them back if possible to the path of duty; if differences arise between brethren, see that the gospel order is followed speedily, that the matter be adjusted and settled in privacy before it be known abroad and the cause suffer loss. (Siler 1887, p. 401)

The adoption of pastors soon led to the adoption of programming. What had begun as a reaction to the formalism of unprogrammed worship led to a Spirit-led pre-programming. The Quaker sense of spiritual intimacy was maintained through periods of open worship.

If the pastoral system did not always work as well as had been hoped, it was because the Quaker infrastructure to support it was under-developed. First, there were no existing Quaker pastors nor the means to train new ones. Pastors often had to be imported from other traditions and learn their Quaker tradition retrospectively. Second, new waves of converts would not always bring in an immediate increase in income. Not only did this result in poor or appalling pay for the pastors but it also meant that Meetings might create a 'circuit' to share the costs, thus diminishing the effectiveness of the position with any one group.

For conservative (anti-pastoral) Friends, these revivalist innovations were beyond the pale. Silence was a symptom not of inactivity but of the all-important expectant waiting; waiting all but disappeared in the new outward forms. Separations took place in Kansas, Canada, Iowa, and Indiana (Western Yearly Meeting) (Fig. 2.6). Dorland quotes the Kansas Conservative epistle from 1886: 'Keep low, keep quiet, mind our own particular calling, our inward condition, and feel the Lord inwardly as the rock and sanctuary where none can make afraid' (Dorland 1968, p. 256). The emphasis on the inward is deliberate. Earlier innovations, such as the acceptance of grave-stones and the move away from plain dress and speech, had shifted Quakerism into a more outward and more worldly faith. Plain dress and plain speech, whilst being themselves outward forms, had nevertheless symbolised the denial of the outward. They represented the curtailment of the cataphatic (an outward approach to God), the exact opposite of the music, emotion, and human leadership of pastor-led revival meetings. These Conservatives were Gurneyites but still wedded to 'the hedge' and the idea of a peculiar people or winnowed remnant. They did not seek conversion or expansion, and falling numbers were the logic of purity surrounded by a corrupt and corrupting apostate world.

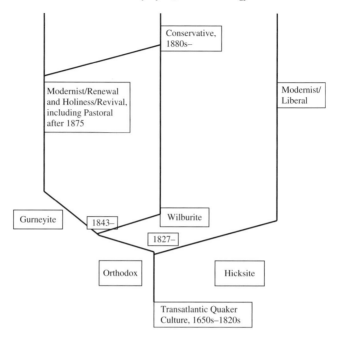

Fig. 2.6 The Pastoral/Conservative separations

GURNEYISM IN BRITAIN

The pastoral system was never seriously contemplated in Britain. Whilst the American Quakers Hannah Whittal Smith and her husband Robert Pearsall began the revivalist Keswick Convention, Revivalism was not part of the evangelical culture in which British Friends were embedded. British Quakerism also did not attract huge numbers of converts in the second half of the century but rather kept them separated from establishment Quakerism in Sunday evening home mission meetings. However, the same liberalising tendencies around testimony took effect in Britain as they had in North American Gurneyism. In 1850, Quakers in Britain could erect gravestones as long as they were all of an equal height and only gave name and dates. After 1860, endogamy was abolished as a rule and Quakers could marry other Christians without fear of disownment. In 1861, the latter part of the fourth query on plain dress and plain speech was dropped. Across nineteenth-century Quakerism, outward plainness was replaced by a commitment to simplicity (Frost 2003, pp. 37–9).

Whilst many Evangelical Friends had maintained a testimony to plainness – Gurney talks of removing 'looking glasses' in 1844 (Isichei 1970, p. 153) – they were more permissive of the world. Changing attitudes to music between 1820 and 1870, Isichei notes, were an explicit barometer of this more world-accepting stance. From 1832 Quakers were eligible to stand as Members of Parliament in Britain and Joseph Pease was elected that year. Quakers, ripe from the success of ecumenical campaigning against the slave trade, began to feel they had a wider role to play in civil society. This honeymoon with the state was to last over eighty years, reaching a crescendo during the 'Quaker renaissance' of 1895–1910, before the violent rupture caused by the Conscription Act in 1916. Joseph Sturge's mission to the Emperor of Russia in 1854 to try and avert the Crimean War, to the disgust of *The Times* newspaper, epitomised this new sense of civic possibility (Isichei 1970, p. 221).

In Britain, the Quietist remnant felt Quakerism and thus the pure true church threatened by the 'worldly' reforms of the 1850s and 1860s. For the evangelicals, the true church lay across the different brands of evangelical Christianity and did not reside in a single group. Paradoxically then, the need to continue Quakerism mattered less soteriologically, but nevertheless led to reforms to make Quakerism more relevant and accessible. For them 'the hedge' between Quakerism and the world was an impediment to conversion. For the Quietists, it was a crucial barrier between themselves and the apostate. Elizabeth Isichei reports one Friend who claimed he would rather 'die as a dog in a ditch than say "you" to a single person' (1967, p. 171) (see Box 14 on the ultra-conservative Irish 'White Quakers'). After the reforms, annual conferences of Conservative Friends gathered for mutual support and to discuss the state of the Yearly Meeting. Daniel Pickard was one notable leader of this group, John Sargent (1813–83) another. Sargent had been living in Paris, a birthright Friend who had had a strong

---

Box 14 White Quakers

James Gregory's research on the White Quakers of Ireland outlines an ultra-conservative group, led by Joshua Jacob and Abigail Beale, emerging in the 1830s, forming a small but visible and distinct group over fourteen years from 1840. Jacob was disowned in 1838 having preached against 'backsliding and mammonism' (Gregory 2004, p. 70) and proceeded to dispose of furniture and worldly goods and only wear undyed (white) clothing. These were ultra-quietists who strongly denied scriptural authority and who undertook acts of humiliation and hardship to break their own will.

convincement experience in 1838. He refused to carry a letter for it would defraud the Crown of its 'revenues and customs' (Isichei 1970, p. 53) and insisted on the plain dress and speech. Sargent moved back to Britain in 1851 and in 1864 started a Meeting in Fritchley, Derbyshire, without the permission of the local Monthly Meeting. He wrote: 'As to asking consent to open a meeting here, we are not at the present time feeling easy to do so, and thus show an allegiance to their authority, that of the present back-slidden organisation' (Isichei 1970, pp. 54–5). Why ask for authorisation from the group to which you had set up an alternative?

In 1868, Sargent travelled to visit the Wilburite Friends in the United States, and he came back affirmed in his desire to separate from the larger body. In 1868, Fritchley General Meeting began a one-hundred-year separation from London Yearly Meeting. This was not a move supported by all of the Conservative tendency and Sargent's fervour and personal determination to separate was questioned as suspect (Isichei 1970, p. 55). Most of the Conservative group stayed within the Yearly Meeting. However, unlike other small schisms, Fritchley was sustained by the fact that a number of the separatists came to live in the locality and operated businesses there: one visitor commented 'They . . . utterly resist being guided by Reason, except in matters of buying and selling, at which they are very sharp' (Isichei 1970, p. 56).

Friends in Bournbrook, Birmingham, joined Fritchley General Meeting in the 1880s, also operating a school in Tiverton Road. However, Fritchley Friends refused to travel to Birmingham for Monthly Meeting, insisting instead that the Friends from Bournbrook come to Derbyshire (Lowndes 1980, p. 42). In 1906, Bournbrook separated from Fritchley, concerned over the increasing permissiveness of the group. They suffered the loss of their school through fire in 1910 and emigrated *en masse* to Canada between 1904 and 1913. There they set up Halcyonia Monthly Meeting in Saskatchewan (Lowndes 1980, pp. 257–72). Fritchley Friends gradually dropped their hedged life – the last bonnet wearer there died in 1933 – and they rejoined London Yearly Meeting in 1968.

THE WATER PARTY

In Britain by the 1880s, evangelicalism was the dominant mode of Quakerism. It was a more relaxed and more ecumenical religion than its Quietist predecessor, but still wary of 'the world' as the following quotation from the 1883 book of discipline on reading reveals:

It behoves us to exercise a sound discretion as to what publications we admit into our houses; that neither we nor our children may be hurt by that reading which would tend in any degree to leaven our minds into the spirit of the world, and to unfit us for the sober duties of life. (*Book of Christian Discipline of the Religious Society of Friends in Great Britain*, 1883, p. 115)

Newman claims that David Bebbington's list of central features of evangelicalism fitted mid-nineteenth-century Quakerism: emphases on conversion, activism (political and philanthropic work), the authority of the Bible as central, and the doctrine of substitutionary atonement (2005, p. 237). The separations of the later nineteenth century were all departures from different aspects of this list but can be grouped into those to do with practice and those to do with authority. The doctrine of the inward Light remained problematical for the whole of the century. Shackleton's and Barnard's insistence on its total sufficiency, mirrored in some way by Hicks, carried on in some part through the Wilburite tradition and found itself resurrected in Conservative reactions to evangelical innovation. As each side of the authority debate either stretched its theological boundaries a little further, or simply reiterated its position in a new period, separation and controversy seemed to follow.

The ordinances were the main remaining difference between Revival Friends and other Christians, and it was perhaps inevitable that they would become an issue. As the emphasis on inward experience was questioned, the traditional Quaker view on inward baptism and communion was also questioned. A further challenge came from the explicitly 'meantime' emphasis of nineteenth-century Quakerism. When 1 Corinthians 11:26 tells its readers to break the bread 'until the Lord come again', it is easy to see how some felt that Barclay and Gurney, with their alternative readings of this passage, had got it wrong and that it should be taken more literally. From a meantime perspective, memorial is key to anticipation. As identity became primarily Christian rather than Quaker, sectarian interpretations seemed less relevant. As early as 1879, the English Quaker Helen Balkwill, a friend of Hannah Whittall Smith, became convinced that water baptism was required of all Christians (Hamm 1988, p. 130).

David Updegraff was the main leader of the campaign for water-toleration, known as the 'water party' or the Waterites. He and his followers argued that water baptism, as symbolic of the new life rather than a mark of salvation, was commanded by Christ. They argued, curiously, that early Friends had tolerated water baptism. As with parts of the pastoral debate, the question arose as to the nature and aim of worship – was the spiritual to be found inwardly or outwardly? The final element to the debate was the balancing of tradition and conscience. Updegraff did not seek to change Quaker practice for all Friends but rather sought toleration. He asked for charity, love, and toleration, not 'cruel persecution'. He had little success and was rebuked at Indiana Yearly Meeting in 1879. Only in his home Yearly Meeting of Ohio did he establish any degree of support and remain unchallenged. He was baptised in 1884 and other Quakers came to Ohio to be baptised. This only strengthened resistance elsewhere. In 1885, New England and New York said anyone baptised could not remain a minister. This became the issue – could ministers be baptised and retain their certificates of service and their membership? Ohio stood alone but in so doing divided the Revivalist wing of Gurneyism. Hamm notes that, curiously, many of the Waterites were birthright Friends whereas the anti-water party was made up of converts.

The opposition was worried about the loss of the final Quaker distinctives, and the criteria for who was a 'real' Quaker were again in debate. For the Waterites they saw anti-revival sentiment manifest itself in a new way, the unsanctified attempting to rid the Society of its most dedicated servants (Hamm 1988, p. 135). Ohio Yearly Meeting uncharacteristically took a vote on the issue, with Updegraff's position upheld 198 to 183. There was a call for separation but it never came as the main moderate opponent, John Butler, died later that year. Hamm notes that opposition more widely was systematic and methodical. The 1885 and 1886 statements of opposition were reaffirmed at Yearly Meetings in 1887 and when Calvin W. Pritchard, editor of the *Christian Worker* (the Evangelical Quaker journal) took a tolerationist view, the anti-water party bought up enough stock in the magazine to force him to change his view or resign (Hamm 1988, p. 136).

THE RICHMOND CONFERENCE AND DECLARATION

In September 1887 a conference of all Gurneyite Yearly Meetings including London and Dublin was called to meet in Richmond, Indiana. The conference adopted a 'Declaration of Faith'. In some ways it can be seen as a pinnacle of the revival with little mention of the inward Light but it was essentially moderate, a Renewal or modernist document, aiming to bring harmony and unity. Critically, albeit deep into the document, the Declaration affirmed the traditional opposition to outward baptism. Its statements on sanctification were also moderate rather than Holiness or Revival in their emphasis. Conservative and Holiness Friends were unhappy with the Declaration. Kansas Conservatives and Philadelphia Wilburites considered it apostate because of its attitude to the inward

Light. At the other end of the spectrum, Updegraff and Ohio Yearly Meeting were isolated, and criticised the Declaration as a creed. London, moving into a new and distinctive theological emphasis (see p. 118 below), refused to adopt the statement even though the British Friend Joseph Bevan Braithwaite had been one of its main drafters. At London Yearly Meeting in 1888, Edward Grubb claimed it was too much like a 'paper union' (*The Friend* 28, 1888, pp. 162–3), although more evangelical Friends also opposed a formal adoption of the statement (Kennedy 2001, pp. 114–15).

Towards the end of the Richmond Conference, William Nicholson suggested a central authority for Yearly Meeting, each sending delegates in proportion to their size, as a way of stemming further disunity. Hamm suggests the idea was met with extreme caution at first, each wing fearing domination by the other, and the whole seeming most unquakerly (1988, p. 138). But the idea gained ground and regular meetings of the American Gurneyite Yearly Meetings (excepting Ohio) would in time become constituted as Five Years Meetings (and ultimately Friends United Meeting), a legislative body with a uniform discipline.

MODERNIST QUAKERISM

BRITISH MODERNIST QUAKERISM

In the 1860s, a new aspect of Quakerism emerged which was to form a renewed basis of modernist (anti-holiness) Quakerism at the turn of the century. David Duncan, a Friend from Manchester, England, began to cause further controversy in the Manchester Mount Street Meeting of Crewdsonite fame. Unitarianism had been a reason for disownment earlier in the century but Isichei characterises Duncan and his followers as of Unitarian sympathies (1970, p. 28). Their main emphasis, however, was on freedom of thought, and critically as part of this the rejection of biblical infallibility and the substitutionary view of the atonement. At the same time that Sargant and Pickard were holding small gatherings of Conservative Friends in Britain, Duncan was giving expression to 'higher criticism', the inadvertent fruits of the liberalising attitudes of Evangelical Quakerism and its greater openness to the world. Whilst considered heretical in 1870, Duncan's views would be mainstream in British Quakerism within thirty years and would in turn offer a revitalised emphasis to moderate Quakerism in the USA. For example, they rejected the eternal punishment of the wicked. As feared by the Evangelicals, they

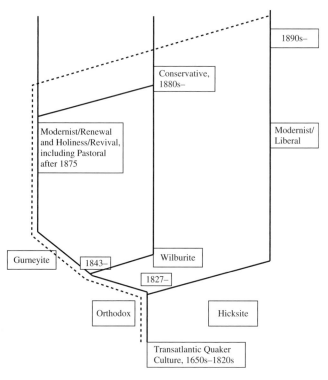

1890s–

Conservative,
1880s–

Modernist/Renewal
and Holiness/Revival,
including Pastoral
after 1875

Modernist/
Liberal

Gurneyite   1843–   Wilburite

1827–

Orthodox   Hicksite

Transatlantic Quaker
Culture, 1650s–1820s

Fig. 2.7 The American separations and the place of British Friends (London Yearly
Meeting represented by dotted line)

could see that the ideas of the inward Light and continuing revelation fitted
well with their sense of increasing knowledge. Duncan was eventually
disowned for his views but died before he could appeal. Eleven of his
followers resigned and set up a separate meeting, which continued into the
1870s with an attendance of about thirty. For two years, they published
The Manchester Friend (Isichei 1970, p. 63).

   In Britain, the shift from evangelical to modernist (Liberal Quaker)
thinking was one of intellectual change, rather than one of liturgical form
(Fig. 2.7). Worship remained unprogrammed, and the positions of Elders,
Overseers, and Ministers, whilst eschewed by Duncan's followers,
remained. What altered was the understanding of the basis and inspiration
for Quaker worship and service. These new Liberals were the daughters and
sons of Evangelical Friends. Whilst they critiqued the religion of their
parents, there was not the schismatic impulse found amongst Friends in
the United States. London Yearly Meeting was smaller, interwoven

dynastically, and bounded by continuing peculiarity. In 1864, the smallest membership since the 1650s had been recorded. Whilst these Friends were optimistic in their 'whig' version of progressive history, they could not afford the limitless sense of right and wrong of separatists; equally, they probably did not feel it necessary: as Isichei notes, 'one of the most striking aspects of the intellectual history of Victorian Quakerism was the rapidity and completeness with which liberal theology spread' (1970, p. 39).

After the Duncan controversy, the next obvious landmarks of the move to Liberal Quakerism were the publication of *A Reasonable Faith* in 1884 and *The Gospel of Divine Help* in 1886. The first of these was published anonymously, for fear of the consequences. The second, by Edward Wordsell, cost him, he claimed, a headship of a Quaker school (Isichei 1970, p. 40). However, the rejection of the Richmond Declaration came in 1888, partly a reaction to content as well as form. In 1892, John Wilhelm Rowntree (Plate 9; and see Box 15) called for the Society to address itself to the needs of its younger members (he was twenty-four at the time) and in 1895 a conference was held at Manchester to discuss the relationship of the Society to modern thought. This attracted about 1000 Friends and the presentations marked a watershed in the acceptability of the public expression of Liberal theology. In the years that followed, hugely popular Summer Schools were held in Scarborough and Birmingham, and in 1901 at Haverford in Pennsylvania. In 1903 a permanent study centre called Woodbrooke was opened in Birmingham. As Isichei points out:

The liberal theology which silently and invisibly became an orthodoxy among Friends was destined to remain so. The reaction which is associated with the names of Barth and Niebuhr, which began to affect English church members in the 1930s, had no influence on Friends. In 1940 Charles Roden Buxton told his brother that he had been reading Barth, but was uninfluenced – otherwise 'I should have had to leave the Society of Friends'. (Isichei 1970, p. 41)

GURNEYITE MODERNISM

Whilst the accession of Liberal theology in Britain was rapid and complete, the situation in America was obviously more complex. Rufus Jones (1863–1948) (Plate 10; and see Box 15) from South China, Maine, had become the editor of the *American Friend* when in 1894 it became the national Gurneyite Quaker journal, succeeding the *Friend's Review* of Philadelphia and the *Christian Worker* of Richmond. It had an open

Plate 9 John Wilhelm Rowntree

editorial policy with the exception of pro-water articles. However, after 1897 and his meeting with J. W. Rowntree, Jones adopted a more modernist editorial policy. This was more accepting of evolutionary theory, higher criticism, progressive revelation, and the authority of the inward Light. It portrayed Quakerism as essentially mystical and gave primary authority to experience. There was less emphasis on the atonement and original sin, and more on the distinctives of Quaker history.

Box 15 J. W. Rowntree (1878–1905) and Rufus Jones (1863–1948)

J. W. Rowntree was the leading architect of Liberal Quakerism in Britain, despite dying prematurely in 1905. In 1897, he was on holiday in Switzerland and met there the American Friend Rufus Jones. Rufus Jones was on holiday with Rendel Harris, the British Quaker academic who later became the first director of studies at Woodbrooke, the Quaker study centre in Birmingham, and they knew the 'Rowntree party' was staying in Murren so they measured their days walks off to arrive there for the weekend. They organised a Quaker Meeting in the hotel on Sunday morning and Harris ministered using the Pre-Raphaelite Christina Rosetti's poem about how love is at the basis of anything of long-term value.

> What is the beginning? Love. What is the course? Love still.
> What is the goal? The goal is love on the happy hill.
> Is there nothing then but love, search we sky and earth?
> There is nothing out of love hath perpetual worth.

Jones claims he found the love that was to have 'perpetual worth' in his friendship with JW (Allott 1994, p. 47). They immediately formed a deep friendship and talked most of the rest of the day. The next day they started walking up the Schilthorn at 2 a.m. to arrive at the summit for breakfast, which their guides had carried for them. JW had a problem with his sight and Rufus Jones walked by his side whilst they climbed, talking more as they went. They had breakfast at 8 a.m., then came down the mountain on burlap sacking. Jones recounted:

> It was a day of continual thrills – my first experience on a high snow mountain – but greater than the joy of climbing or of seeing sunrise on the Jungfrau or of plunging down a mountain top into space was my highborn joy as I went on discovering the remarkable character and quality of the new friend who was walking by my side. We both knew before the day was over that we were to be comrades for the rest of life. (Allott 1994, p. 48)

Together, these two would refashion British and East Coast American Quakerism and their legacy still informs the kind of Quakerism most familiar in Europe. The two became companions for the rest of their lives and fittingly, although sadly, Rowntree was to die in America with Jones by his bedside. They are buried next to each other at Haverford.

For the Revivalist Friends, this resurrection of denominational distinctiveness, the questioning of biblical authority, and the centrality of the atonement were deeply worrying. The modernist Renewal Friends were not dismissive of the Bible; their upbringing meant they knew it intimately.

Plate 10 Rufus Jones (carbon print from pencil sketch by Adelaide Newman)

Rather, they were now meticulous in their study of it. They were consequently anti-credal and non-dogmatic. Instead they emphasised the freedom to follow new paths and to receive new guidance from God. The life of Christ was an exemplar. Salvation lay in mystical union with God (Hamm 1988, p. 150) (see Box 16).

Jones, a teacher at Haverford, had key allies at the other Quaker colleges, Elbert Russell at Earlham, and Mary Mendenhall Hobbs at Guilford. Jones, however, was the key architect of the transformation of Quakerism. He aimed for a new reliance on tradition and history, the understanding of Quakerism as essentially about group mysticism, and a commitment to the

---

Box 16 Beanite Quakerism

Joel and Hannah Bean were Renewal Friends in Iowa but found themselves under attack in 1881 at their own Yearly Meeting from visiting Ohio Revivalist David Updegraff. When Updegraff was given a returning minute of gratitude from Iowa Yearly Meeting, the Beans felt rebuked. In 1882, they sold up and moved to California, claiming 'we need rest and change' (Hamm 1988, p. 139). They transferred their membership to Honey Creek, a Holiness Quarterly Meeting under the care of Iowa Yearly Meeting but found some refuge in a sympathetic Monthly Meeting in San Jose. Fuelled by opposition from back in Iowa for 'unsoundness', San Jose soon found themselves a minority within the Quarter and the Quarterly Meeting dissolved the Monthly Meeting and removed the membership to another Monthly Meeting. The Beans built a small Meeting House in College Park whilst the Revivalists established San Jose Friends Church. In 1893, the Beans were deposed from the ministry for being able to affirm only eight of nine points of doctrine. College Park adopted a five-point statement of faith, rooted in the leadership of the Holy Spirit and modernist in its outlook on the world. Remaining unprogrammed, and with its emphasis on the inward Light, this modernist branch of Gurneyism would ultimately underpin modernist Liberal Quakerism in California and the Pacific Northwest.

---

social gospel; he hoped he could unite the different persuasions around this renewed vision. If Quakers only understood their past, they would disagree less. Some of the leading Liberals were pastors but all were anti-revival and anti-emotionalism: Russell caused controversy when he failed to take part in a 'handkerchief salute to loved ones looking down from heaven' (Hamm 1988, p. 155); 'Mary Hobbs thought revivals "disgraceful"' (Hamm 1988, p. 156).

Renewal modernists began to dialogue with Hicksites and, in 1904, Jones supported a move by London Yearly Meeting to send an epistle to all Yearly Meetings, not just Gurneyite ones. In 1905, he attended a Hicksite Yearly Meeting. Joint Meetings for Worship became common after 1900, according to Hamm (1988, p. 156); indeed, Jones' later work would be very much directed to bridging the divisions, particularly through service. Post-millennial in its theology (see p. 108 above), the social gospel was crucial and centred on temperance and prohibition, and prison and educational reform. Their optimistic sense of human progress envisioned society getting better and better.

Hamm claims that between 1900 and 1910, modernist and Holiness Friends battled for the future of Gurneyite Quakerism. He identifies three distinct periods: a crystallisation of the two sides between 1895 and 1900, the development of a Holiness infrastructure between 1900 and 1905 to match the positions of power held by Jones and Russell, and the attempt by Holiness Friends to purify the Society after 1905 (Hamm 1988, p. 166). It was battle of the elites with most uninterested or unaware.

The Holiness wing, whilst more reactionary after the mid-1890s, maintained its earlier position. Many of the Holiness leaders had died or joined other groups but new leaders emerged, notably J. Walter Malone (see Box 21 below). Malone set up the Friends Bible Institute in Cleveland and a rival journal to the increasingly Liberal *American Friend, Bible Student*, later *Soul Winner*, later *The Evangelical Friend*. The latter journal, begun in 1905, went into open war with *The American Friend*, the two trading editorials. West of the Appalachians, only Indiana Yearly Meeting had modernist sympathies and the Holiness Friends looked to over-ride those and get Russell removed from Earlham.

However, the Holiness cause would be ultimately undone from within its own ranks, resulting from the spread of Pentecostalism and the idea that there was a third blessing following sanctification, that of the gift of tongues. Holiness Friends became divided over the extreme emotionalism of Pentecostal worship. The leaders in Cleveland decided that the idea that all would receive this third blessing, and that it was the only sign of true baptism, was unscriptural. Ohio Yearly Meeting met in emergency session to denounce it and disown the Pentecostalist advocate, Levi Lupton, but Holiness Friends were not united in the condemnation. Jones took the initiative and attacked Pentecostalism and the Holiness division over it. By mid-1907, Jones had secured a victory for his modernist outlook: one correspondent wrote to him while he was on a decisive speaking tour in that year, 'you have got them whipped for all time now' (Hamm 1988, p. 172). In October 1907, Five Years Meeting convened, and the modernists carried the day.

HICKSITE MODERNISM

The Hicksites had not had a problem moving with the intellectual times. Their emphasis on form rather than doctrine led to separations of 'Progressives' over ecclesiology and political attitudes but they had generally adopted a modernist rationalist approach by the 1870s (Hamm 2002). Thus, on both sides of the Great Separation, modernism was to emerge as common ground which would later help build bridges and lead to reunited

Plate 11 Lucretia Mott (print)

Yearly Meetings. Where Five Years Meeting Yearly Meetings had a Renewal emphasis rather than a Revival one, modernism emerged as a dominant force, leading to an explicit or implicit Liberal approach to Scripture. The Hicksites were ahead of the Gurneyites in the transition of their thought, but only by about thirty years. Hicks himself had been an anti-literalist and had contended that Scripture could only be understood with the help of the inward Light, and in 1828 Hicksites were divided over the nature of the Bible. Some were free-thinkers, similar to the New Lights (see p. 84 above) in their ideas; others held views akin to the Orthodox party on scriptural authority. Lucretia Mott (Plate 11; and see Box 17) wrote as early as 1838: 'it is quite time that we read and examined the Bible more rationally in order that truth may shine in its native brightness' (Hamm 2002, p. 186). It was this division that had been erased by the 1870s as the

---

Box 17 Lucretia Mott (1793–1880)

Born Lucretia Coffin, she married James Mott at the age of eighteen. Lucretia Mott worked tirelessly for the abolition of slavery, joining with those outside her own Hicksite tradition to do so. She co-founded the Philadelphia Female Anti-Slavery Society, which was interracial and interdenominational. In 1840, she travelled to London to attend the World Anti-Slavery Convention. She was denied a seat as she was a woman and this led her, with other Quaker women, to organise the Seneca Falls Convention for women's rights of 1848. Mott was also an advocate of peaceful non-resistance, Native American rights, temperance, and prison reform (Bacon 2003, p. 186).

Box 18 Progressives

The Progressives were Congregationalist in ecclesiological terms and more involved in political reform, even where it meant involvement with 'the world'. The Congregationalism was a reaction against the discipline imposed by the Elders, a paradoxical situation for Hicksites who had reacted in the same way against the Orthodox. Dorlund states that ten new Yearly Meetings were set up by separation after 1848 (1968, p. 163). As usual, mutual disownment followed schism. Their political interests were particularly concerned with anti-slavery and women's rights, but also pacifism, temperance (shared throughout the Quaker world at that time), Native American rights, and the abolition of capital punishment. Separate men's and women's meetings were abolished, as were Elders and recorded ministers. The group at Waterloo in New York articulated their ideology in its 'Basis of Religious Association'; and the group there also initiated the first women's rights convention at Seneca Falls in 1848. In time, they lost their Quaker identity and Quaker form of worship, and changed their name to the Friends of Human Progress or Friends of Progress. Some became spiritualist. Most groups died out by the end of the nineteenth century but some such as Longwood, Pennsylvania and Vineland in New Jersey carried on to the middle of the twentieth century (Hawkes 2003, pp. 228–9).

(Thomas Hamm's work on the Society for Universal Enquiry and Reform reveals another version of this Progressive Quaker ideal. Here, Hicksites and others interested in immediate abolition of slavery (called Garrisonians after William Lloyd Garrison), or Ultraists, proclaimed a new type of society altogether without any coercive power, the abolition of private landholding, and a co-operative communitarian economic system with full equality for women. Technology would be used to help the workers, and new education systems and better diet would help give mental and physical preparation to live in this idealised world. Corrupt religion would be replaced by a pure Christianity, a post-millennial agenda to usher in God's Government. They founded eight communities, three in Ohio, four in Indiana, and one in New York. None lasted longer than four years (Hamm 1995, p. xvi).)

Box 19 Native Americans

Friends, from the start of their time in the American colonies, attempted to create positive and peaceful relations with the Native Americans. There are stories of Quaker worship and testimony influencing Native American attitudes towards this particular group of settlers (as also happened in New Zealand with the Maoris). In the eighteenth and nineteenth centuries, Quakers worked to observe treaties and revise unjust ones and advocated a peaceful approach towards Native Americans. In 1869, under President Grant's Peace Policy, Quakers, amongst other churches, were asked to oversee Government agencies. For almost twenty years, both Orthodox and Hicksite Friends fulfilled this role and set up committees on 'Indian Affairs'. In the twentieth century Friends were again concerned about, and campaigned for, Native American Rights in the USA and Canada. In the mid-nineteenth century, Orthodox Yearly Meetings became interested in mission work, and in the 1880s Meetings were established amongst Native Americans in Oklahoma and Kansas (Densmore 2003, pp. 190–2). At least one group remains today.

Radicals outlived the Conservatives and as a new generation of leaders emerged (Hamm 2002, p. 187).

By the 1880s, Hicksite Friends had achieved a new consensus about their faith . . . They openly described themselves as *liberals*, in sympathy with Unitarian and liberal movements in other Protestant denominations. (Hamm 2003, p. 46)

In common with the Liberals who would emerge in Britain in the following decade, Hicksite Liberals emphasised religious experience as primary in terms of religious authority above Scripture and doctrine, were cautious about scriptural doctrine such as the atonement, and emphasised openness to new ideas and a theology of progressivism (see Box 18) (Hamm 2003, p. 46). Symbolic of this new thinking was their commitment to education (p. 46) and politics. Engagement with the world had been a moot point on both sides of the Orthodox/Hicksite split. Rachel West illustrates this well in her article on Rachel Hicks, who married a nephew of Elias Hicks, and who was bitterly opposed to the worldly alliances set up by Lucretia Mott even though both of these Hicksites were vehemently opposed to slavery (West 2001). Mott appeared to occupy a position close to that of the Progressives (see Box 18).

Anti-slavery and the rights of women were increasingly linked in the 1830s and 1840s as women anti-slavery campaigners, such as the Grimke sisters, met with opposition. The Progressive Quaker Mary Ann McLintock (1799–1884) and her daughters, and modernist and radical

Hicksite Lucretia Mott, met with two other women Friends and the non-Quaker Elizabeth Cady Stanton to organise the Seneca Falls Women's Rights Convention, which was held in 1848. The Convention resulted in the call for suffrage and a number of resolutions including 'A Declaration of Sentiments' modelled on the United States Declaration of Independence. These ideas too were taken up by Hicksite modernists as normative after the 1880s.

SUMMARY

By the end of the nineteenth century, the varieties of Quakerism were well established and well delineated. All but the most conservative had denominationalised and had become a respected part of the Christian and societal landscape, and modernism was an influence in all the traditions to a lesser or greater extent. Quakers continued to build a reputation for their social witness and business acumen and came increasingly to enjoy this reputation, as they became less cautious about 'the world', including the rest of Christianity. The twentieth century would see further theological innovation of the Quaker tradition in the form of Liberal Quakerism, huge mission success amongst Evangelical Friends, as well as a continuing sense of 'family resemblance' which, in some cases, would lead to the reunification of some of the American Yearly Meetings.

CHAPTER 3

Quakerism in the twentieth century

This chapter considers twentieth-century Quakerism in terms of Liberal Quakerism and also the mission movement as the two main arenas of Quaker development within the century. The chapter ends with a summary of the different strands of present-day Quakerism and a numerical overview of different types of Quaker.

LIBERAL QUAKERISM

While Edward Grubb lucidly critiqued Barclay's influence on Quietist Quakers, reducing human agency in the interaction with God and diminishing the role of teaching (1908, p. 85), J. W. Rowntree wanted an active social Quakerism. He claimed that 'the Society of Friends so far from leading as it did in the seventeenth century, has been an unintelligent spectator of the greatest revolution in religious thought since the time of the Reformation' (1906, p. 241).

We stopped thinking in the seventeenth century. The thought-stuff of Fox, Penington and Barclay was never properly worked out. We never understood the Inward Light. We . . . set up an idolatry of the past, grew into formalists . . . repelled fresh thought by discipline instead of argument, and finally accepted a compromise with mid-Victorian Evangelicalism . . . The Society of Friends as a separate organisation will speedily disappear . . . who can rouse enthusiasm upon a cry of 'no baptism', and 'no supper', 'no paid ministry', and 'no singing'? These negations do not touch the heart of the modern questions which exercise us, it is impossible to maintain a fellowship upon negative distinctions, or to gather a people round a system of worship, however primitive or simple. (1906, pp. 243, 246)

Davie (1997, pp. 67–72) sets out a list of features which characterised the Liberal Quakerism which emerged in Britain and parts of America at the end of the nineteenth century. Theologically, there were four main motifs to the modernist vision:
1 that experience was primary
2 that faith needed to be relevant to the age

129

3 that Friends were to be open to 'new Light'
4 that new revelation had an automatic authority over old revelation and
   that God's Truth was revealed to us gradually over time: the idea of
   'Progressivism'.

EXPERIENCE AS PRIMARY

Modernist Friends imagined that they were reclaiming original Quakerism
but in fact they were to establish in its Liberal variation the biggest
departure from the rest of Quaker tradition to date. Early Friends had
indeed placed the experience of divine revelation as primary but Fox also
commented that it was always confirmed by Scripture even whilst he was
not looking for such verification (see p. 21 above). To place authority in
experience alone was new. How believers know what is of God is a critical
question for all religious groups. For these Friends, their experience was to
tell them. And should it need further verification, the experience of a wider
group was to suffice. Theological reliability comes in numbers or collective
experience for these Friends.

QUAKERISM AS RELEVANT TO THE AGE

At the same time, Friends wanted to have a faith that was relevant to the
age. Like their evangelical parents, they rejected the Quietistic preference
for the 'hedge'. They had no wish to reverse the reforms of the 1850s and
1860s. After 1870 in Britain, and only then, Friends could finally live as full
citizens without compromise. They could join the professions and attend
all universities. They enjoyed the freedom and status of this new citizenship and wished to celebrate education. *The Friend*, the weekly Quaker
periodical which had begun in 1843 as an evangelical journal, in counterpoint to the more conservative *British Friend* begun the same year, would
regularly carry reports of all that was good that had been said about
Quakers. The period 1895–1910 has been called the 'Quaker renaissance'
(Phillips 1989, p. 3). Brian Phillips' work portrays a rather vain movement,
proud of its past and its potential future as the nonconformists of the
nonconformists (Phillips 1989, p. 53), a civilising influence in the world
alongside empire.

   In one editorial, *The Friend* reported that a Methodist preacher had
claimed that Jesus would surely have been a Quaker. The Editor commented that whilst Friends themselves could never have made the claim,
the truth of it could not be doubted. Phillips characterises this period as

one of a 'Parade Society', one of show, of Quakers, sometimes naively, feeling they were a force to be reckoned with (1989).

Whereas John Bright, the famous British Quaker Member of Parliament (MP), had rejected service as a Quaker Elder as he was also a politician, the Quakers of the end of the century had no concerns about worldly involvement sitting alongside their spiritual lives. Woolman was celebrated as a Quaker role-model, back in fashion after the Evangelical distrust of his reliance on the inward guide. In 1906 a parliamentary election landslide for the Liberal Party included nine Quaker MPs. Phillips has described the stance of the Quaker renaissance as based in hubris or folly (2004), but it was also one rooted in a 'whig' view of history as progress and the Friends who lost most of the hedge in the 1860s were never to rebuild it. British Friends increasingly tolerated the state as the state increasingly tolerated the Quakers.

When Edward VII died in 1910, Friends found that Yearly Meeting coincided with his funeral. There had already been correspondence in *The Friend* over how large hats worn at Yearly Meeting should be. Now there was a division about whether Friends should wear mourning dress. Friends had become very much more worldly only a century after the 1802 book of discipline had so strongly proscribed mourning habits. The question was the extent to which Friends were part of 'the nation united in grief'.

In 1997, these questions of how far British Quakers were part of the nation were rehearsed after the death of Diana, Princess of Wales. Two articles appeared in *The Friend* offering sympathy to her two boys and the Clerk of Meeting for Sufferings independently wrote to the boys offering them the condolences of the Religious Society. As one Friend responded in part:

We Quakers, who look back on a long tradition of dissent and 'swimming against the tide', have we lost our ability to examine popular movements, and to resist pressure to conform to a mass emotion, even idolatry? Have we exchanged our traditional moral rigour for a more modern and conventional easy sentimentality? We have a testimony to equality: the death of a celebrity is not more important than any other. (Letter to *The Friend*, 19 September 1997)

OPEN TO NEW LIGHT

Today Liberal Friends take the idea of being 'open to new Light' as normative. It is enshrined in the current British discipline as being 'open to new light, from whatever quarter it may come' (*Quaker Faith and Practice*, 1995, Advice 7). The 1931 Yearly Meeting invented it (Punshon 1989, p. 15) and it accommodates corporate as well as individual innovation. In contrast, Fox was strongly opposed to random incursions of 'new Light', as the John Perrot example shows (see p. 45 above).

PROGRESSIVISM

Progressivism, which Isichei finds emerging within British Quakerism from 1874, is the idea that 'God's truths are timeless and unchanging, but God's revelation of them to humanity is gradual' (Isichei 1970, p. 36), appropriate to the age. Innate to this idea is a chronological authority to revelation, i.e. that new revelation automatically has a higher authority than old. From the details of the Perrot case, we can see that this was not the case early on. This idea of progressive revelation allowed Liberal Friends to co-opt new ideas such as those regarding evolution or higher criticism (which was calculating how the Bible was put together and by whom it was written) without sensing a tension between tradition and innovation. It could explain new ideas in terms of a divine invitation to new knowledge, newly appropriate to the human condition. This also fitted well with a view of history as being about progress, and complemented the optimistic view of humanity and of civilisation affirmed by the emphasis on experience and the Liberal reclamation of the idea of 'that of God in every one' (Isichei 1970, p. 34).

This renewed emphasis on Light can also be seen as directly opposite to the Evangelical trend away from the idea of the inward Light as unscriptural and prone to a theological fragility, a susceptibility to feelings. Crewdson had questioned it very publicly in 1835 and had left the Religious Society as a result. By 1861, it was being questioned within London Yearly Meeting (see p. 95 above). However, as with the Liberals' other reclamations of the Quaker past, this idea was also transformed. In contrast to Barclay's clear sense that conscience and the Light were distinct and should not be confused (see p. 59 above), the Liberals co-opted conscience as a spiritual faculty and as the very faculty in which the Light operated. They also rejected the idea of original sin (Isichei 1970, p. 34), emphasising instead the idea of the seed of God in the heart, a kind of original blessing or an innate Godliness, which in turn would accommodate the growth of the popular idea of the inner Light rather than the inward Light of earlier generations. 'Inward' implies that the Light comes from beyond, as if through a keyhole. It is a dualistic concept and sets the Light up as separate from humanity. 'Inner' situates the Light inside the individual and can be used to accommodate more monist interpretations of how God works with humanity. 'That of God in every one' changed its meaning, from the ability of everyone to turn to the inward Light of Christ to a sense that a piece of the Divine resides in everybody

(Dandelion 1996, p. 268). The 'inner Light' is mainly a twentieth-century invention along with much of normative Liberal Quakerism and has been wrongly imputed to earlier generations by countless scholars. It is only in the subtle details of the meanings of these look-alike terms that the real revolution in thinking becomes apparent. The term 'inner Light' was used in the 1870s by Joseph Binyon Forster, David Duncan's ally, but became normative through the influential writings of Rufus Jones who used it interchangeably with 'inward Light' in his twentieth-century writings. Its use has helped accommodate theological change within the Liberal tradition as well as adding to the misunderstandings between the different branches of Quakerism. Phillips writes of the 1910 London Yearly Meeting which clashed with the funeral of Edward VII:

When these 'well-fed, comfortable and self-sufficient' Quakers arrived in London in May, 1910 for their Yearly Meeting, they found that the occasion of the Society's annual national gathering had the misfortune to coincide with the very day of the King's funeral. As *The Friend* reported soberly: 'The King's funeral had a practical effect which touched many Friends. Lyons', and most of the other restaurants, were closed all day; the ABC's were open part of the day, so that many Friends had difficulty in finding the physical refreshment that they needed. The restaurants which were open in the immediate neighbourhood were soon cleared out, and after the afternoon sitting Friends were seen to be rambling about the streets in search of a place where they could have some tea.' The confused and rambling Friends of this account – rendered temporarily insecure in the absence of expected provisions, were to face far greater instabilities and trials in the years just ahead. The search for the last Edwardian cup of tea was but a preamble to a more arduous search for an authentic twentieth-century Quaker identity, and for the soul of the Society of Friends itself. (Phillips 1989, pp. 346–7)

THE SHIFT TO PLURALISM

The importance of the four characteristics of modernism is that they both represent a deviation from erstwhile Quaker theology and also are difficult to regulate, lacking as they do any external accountability beyond the collective interpretation of pure experience. They are tied to nothing in terms of doctrine, to no particular text, no particular rendering of the tradition. Whilst based on interpretations of the past, they allow and accommodate a Quakerism potentially forever on the move.

The Liberal Quakerism of the early twentieth century was part of a wider liberal theological movement of that time. It was followed by a distinctly different form of unprogrammed Quakerism in the period after the Second World War, not only in Britain but also, to a lesser extent, throughout the rest of the Liberal Quaker world. Martin Davie has charted the shift as being one from 'conservative' to 'radical', most visibly seen in the move from a Liberal Quakerism which assumed Christianity to one in which it did not matter. As early as the 1930s, Rufus Jones was apparently asked whether you had to be a Christian to be a Quaker. His answer is not known for certain, but the question itself is more interesting. In 1966 at London Yearly Meeting, British Friends rejected draft membership regulations as too doctrinally Christian. One Friend 'appealed for a place in the Society for those who, like himself, were reluctant to define their attitude in terms only of Christian belief' (*The Friend* 124 (1966), p. 672). Davie (1997) cites Janet Scott's 1980 Swarthmore Lecture *What canst thou say? Towards a Quaker Theology* as symbolic of this shift. When faced with the question as to whether Quakers need be Christian or not, Scott answers that it does not matter: 'what matters to Quakers is not the label by which we are called or call ourselves, but the life' (1980, p. 70).

The set of four characteristics of Liberal Quakerism, described above (experience as primary; faith relevant to the age; open to new Light; progressivism), underpinned by a rationalist modernist approach that could accommodate higher criticism and Darwinianism, meant that it was not tied to any text or any tradition. That set of characteristics, so rooted in experience and its interpretation in changing times, each new revelation with more authority than the last, allowed and then encouraged Liberal Quakerism to be a religious enterprise always on the move. The term 'liberal-Liberal Quakerism' is used here to describe this pluralistic and consequential modification of earlier Liberal Quakerism.

LIBERAL-LIBERAL QUAKERISM, CHRISTIANITY, AND THE SECOND COMING

For liberal-Liberal Friends, theology has become a story (see p. 145 below), God an option. Key parts of the tradition can be, and have been, questioned as new sets of individual experiences/interpretations modify collective popular belief and over time. The collective orthodoxy is reframed by each generation in a revised book of discipline. Liberal-Liberal Quakerism is one in which belief is pluralised, privatised, but also marginalised: it is not seen as important. This kind of Quakerism is held together by an adherence to form, by the way the group is religious, not by what it believes. There are Muslim, Hindu, Sikh, and Buddhist Quakers (Huber 2001), theist and non-theist (Rush 2003), agnostic and atheist. The second coming, for most, is no longer part of their story. The British book of discipline contains the following:

The first Friends had an apocalyptic vision of the world transformed by Christ and they set about to make it come true. The present generation of Quakers shares this conviction of the power of the spirit, but it is doubtful whether it will transform the world in our lifetime, or in that of our children or children's children. For us it is not so important when the perfect world will be achieved or what it will be like. What matters is living our lives in the power of love and not worrying too much about the results. In doing this, the means become part of the end. Hence we lose the sense of helplessness and futility in the face of the world's crushing problems. We also lose the craving for success, always focusing on the goal to the exclusion of the way of getting there. We must literally not take too much thought for the morrow but throw ourselves whole-heartedly into the present. That is the beauty of the way of love; it cannot be planned and its end cannot be foretold. (*Quaker Faith and Practice*, 1995, 24.60)

In terms of the chart, outlining where Friends are between meantime and endtime, Liberal Friends have fallen off (Fig. 3.1). For those without a first coming a second coming makes no sense.

In the mid-1990s I suggested that Friends in Britain are post-Christian, in that many use alternative ways of describing their spirituality (1996, p. 178). Ten years later, Rosie Rutherford asked over 1000 Friends whether they

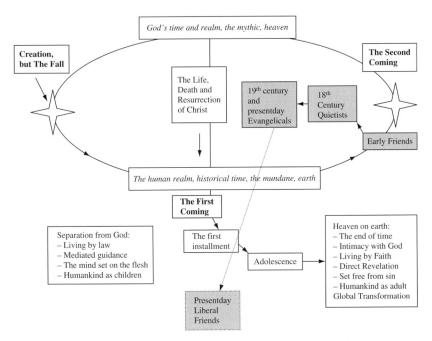

Fig. 3.1 A biblical understanding of time and Liberal Friends

describe themselves as Christian: 45% responded that they do. However, at the same time, recent work by Kate Mellor has located Meetings where almost 90% of Friends have claimed to be Christian, with the term defined as they wish. My 1989 survey found that 39% of British Friends claimed that Jesus was an important figure in their spiritual life with a further 32% for whom it varies. Thus, at any one point, as many as 71% could answer in the affirmative. Rutherford's statistics are very similar (personal communication). A study of Swiss Friends gave a figure of 51% for whom Jesus was an important figure in their spiritual lives, with 25% for whom it varies (Nancy Krieger, personal communication). No comparable work has yet been undertaken for Liberal Quakerism in the USA.

THE BEHAVIOURAL CREED

Eleven reasons for not adopting a credal system of belief come easily and readily to Liberal Quaker groups. These can be grouped into five categories as follows:

1 The limitations of language.
   (a) Religious experience is beyond linguistic codification and definition.
   (b) Credal statements demean, in their limited linguistic form, the depth of religious experience.
2 The limitation of God's Word.
   (c) Credal statements operate to close off new religious expression and revelation.
   (d) Credal statements encourage a complacency of attitude to religious life by giving an impression of finality and surety.
   (e) Credal statements take on an authority of their own, belying the authority of God.
3 The limitation of Quakerism.
   (f) It would be impossible, inappropriate and dishonest, because of the diversity of individual belief, to adopt a credal statement.
   (g) Credal statements, even if possible, would misrepresent the nature of Quaker religion.
4 The exclusive nature of credal statements.
   (h) Credal statements operate (i) to exclude those outside the group, and (ii) to alienate those within the group, who cannot subscribe to them.
   (i) A credal statement would separate the group from those of other faiths by identifying the group with one particular faith.

5 The practical points.
  (j) There is no structural need to adopt a credal statement, e.g. as a basis for Membership.
  (k) There is no mechanism for adopting a credal statement.

What is interesting is the way Liberal Quakers collectively agree and affirm these eleven values. Ambler has described the following six advantages of creeds:

(a) express faith in memorable words;
(b) educate new members and the young;
(c) symbolise unity;
(d) define and defend the faith in relation to other beliefs;
(e) maintain authority and discipline;
(f) provide a church with a public identity. (Ambler 1989, p. 11)

Even when faced with these advantages, Liberal Friends affirm their opposition to creeds. If pushed, they resist more firmly. In other words, Liberal Friends collectively agree that they do not have creeds. I have called this paradoxical collective affirmation of belief in not having creeds a 'behavioural creed' (Dandelion 1996, chapter 3). In other words, a credal attitude to form or practice exists, visible through its opposition to more traditional kinds of creed.

If we take the eleven reasons against credal systems of belief and apply them to attitudes to Quaker worship, the keystone of Liberal Quakerism, we find that the opposition falls away. Liberal Quakers do not feel concerned that maintaining a similar system of worship for 350 years demeans the experience of worship, undermines progressive revelation, or leads to complacency and a false sense of surety. These Friends do not feel silent worship misrepresents Quakerism and its diversity or inappropriately links Quakerism with particular faith. If it excludes those outside the group or alienates those within, this does not seem to concern these Friends. Orthopraxy is used as a basis for Liberal Quaker commitment and membership. Prescriptive passages on practice form part of the Yearly Meeting book of discipline. In other words, the concerns over the consequences of belief creed are not present when Liberal Friends think about their adherence to a particular form.

THE QUAKER DOUBLE-CULTURE

This contrasting pattern, of a permissive approach to belief content and a conformist and conservative 'behavioural creed' comprising a 'double-culture', is sociologically fascinating. First, it is the behavioural creed, the way in which Quakers are religious, which acts as the social glue. Second, more detailed research may be able to show that the two aspects of the double-culture operate in inverse relationship, so that when one is weak or permissive, the other is strong. Thus, we could identify a proto-behavioural creed in the Quietist period. The peculiarities were the outward mark of the inward Quaker spirituality and they operated as a boundary marker of who was in and who was out of the group. The Evangelicals with strong belief content felt able to abolish the peculiarities and relax the behavioural creed surrounding worship, even in some cases replacing traditions such as unprogrammed worship. The Liberals with a permissive attitude to belief regrouped, according to Kennedy (2001), on the peace testimony and latterly on process rather than belief content.

In terms of the sect/denomination typology discussed above (see pp. 80–1), it can be argued that liberal-Liberal Quakers operate as both. The permissiveness afforded to belief content places low demands on participants: there is nothing to learn or get right, and no requirement for a confession of faith or conversion narrative. At the same time, participants are required to learn the rules of worship and 'Meetings for Business' (see p. 217 below). These collective acts are by default more public and more central to Liberal Quaker identity. When these Quakers answer that 'dread question', 'what do Quakers believe?' with a list of negatives: 'we do not sing hymns', 'we do not have outward sacraments', 'we do not have a separated priesthood' (Dandelion 1996, p. 302), it looks as if they are avoiding the question. They are actually answering the question they think is being asked, 'What is at the core of your religion?' In other words, what defines you as a particular set of believers? Silent worship, in its open and inward form, is what defines this form of Quakerism. It is the means to the experience, central to the Liberal Quaker project. We will see below how this difference in definition is one of the differences between Liberal and Evangelical Friends (see p. 242 below).

The twin cultures are also played out in attitudes to leadership and responsibility. The flat ecclesiology (see p. 205 below) contains within it temporary and rotating roles collectively agreed and assigned by the group. In Britain, the main roles are Clerk, Elder, and Overseer. The Clerk manages the business of the Meeting, the Elders help nurture the worship life, and Overseers have responsibility for helping with pastoral care (the term 'Overseer' is avoided in many US meetings because of its slavery connotations). The more public roles of Clerk and Elder have their duties firmly related to the form of the group. For example, an Elder might interrupt an overlong ministry (that is one which went against the behavioural norms of the group) but could not intervene in terms of content, that aspect accommodated by the liberal belief culture. Similarly Clerks' duties are clearly delineated within the book of discipline to apply to process, not content. Only the unofficial leadership of 'weighty Friends', those whose words carry weight, influences belief content. Here charismatic authority is given by other group members: influence in some ways is self-selected. Attempted resignations which emphasise a crisis of faith or doubt are unlikely to be successful. They do not contradict the liberal belief culture in which doubt is valid (*Advices and Queries*, 1995, no. 5). When one Friend criticised 'Nominations Committees' (who 'discern' the names for those appointed to roles) as 'undemocratic', a tension was exposed between the individual and the behavioural creed. No longer seeing itself as the true church, the Meeting encouraged this Friend to go elsewhere as there seemed to be so large a gap in understanding of the fundamentals of the faith. In a group which places so much emphasis on continuing revelation, individuals resign not only because they feel disenchanted generally but because they feel left behind a group on the move. Equally they can feel 'left ahead', that the group is moving too slowly in spite of being 'open to new Light'. Each of these three types of resignation operates in each aspect of the double-culture, belief and practice (Dandelion 2002).

TESTIMONY

Testimony falls interestingly across the double-culture. During the 1991 Gulf War, there were many views as to what the best course of action should be. In other words, what did the 'peace testimony' mean in this context? One suggestion was to assassinate Saddam Hussein as the path of least suffering. In this example, the twentieth-century shift from a 'testimony against war' to a 'testimony for peace' had raised questions of interpretation, 'peace' being a far broader and more diffuse concept than 'against war'. Jung Jiseok, building on the work of Elaine Bishop, cites the move between the two testimonies as being a shift from a particular concept to a diffuse one, from a conservative notion to a radical one, from a prescription to an option, and from being a testimony rooted in Christianity to one rooted in a variety of spiritualities (Jiseok 2004). Whilst Friends have always enlisted in any major war, they have also been disowned for so doing, as in the case of the Free Quakers (see p. 52 above), or only conditionally accepted. For example, a man by the name of Purdey wished to join New York Yearly Meeting in the 1930s but openly expressed his difficulty with the peace testimony. He was admitted to membership on the

---

Box 20 Simplicity and Quaker neo-Luddites

Simplicity replaced 'plainness' as the governing criterion for style and consumption in the nineteenth century. This accommodated the move away from
the 'peculiarities' as Friends argued they could maintain simplicity inwardly
without outward display. Simplicity, however, is a more diffuse concept than
plainness and Friends today can interpret this aspect of testimony very differ-
ently. One Friend may decide to cycle everywhere, another may buy an
expensive car because of its greater longevity over a cheaper model. In
America, some Friends have been attracted by the neo-Luddite gatherings
and resistance to 'unnecessary' technology.

---

basis that he needed to acknowledge that this testimony had always been
part of Quaker tradition and that he would not try to change the Society.
This was known for a time locally as the 'Purdey Principle'.

Today, in the liberal-Liberal setting, Friends interpret the beliefs associated with the peace testimony individually. What is interesting is that the
testimony itself, seen as part of the Quaker tradition dating back to 1660 (see
p. 43 above), is never questioned. It has become an aspirational principle, a
shift away from the use of testimony as rule of the eighteenth century and
away from the idea of testimony as consequence amongst the earliest
Friends. Some Friends join in spite of not agreeing with the peace testimony
but it is not challenged as foundational for most Quakers and indeed it
remains one of the three main shared elements of worldwide Quakerism, as
we will also see below (p. 246). In this way, attitudes towards testimony
reflect both sides of the liberal-Liberal Quaker double-culture. (Box 20
outlines the similar example of the testimony on simplicity.)

LIBERAL FRIENDS AND THE WORLD

The days of Elders visiting the homes of Friends on matters of theology
and lifestyle are gone, and disownment is now rare (see p. 238 below). The
reform of the peculiarities by Evangelical Friends left open the possibility
of private life after 1860. The Quaker could leave the Meeting, invisible and
inaudible as such to the world, given the loss of plain dress and plain
speech, and head home to a non-Quaker spouse. In the following period,
Meetings increasingly stepped back from exercising authority outside of
the Meeting House. Ultimately, it was left to the individual Friend how
much he or she shared with the Meeting of life outside of 'Quaker time',
the time Friends come together explicitly as Quakers. This is generally true

Fig. 3.2 Liberal Quakers and the world

of all Quaker traditions, although the degree to which certain activities are proscribed varies (see p. 221 below). Some pastors, for example, are told not to drink alcohol in public, and divorce may be beyond the pale. Liberal Friends experiencing difficulties in relationships can feel unsupported. It may be, however, that the Meeting now no longer knows how to act, or whether it can even do so, outside of the routines of Meeting House life. For Liberal Friends, 'the world' has become very small, and there is a question about what, if anything, may now be proscribed by all Friends (Fig 3.2). In turn this problematises how Friends can operate systems of mutual accountability.

SILENCE AND SPEECH

The double-culture also underpins the way in which silence has masked and accommodated the pluralisation of belief within Britain Yearly Meeting and other Liberal Yearly Meetings in the last fifty years. The 'Culture of Silence' (Dandelion 1996, chapter 6) is created through the high value given silence, the low value given language, and the consequent rules about breaking the silence. Superficially, silence marks the boundaries of the collective worship. It is also, in Quaker orthodoxy, the medium through which God's will is heard, voiced, and discerned.

It is through the silence, then, that:

1 God is experienced by the individual, and thus authority for belief in God is given

2 the silent approach to discerning God's will is validated through the fact that participants claim they experience God in the silence

3 God's will is discerned by the individual through 'leadings'
4 ideas of what might constitute God's will are shared and tested through
   ministry
5 action consequent to God's will is devised and accepted through
   Business Meeting decisions
6 the names of those playing roles are thought of (in nominations committee), are decided upon, and are given their authority (the appointment of Officers or committee members by the appropriate Meeting for
   Worship for Church Affairs).

Within the liberal-Liberal liturgy of silence, speech is devalued by consequence of the theological role given to collective silence. Its status is also
diminished by the popular Quaker view on the impossibility, and the
inappropriateness, of speech, to communicate belief. First, words are not
of practical use in expressing spirituality. Leichty conceptualises this view
in theological terms:

God *an sich* is an utterly unknowable *X* and that what we cannot speak about, of
that we must remain silent! Theology is richer and not poorer for this silence. For
then we are unburdened to seek truth about the plurality of religions in the full
face of the many Gods of humankind. (1990, p. 83)

Second, it is not appropriate to try and verbalise religious belief. This view
is based on the premise that the nature of language and the nature of God
are qualitatively distinct. Language limits the understanding of God. It can
also be inappropriate. Hewitt neatly summates the Quaker view:

God cannot be fitted into preformed notions bounded by expression in
words. Faith must allow for elements of radical unknowability and mystery
about God. (1990, p. 757)

Cowie elaborates:

Quakers, in my perception, have arrived at a novel position. The response to any
direct, precise question on faith or morals has to be silence. (1990, p. 7)

In this sense, this Quaker group sets itself apart from both a text-bound
tradition and an oral one.

For many of us, I feel sure, putting 'God' into words at all is to trivialise
the very thing we are seeking to convey … the silence of meeting means
so much to me. Where else can I go to share with others what is beyond
words? (Letter to *The Friend*, 150 (1992), p. 471)

In these ways, vocal expression of belief is devalued. By inference, the free
ministry is properly concerned with that which is not beyond words. God's

word, ministry, is secular in content, if divine in origin. This position of recognising the limitations of expressing religiosity vocally is philosophically fortuitous but is undermined and contradicted by the debates around whether or not Quakers need be theists, Christians, etc.

The value placed on silence devalues speech and also increases attention on the role of vocal ministry (Kelly 1944, p. 12). For all the functions of silence outlined above, ministry is the means by which those functions are expressed. If the will of God is discerned by the gathered collective, it is the vocal ministry which expresses the sense of the message. Vocal ministry is deemed, by definition, to come from God. Present-day Friends are confronted by two challenges. The first is to identify what is and what is not true ministry. The second is to deliver God's word in the right way.

The challenge for the individual Friend is to attempt to determine the legitimacy (whether or not it is from God) of the message prior to its delivery.

Each Friend who feels called upon to rise and deliver a lengthy discourse might question himself – and herself – most searchingly, as to whether the message could not be more lastingly given in the fewest possible words, or even through his or her personality alone, in entire and trustful silence. 'Cream must always rise to the surface.' True. But other substances rise to the surface besides cream; substances that may have to be skimmed off and thrown away before bodies and souls can be duly nourished. 'Is my message cream or scum?' may be an unusual and is certainly a very homely query. Still it is one that every speaker, in a crowded gathering especially, should honestly face. Some of the dangers of silent worship can best be guarded against by its courtesies. (*Quaker Faith and Practice*, 1995, 2.64)

This quotation neatly summarises the problem of discerning the legitimacy of vocal ministry. Zielinski comments:

if there is any doubt in the mind of the speaker as to the value of his message, then he should remain silent. (1975, p. 31)

In addition to discerning whether or not the message is from God, the Friend needs to submit to the cultural and theological rules around when and how the silence can be broken by speech if s/he is not to risk public interruption or a private word from an Elder.

The speaker must always be sensitive to the needs and the spiritual conditions of the worshippers, remembering that through him the united exercise of the group may find a voice. (*Quaker Faith and Practice*, 1995, 2.55)

Seven aspects of normative ministry are readily identifiable. They are: (i) length, (ii) style, (iii) frequency, (iv) timing, (v) content, (vi) thematic association, (vii) linguistic construction. Davies found in a survey of four-teen Meetings that the total length of ministry ranged between 7.5 and 20.25 minutes for a whole Meeting. Individual ministries ranged between 0.25 and 10.25 minutes. Seventy per cent of the spoken contributions were less than three minutes in duration (1988, p. 123). Ministries which are of a length greater than ten to fifteen minutes are subject to public interruption by an Elder.

Friends used to minister in a nasal tone to differentiate between their own words and those of God. Present-day Friends do not mask their own voices in the same way but, just as the stereotype of a priest giving a sermon includes a distinct modulation, Friends subdue their voices. Displays of emotion are rare. Davies characterises vocal ministry as having a 'heavily marked style' (1988, p. 133).

Timing is important too.

> Wait to be sure of the right moment for giving the message ... Beware of making additions towards the end of a meeting when it was well left before. (*Quaker Faith and Practice*, 1995, 2.55)

There are 'right moments' for speech. There are also 'right moments' for other sorts of noise. One movement is a signal for many. Noise levels rise when accompanying breaks in the ritual of silence occur: when one person breaks the silence, to minister, leave, or enter, others take the opportunity to make themselves comfortable for the subsequent return to silence.

Davies talks of 'non-mentionables' or those subjects which 'are just not among the mentionables' (1988, p. 131). He cites insults, contributions which require an answer (such as the making of arrangements), and items which have no relevance or significance to the group (p. 131).

Hubbard has noted how 'the sequence of contributions to a Meeting develops, usually in a fairly logical and associative manner, from one speaker to another' (1992, p. 198). Similarly, Davies has noted that whilst the content of ministry can vary, the normative pattern of ministry is for a series of thematic ministries to add to the opening contribution (1988, p. 129). Key words enter into successive ministries (1988, p. 129).

THE CULTURE OF SILENCE

There are four consequences to the rules around speech and silence in worship. The first is that the correct use of silence and speech is a skill to be learned. Second then, conversely, silence can be misused. In one Meeting, someone from another church used the space to try and persuade Quakers of his superior doctrine (before the Elders asked him to go outside and talk more personally with them). Participants try to minimise differences between their 'performances'. Third, fear of not having learnt the normative style of, or misusing, speech acts as self-censor within worship. Fourth, fear of conflict and ostracism within a pluralistic group where theology is often kept private impedes 'talking-God' outside of the worship event. If theology is not mentioned within ministry, it is even less likely to be mentioned in contributions which lack the divine potential of ministry. It is not only fear of getting the form of ministry wrong which constrains, but fear of expressing ideas which will not be approved of. Quakers learn in silence too. Over half of those who have been involved with Friends for less than three years have not ministered (Dandelion 1996, p. 254). Changes in belief content remain hidden. Figure 3.3 illustrates the operation of the culture of silence.

At the top of the diagram is worship and the use of silence as the basis of the Liberal Quaker form. Quaker religious experience occurs within the silence, and types of individual belief are constructed to help make sense of that experience. Belief may be vocalised in ministry but frequently is not, through either a lack of opportunity or lack of courage (with the silence used as a form of self-censor or defence against ostracism). The lack of regular and explicit vocalisation of belief means that there is no reaction in these terms. The silence operates at this stage of the process as a consequence of (a) silence used as a form of worship, and (b) silence used as a defence. In this way, changes to popular belief, as newcomers enter the group or as participants change the language of the theology, occur covertly. This process is repeatable and changes in individual and group belief remain hidden (silence masks reality) whilst the common form of worship presents a picture of unity.

Thus, the silence operated by liberal-Liberal Friends can conceal diversity, both of personal theology, and of the theology of worship. Whilst the form of worship operates as a means of cohesion for the group, its varying interpretations may at some stage begin to unpick the form. The Meeting for Worship for Business, for example, also based in silence has been traditionally seen as a means to the discernment of the will of God. For those without a God or without a God with a will, this formula becomes anachronistic. Instead, for these Friends, the business method becomes secular, simply a temperamental or political preference. What was once a heretical query, 'why can't we vote?' becomes a legitimate question.

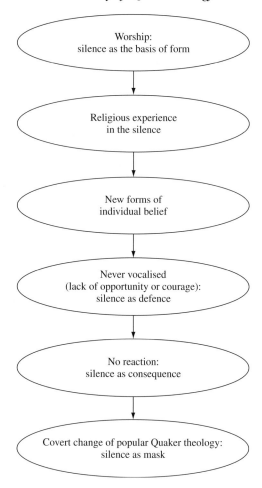

Fig. 3.3 The operation of the culture of silence (after Dandelion 1996, p. 258)

MODELS OF LIBERAL QUAKERISM

To try and understand its shifting dynamics, there have been various attempts to model Liberal Quakerism. In 1992 Fran Taber suggested a dynamic Quakerism in tension between Liberal and Conservative impulses. She argued that this was a healthy Quakerism with spin-offs or aberrations the result of losing the counterbalance (Fig. 3.4 and Table 3.1). In the British context however, the model fell short, as much of what was normative in Britain had been described by her as an aberration.

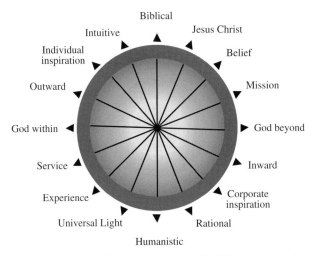

Fig. 3.4 A model of Quaker theology (after Taber 1992, p. 16)

Emlyn Warren focused on the nature of believing within Liberal Quakerism. His three models depict a shift from a Quakerism with a central core of belief in the 1660s, to one with a more diffuse pattern of believing in the 1990s (Fig. 3.5). His projection (Fig. 3.6) is of different clusters of belief affinities operating in the periphery of Quakerism, independent of each other.

This is similar to Gay Pilgrim's model of the future of Quakerism (Fig. 3.7). She uses the term 'heterotopic' to describe the way in which some social groups such as the Quakers have defined themselves by creating dissonant contexts, such as by turning the courtroom into a pulpit (see p. 27 above). She argues that Quakers have maintained unity and identity through their heterotopic stance. Pilgrim argues that for world-affirming Liberal Friends in a Quaker-affirming culture, the heterotopic impulse has become turned inward. In other words, the desire to create difference and dissonance becomes internalised. This results in the celebration and even prescription of mutual difference between participants. The ability to be different has become a normative expectation. She argues that three kinds of Friends have emerged as distinct groupings, akin to Warren's clusters. The first group are exclusivists, who maintain a doctrinal unity, some of whom have left the 'larger body' such as the Yearly Meeting of Friends in Christ (see p. 168 below). The second group is that of the syncretists who manage the Liberal belief culture by continually adding new layers to their

Table 3.1. *A typology of Quaker theology (Taber 1992, p. 17)*

SPIN-OFF or ABERRATION	UNIVERSAL	JESUS CHRIST-CENTRED	SPIN-OFF or ABERRATION
Liberal, vague intellectualism	Affirmation of truth experienced by others	Affirmation of truth as I have experienced it in the context of Christian history	Fundamentalist, exclusive intellectualism
Powerlessness, hopelessness, fatigue (the tired Liberal) Limiting God from powerful action in time	Seeking to embody and express the love of God Affirmation of God as an inhabiter of space unconfined by time	Being empowered by God Affirmation of God as acting in time	Misuse of power, apparent lack of love Limiting God's actions to a particular context
Limitation of God's actual transformation of our lives Focus on psychic	Immanent-God as expressed in creation Intuitive	Transcendant-God as greater than any expression we can know Intellectual system of theology	Limitation of God's actual transformation of our lives Association of psychic with demonic
Inability to put experience in words with any strength Lack of clear relation to God	Felt, sensed, experienced, uncontainable in words God understood as beyond personhood	Verbally explained God understood as personal	Rigid exclusive to creed Limited nature of relation to God
Relationship confined by the limitations of my own viewpoint	'Spiritual' relationship to God. Inward Light as impersonal presence	'Personal' relationship to God	Relationship confined by the limitations of my own viewpoint
Life of Christ is without power for me There is nothing intrinsically unique about the Jesus of history	Life of Jesus Christ as example, model, source of teaching Jesus as God-filled or inspired revealer	Life of Jesus Christ as unique, and essentially relevant to me Jesus Christ as son of God and redeemer	Those who don't know Jesus Christ are benighted Those who do not connect with the Jesus of history are lost
God's action so generalized as to lose force	God acts everywhere, at all times, whether we are aware of it or not	God acts in this specific time and in this specific way	God's action in other ways is not perceived

Tendency to have fuzzy, ineffective concept of God	Mystical-experiencing God	Theological-thinking about God	Tendency to confine God to the ways we have described God
Hope diffuse, ungrounded	Hope	Faith	Faith narrowly focused, brittle
I'm OK, you're OK, we're all OK	Appreciation of others' viewpoint	Concern for others' spiritual welfare	Judgement and control of others
Religious so ineffectually communicated that its reality seems unclear	Religious experience as ultimately indescribable	Religious experience described	Religious experience prescribed
Equalising all experience – all of some value – no sense or criteria of maturing	Appreciation of others' experience	Evaluation of others' experience	Discounting of others' experience
Emphasis on proclamation equated with underestimating importance of material needs	Social action	Proclamation	Emphasis on social action equated with lack of essential grounding in faith
Failure to communicate the ground out of which action comes	Social action	Proclamation	Failure to translate faith into action

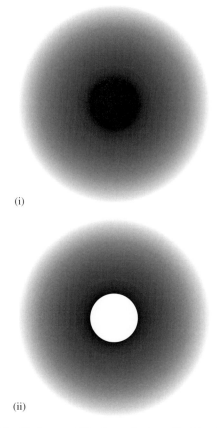

Fig. 3.5 Models of influence of Quaker orthodoxy: (i) 1660s, (ii) 1990s (after
Dandelion 1996, p. 287)

theology but also uphold the conservative and conformist behavioural creed. The third group is that of the individualists who follow a self-serving path through Quakerism. These last two groupings correspond partly to my division of Friends into corporatists, who uphold the Yearly Meeting discipline, and congregationalists and individualists, those who ignore the Yearly Meeting, believing in local or individual authority respectively (Dandelion 1996, Foreword).

In my analysis the main problem with these models is that they over-emphasise the place of believing. It is the behavioural creed which remains definitional for Liberal Friends (see p. 137 above), with belief, 'belief stories' of semi-realist interpretation, marginal and individual. Only the

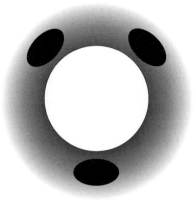

Fig. 3.6 Projected model of Liberal Quaker belief in the 1990s (Dandelion 1996, p. 299)

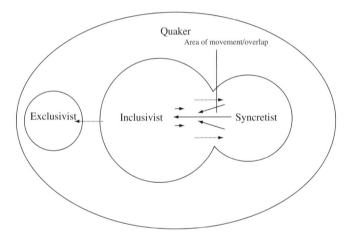

Fig. 3.7 Pilgrim's model of the heterotopic impulse within British Quakerism
(Dandelion 2004, p. 219)

idea of 'that of God in everyone' is shared, acting as (i) an underpinning of
form (e.g. the free ministry), (ii) an underpinning of testimony, (iii) a
common element of the belief stories, and (iv) a boundary function in that
anything which transgressed this idea would be challenged. Its meaning,
what the 'that', the 'God', and the 'everyone' means, nevertheless remains
individual.

The additional boundary function to Quaker identity not identified in
this model is the idea of the 'absolute perhaps', the prescription of seeking

as the normative mode of belief, a rigorous and conformist aspect of the otherwise liberal belief culture which ultimately makes liberal-Liberal Quakerism less permissive than it first appears (Dandelion 2004b). In other words, Liberal Quakerism is held together by *how* it believes. The set of characteristics that allowed this kind of Quakerism to be forever on the move have become normative. The possibility of difference has become a prescription. The ideas of progressivism and of being open to new Light have become translated into the idea that the group cannot know Truth, except personally, partially, or provisionally. Thus liberal-Liberal Quakerism is not just about the possibility of seeking, it is about the certainty of never finding. I have suggested that Friends of this kind are a Seeker C type, that they can seek anywhere where they are sure they will not find (see Box 3 above). All theology is 'towards', a 'perhaps' kind of exercise. In a rational philosophical understanding of the nature of religion, these Friends have decided that religious truth claims are problematic, perhaps even neither true nor false but meaningless. From outside the religious enterprise they are sure of this. In other words, they are absolutely certain (rationally) that they can never be certain (theologically). They operate a doctrine of the 'absolute perhaps' and they operate it in a prescriptive way. In other words, these Friends are zealous, even fundamentalist, about their theological stance (Dandelion 2004b). Those who find theological truth or who wish to share it with the rest of the group will feel increasingly uncomfortable. One of the ironies for such a permissive group is that this position holds that any group or any individual who claims to have found the final truth, for all people or for all time, is wrong. All religious groups have to be partly wrong theologically: liberal-Liberal Quakers know this only from outside of that epistemological difficulty of theology.

So, ecumenically, liberal-Liberal Quakers are in an interesting position. They believe in a very different way from most religious groups and hold belief as a category in a very different esteem, but they also tend to judge down all those groups who do place belief as central and who think theology can be or is true. The 'absolute perhaps' is the defining character-istic of the liberal-Liberal Quaker and is the key difference between these Friends and the whole of the rest of Quakerism, worldwide today and historically.

Wildwood's model depicts Quakerism as straddling the worlds of Christian theism, and multi-faith and new age spiritualities and the area of overlap between the two. Historically, Liberal Quakerism has shifted away from Christian theism in the last fifty years but Wildwood contends that at present the group straddles both worlds. This contradicts the work of Linda Woodhead and Paul Heelas who in their work on the town of Kendal identified Quakerism as part of 'religion', i.e. emphasising the sacred as transcendent or 'other', rather than 'spiritual', where the sacred is part of the subjective (Heelas *et al.* 2005, p. 6). In Wildwood's analysis, Woodhead and Heelas are right to include Quakerism at the experiential end of religion (2005, pp. 21–2) but wrong not to have it overlapping into their 'holistic milieu'. Theologically or devotionally, Quakers need to address how to live in this multi-faith world whilst those who are more exclusivist, in Pilgrim's terms, leave from either side. Pilgrim's syncretists and individualists can lie at any place on the spectrum but those believing in a corporate structure based on divine guidance are likely to be grouped more towards the traditional end, with more diffuse spiritualities towards the innovative end. The model is helpful too in letting us see that whilst particular theologies within Liberal Quakerism may not be distinct from those of other Christians or Buddhists, this form of Quakerism as a whole transcends any single faith definition or identity. Wildwood's model also leaves open the question of what constitutes the nature and boundary of Quakerism. It can thus accommodate Pilgrim's idea of heterotopia, mine of the 'absolute perhaps', or Collins' idea of 'plaining', a deeply enculturated construction of 'the plain' as a counter-cultural aesthetic impulse in everyday Quaker life (1996)(see pp. 66–7 above).

Liberal Quakerism remains a distinct and changing tradition within Quakerism. It operates in a unique way amongst religious groups in its emphasis on form rather than belief and consequently transcends many of the philosophical and theological problems associated with more doctrinal churches. It is also highly attractive to those who perceive the spiritual life as a journey rather than a destination. Similar in some ways to early Friends, it is also radically different in others and probably represents the biggest deviation from early Quaker tradition to date.

MISSION AND WITNESS

Most of Quakerism around the world has its roots in the twentieth century, owing to the mission work of those Yearly Meetings revitalised through the evangelical revivals and the interdenominational Holiness movement. Liberal Quakerism revitalised itself too, but Evangelical Quakerism turned the revitalisation into an intensification of mission work rather than primarily philanthropic activity, or internal renewal.

Through the 1850s and 1860s, affirmed by 'the great commission' found at the end of the book of Matthew (see p. 230 below), Home Mission initiatives were started by Evangelical Yearly Meetings including Britain, although not always without opposition from more Quietist or Conservative Friends. In Britain, pastoral concern for other Friends was added to missionary concern for non-Friends and the Home Mission Movement and the Adult School Movement provided programmed evening worship and literacy classes respectively.

In the 1830s, Daniel Wheeler, who had served two Russian Emperors in reclaiming 2700 acres of marsh land for cultivation, left his family in Russia and prepared to set sail for Australia, New Zealand, and the Pacific Islands. With a temperance crew, the *Henry Freeling* was not only paid for by a Yearly Meeting committee but stocked with bibles and tracts (Brodie and Brodie 1993, pp. 37–46). The four-year journey Wheeler and his son Charles made was a very early example of nineteenth-century Quaker foreign mission. Whilst early Friends had travelled extensively on such journeys, it was in the 1860s that renewed attention was given to overseas mission fields, 'mission' being variously emphasised as conversion and/or educational work. In Britain, the Friends Foreign Missionary Association was set up in 1868, following correspondence initiated by a Newcastle Monthly Meeting Quaker, George Richardson, in *The Friend*. Work focused on Madagascar, India, and Ceylon and, from the 1880s, China. London Yearly Meeting had thirteen missionaries in China in 1901, thirty-nine by 1916. Working in the Szechwan Province, Quakers set up schools and hospitals.

In the United States, the settling of the frontier and the increasingly local organisation of Friends' activities, as opposed to the transitional practice of Meetings being under the care of remote parent Yearly Meetings, allowed in turn a greater national co-ordination of efforts directed overseas as Meeting administration became less unwieldy.

ASIA

Arriving in 1866, Rachel Metcalfe was the first British Quaker missionary to India and in 1907 Mid-India Yearly Meeting was started. The Friends Foreign Missionary Association also founded Bhopal Monthly Meeting. After 1890, Esther Baird of Ohio Yearly Meeting ran mission work in the Bundelkhand district, resulting in the Yearly Meeting there. Nepal became a related mission field in 1994. In 1887, Esther Butler from Ohio Yearly Meeting (Gurneyite) led a women's mission to women in Nanjing for a

---

Box 21 The Malones

In 1892, Emma (1860–1924) and Walter (1857–1935) Malone co-founded the Christian Workers Training School for Bible Study and Practical Methods of Work. This became the Cleveland Bible Institute and Training College and in 1957 was renamed Malone College when it moved to Canton. The Malones were Holiness Friends, dedicated to practical help of the poor and marginalised alongside evangelism. They published the *Christian Worker* but merged this with the Philadelphia-based *Friends Review* in 1894 to form the *American Friend* in 1894, with Rufus Jones as Editor. After Jones' conversion to a modernist position (see Box 15), the Malones eventually set up the *Soul Winner* in 1902, which became the *Evangelical Friend* in 1905. The Bible Institute was successful in recruiting and training a high calibre of Friend, and by 1907 missionaries from the school were serving in Brazil, China, Cuba, India, Jamaica, Japan, Kenya, Mexico, South Africa, and Venezuela. John Oliver writes: 'In no small part, the fact that most Friends today live outside Europe and North America is due to Walter and Emma Malone' (2003, p. 163).

---

decade and remained in China until her death in 1921. Twenty-five to thirty-five missionaries served in the area, and by the 1930s 300 local Friends schools and hospitals had been started. Many of the missionaries suffered imprisonment after the Revolution in 1949 and buildings were confiscated. After that period, Ohio Yearly Meeting began mission work in Taiwan in 1953 and twenty-six missionaries have served there. Women from Philadelphia Yearly Meeting began a mission in Japan in 1885 which resulted in a Quaker school, started in 1887, and from 1917 a Yearly Meeting.

AFRICA

Arthur Chilson and Willis Hotchkiss, graduates of Cleveland Bible Institute (see Box 21), and Edgar Hole, a Trustee, were supported by the Board of the Friends Africa Industrial Mission to travel to Kenya in 1902. This Board was later brought under the American Friends Mission Board of Five Years Meeting. London Yearly Meeting had maintained a small mission in Pemba, off the coast of East Africa, to set up a freed slave colony from 1896 but it was in Kenya that Quakerism was to prove so popular. Today, a third of all Quakers in the world belong to one of the sixteen Yearly Meetings there. These three men took the first passenger train from Mombasa to Port Florence (later Kisumu) and began their work at Kaimosi (Mombo 1998, p. 82):

Plate 12 Lirhanda Friends Meeting House, Kenya

Evangelization proceeded slowly; by 1906 there were only five converts, and only 50 members by 1914. This was partly due to difficulties in communication and partly to the missionaries' attitude to the local culture, which they saw as inimical to the Christian faith. (Mombo 2003, p. 78)

In particular they challenged the local prohibition against women eating chicken (p. 78) and prescribed monogamy rather than polygamy, which often resulted in great hardship and ostracisation for the second and third wives of converts (Mombo 1998, pp. 135–42). The missionaries translated the Bible into Llogooli, one of the tribal languages, but this signalled a cultural domination of this language group which Mombo claims later caused schism (2003, p. 78). From the middle of the 1920s, Quaker converts created their own villages, assimilating western mission culture (Plate 12). As Kenya reacted against British colonial rule, so local Quakers began to wish for greater independence and in 1945 Five Years Meeting approved the establishment of East Africa Yearly Meeting. It gained full independence in 1962. After 1980, the Yearly Meeting began to divide, as a result partly of size, partly of ethnic tensions (Mombo 2003, p. 80).

Plate 13 Friends Meeting House, Achimota, Ghana (built in 1934 at a cost of £50)

Mission work in Central Africa (Burundi, Rwanda, and Congo) started later. Mid-America Yearly Meeting started Friends Africa Gospel Mission in Burundi in 1934, and in 1984 Burundi Friends Church became its own Yearly Meeting. In the same year, Burundi Friends began mission work in Congo, and two years later work began in Rwanda. All are part of Evangelical Friends International (EFI). In 1999, EFI-Africa region opened the Great Lakes School of Theology in Burundi and since 2001 a Reconciliation Centre has operated to help heal the civil disturbances of the 1990s.

Quakerism in Ghana started as a result of expatriates and local residents (Plate 13).

CENTRAL AND SOUTHERN AMERICA

Iowa Yearly Meeting re-established Quakerism in Jamaica from 1881 and began mission work to Cuba in 1900. California Yearly Meeting (now Southwest) sent missionaries to Guatemala in 1902. Ruth Esther Smith (1870–1947) arrived in 1906 and became the lead missionary for work in Central America. Many meetings began in Guatemala and Honduras. Berea Bible College, now Berea Seminary, opened in Guatemala in 1921.

Central Yearly Meeting began its mission work in Bolivia in 1919, Oregon (now Northwest) Yearly Meeting in 1930. The Central Yearly

Meeting mission divided, so there are now three groups of Evangelical Quakers. There is also a small unprogrammed group in Bolivia. Oregon Yearly Meeting missionaries began work in Peru in 1961.

Much of the mission work was carried out by men, or by men in the more public roles with women in support. Mombo argues that Gurneyite Quakerism was ambivalent towards the public role of women. 'Separate Sphere' ideology was more prevalent there than in the Hicksite tradition, and when pastors were introduced these were usually men (see Box 22). There were some women missionaries including: Sybil Jones (aunt to

---

Box 22 The reality of spiritual equality

The twentieth century saw the first fully united men's and women's Yearly Meetings in Britain and elsewhere. Since the 1670s, men and women Friends had held separate Business Meetings and had developed particular areas of decision-making, typically gendered. Many old Meeting Houses still have the shutters which could be lowered to separate the two Business Meetings. The idea of spiritual equality remained but political equality was less apparent. The London Women's Yearly Meeting only began in 1784. Isichei notes that whilst some women ministers did exert influence over the men's Meetings, 'all important decisions, both at the local and national level, were made without any reference to the opinions of the women's meetings at all' (1970, p. 108). Only towards the end of the Victorian period did women start to question the separation. In 1896 Men's Yearly Meeting decided that women should be able to serve on Meeting for Sufferings and that important decisions at Yearly Meeting should be considered jointly. The first fully united Yearly Meeting was not until 1909.

Isichei estimates that attendance at Men's Yearly Meeting was between a fifth and a third of the male members. However, only about a twelfth of these actually ministered, and about seventy or so Friends grouped around the Table (where the Clerks sat, but also used as a collective term for the Clerks) seemed to speak regularly. Josiah Forster spoke seventy-nine times over a seven-year period (Isichei 1970, p. 80). The average age of those who spoke twenty times or more was 60.7 (p. 81). By 1900, however, contributions were coming from a wider range of people of a wider range of ages.

Elizabeth O'Donnell argues that Quaker women of the nineteenth century were not proto-feminists and that indeed some of the most radical in her sample from Newcastle Monthly Meeting left the Religious Society of Friends (1999). Pam Lunn's work on Quaker responses to the Suffragette movement also suggests a political conservatism (1997).

Plate 14 'Ladies Lesson': Deborah A. Rees teaching in Kenya. She served as a missionary in Kenya from 1904 to 1926, working primarily with other women.

Rufus Jones) who went to Ramallah, Palestine and Brummana in the Lebanon in 1867; Esther Frame and Elizabeth Comstock; Esther Butler; Esther Baird. However, Mombo notes that where missionary teams were mixed, women were usually in subordinate roles (1998, p. 73). This model of subordination was carried over into the mission work itself, with much of the cultural change required of converts by the missionaries focusing on women's lives (Mombo 1998) (Plate 14).

Starting in Indiana, and building on the success of the Women's Home Mission Association, Women's Foreign Mission Associations were established in thirteen Yearly Meetings in the 1880s, with their own journal, *Missionary Advocate*, and argued for the importance of women working with women (Mombo 1998, p. 72). In 1890, they formed the Women's Foreign Missionary Union of Friends in America (WFMU). In 1894, Five Years Meeting established its American Friends Board of Foreign Missions to co-ordinate all the work being run by individual Yearly Meetings. Mombo argues that FYM seems to have ignored the WFMU, and in later discussions about the relationship between the two bodies some male Friends were dismissive of the idea of working side by side with women as equals. They continued as separate bodies, and WFMU changed its name to the United Society of Friends Women in 1948, and in 1974 to United Society of Friends Women International (USFWI) as women from Yearly Meetings in East Africa and Jamaica became involved.

PEACE AND SOCIAL WITNESS

Quakers have rarely been politically radical beyond the confines of their class status, and those who tried, like Woolman, were usually censured for their activism. Retrospectively, social pioneers such as Woolman and Elizabeth Fry and the founders of Oxfam have been readopted as Quaker pioneers but these prophets were not always heard in their own time, or given official support. One third of eligible British Quaker men joined up in the First World War, but Thomas Kennedy has argued that between the World Wars those who had taken the absolutist position on conscientious objection became the 'weighty' leaders and that the collective reaffirmation of the Quaker opposition to war in turn renewed London Yearly Meeting and gave it a new sense of purpose. In 1918, Friends in Britain adopted 'Foundations of a True Social Order' (*Quaker Faith and Practice*, 1995, 23.16), the closest the Yearly Meeting ever came to an anti-capitalist stance. When the Great Strike came in 1926, influential Quakers rushed to depict the 1918 statement as overhasty or as going further 'in some directions than the Society ought to go ... further than truth requires or permits in the direction of Socialist and even Communist principles', as H. G. Wood put it in the *Friends Quarterly Examiner* (1927, p. 288).

Those who sought appeasement before both World Wars may now be seen as naïve (Phillips 2004) but were attempting to live out their testimony against war and their modernist optimism in human nature. Rufus Jones was part of a mission to Germany in 1938 to try to secure the safe passage of Jews to Switzerland. The small group achieved the agreement of the Gestapo but the Second World War broke out before the plans could be carried through (Vining 1958, pp. 280–93).

The First World War saw the creation of the independent Friends Ambulance Unit which offered an alternative to combatant service (see Box 23). It was active again in the Second World War and continued until 1959 when 'National Service' in Britain came to an end.

In 1917, a coalition of Friends formed the American Friends Service Committee (AFSC) to help co-ordinate Quaker relief work in war-torn Europe. Post-war relief, co-ordinated by the American Friends Service Committee and the Friends Relief Service in Britain, was widespread, with the AFSC being given (by the Quaker future President Herbert

Box 23 Alternative service

In the First World War, British Friends faced with conscription campaigned for the right of conscientious objection. Some argued their cause before tribunals, others were imprisoned for refusal to register their objections. Others formed the Friends Ambulance Unit (FAU) which allowed Friends and others 'alternative service'. The FAU continued its work into the 1950s, helping with relief after both World Wars. It was laid down with the ending of National Service. In America, during World War II, the US government established 'Civilian Public Service' (CPS) camps for conscientious objectors to do useful work in isolation from the wider community. The camps were funded by the Quakers, Mennonites, and Brethren, and a Quaker administered them although the Government had final authority. Leadership for Quakerism after both World Wars often came from those who resisted the most and who were part of these alternative projects.

Plate 15 Friends Relief Service, Austria – Rubland Kinderlandvershickung (KLV). The KLV camps in Austria had been used to house evacuees from Germany and Austria during the war. They were taken over by relief workers for the recuperation of malnourished children from Vienna

Hoover) the task of co-ordinating hunger relief on behalf of the American Government. Feeding programmes were established in France, Germany, Austria, Poland, and Russia (Spielhofer and Gorfinkel 2001; McFadden 2004) (Plate 15). Similar work was undertaken in the Spanish Civil War

(Mendlesohn 2002) and after the Second World War. This led to the AFSC and London Yearly Meeting becoming joint recipients of the Nobel Peace Prize in 1947. British Friends were not sure as to whether to accept but in the end the Harvard scholar Henry J. Cadbury and Margaret Backhouse jointly collected the Prize from the Norwegian King.

Mission, within Liberal and modernist Quakerism, generally turned to service. In Britain, the Friends Evangelistic Band, started in 1919, continued its mission work but gradually became more interdenominational. The Friends Home Mission Committee, as it became in the first years of the twentieth century, became the Friends Home Service Council in 1927 (Manasseh 2000, p. 7). This committee became involved in the late 1920s in relief for unemployed miners, especially in the South Wales communities of Maes-yr-Haf and Brynmawr. Furniture-making workshops and the like were set up to try and provide alternative employment. There was sometimes opposition from those who resented the invasion of English middle-class Quakers, and ideological differences on the committee also meant the work was affected.

By the 1970s in Britain, the successor bodies to those concerned with mission were strictly concerned with peace and social witness work. The Friends Service Council became Quaker Peace and Service in 1979, Quaker Peace and Social Witness in 2001. This shift in the content of service reflected the twentieth-century reinvention of the testimony against war into a 'peace testimony'. After 1907, this is increasingly the term used. Before then, Friends had a testimony against war, not a peace testimony. Elaine Bishop and Jung Jiseok have both worked on the fourfold nature of the shift which took place. First, the change of emphasis shifts away from opposition to war and preparation for war to the advocacy of peace. In turn, secondly, this results in a more diffuse interpretation of the testimony: 'peace' is a far more amorphous concept than 'against war'. Third, under the rubric of Liberal Quakerism, the theology underpinning this aspect of Quaker testimony becomes more diffuse. Fourth, the testimony itself becomes less prescriptive. The large proportion of British eligible Quaker men who joined up in the First World War (about 33% – Kennedy 2001, p. 313) and of American Quaker men in the Second World War (about 50%) were not disowned. When Norman Morrison self-immolated during the bombing of Vietnam in 1965, such extreme protest was contentious. Ingle argues that Evangelical Friends had become similarly permissive, and cites their failure to elder East Whittier Quaker, President Richard Nixon, for ordering that very same bombing (2001). Quaker peace work became professionalised and

Quaker Peace and Service asked enthusiastic but amateur Friends *not* to attempt post-war relief after the Kosovo bombings early in the twenty-first century.

Service work did bring about the fruits of mission. Quakerism in Germany, initiated perhaps by the distribution of Barclay's *Apology* in the 1670s and nurtured in Bad Pyrmont and the Friedenstahl (Peace Valley) by British Friends in the eighteenth and nineteenth centuries (Bernet 2004), was revitalised after the First World War. Quaker Embassies or International Centres, pioneered by Carl Heath, often in tension with relief workers, such as Hilda Clark in Vienna (Spielhofer 2001), helped nurture Meetings in Vienna, Geneva, Berlin, and Paris.

QUAKERS AND POLITICS

Tonsing (2002) and Clark (2003) have explored the role that Quakers in South Africa played in the fight against apartheid. Clark focuses on the role women played and the tensions they faced between maternal responsibilities and the sense of injustice created by the system.

Quaker Members of Parliament have served in Britain, South Africa, Australia, and New Zealand, where a Quaker served as Minister for Disarmament at the start of the twenty-first century. The Friends Council for National Legislation currently lobbies the US chambers of Government on behalf of Friends throughout the USA. Richard Nixon, whilst a President who appeared to do little to end his country's involvement in a number of wars, also pioneered new approaches to Russia and China during the Cold War period, moves that his obituarists linked to his Quaker upbringing. Nixon himself describes a strong Quaker upbringing in a tight-knit Quaker community (Nixon 1978, p. 5). His great-grandmother was used by his cousin, Jessamyn West, as a model for the lead character, Eliza Cope Birdwell, in her novel *The Friendly Persuasion* (1945). He called himself a Quaker but also claimed that he felt the peace testimony could only work if facing a 'civilised compassionate enemy' (Nixon 1978, p. 27). 'In the face of Hitler and Tojo, pacifism not only failed to stop violence – it actually played into the hands of a barbarous foe and weakened home-front morale' (p. 27).

In terms of American Civil Rights, Brian Ward's work illustrates how American Friends Service Committee was concerned to influence public opinion through its radio broadcasts from the 1940s (2005). At the same time, Quaker Meetings were more openly welcoming African Americans as

Plate 16 Abington Friends Meeting House, Philadelphia Yearly Meeting, typical of many
eastern US Meeting Houses (photograph taken in 1929)

members. In the 1960s, individual Friends such as Bayard Rustin and John
Yungblut worked with Martin Luther King Jr.

In the 1980s, Jim Corbett and other Friends joined with those from
other denominations to offer refugees sanctuary from violence in Central
America. Corbett was acquitted in a trial brought by the Government to try
and end the practice of sanctuary.

After the events in the USA of September 11, 2001, Friends were divided
over their support for the Bush administration and its moves to launch a
military campaign in Afghanistan. Some, as has always been the case in
national wars, felt the need to be patriotic or that these were exceptional
circumstances in which the peace testimony was no longer appropriate.
Some Meetings even agreed to hang banners on the Meeting Houses in
support of President Bush. Others adhered to the traditional Quaker
witness for peace. Scott Simon, a Quaker National Public Radio journalist,
shocked other Quakers by publicly urging war. In his defence, he cited
exceptional circumstances and, like the Free Quakers two centuries earlier
(see p. 52 above), asked for ideological freedom within the Society (Simon
2003, pp. 18–21).

Plate 17 First Friends, Richmond, Indiana. This modern Friends church contrasts architecturally with Abington but still resists looking like a 'steeple house'

SETTLED DIVERSITY

EVANGELICAL FRIENDS

By the 1960s, Oregon, Kansas, and Nebraska Yearly Meetings had left Five Years Meeting (FYM). Together with Ohio, never part of that body, they formed in 1965 the Evangelical Friends Association, now Evangelical Friends International (EFI). Mission work has been most successful in Bolivia, Rwanda and Burundi, Congo, Peru, Taiwan, and the Philippines and Cambodia, but has also been effective in India, Hong Kong, and Nepal, and throughout Central America. Churches have also been planted in Philadelphia and Toronto amongst Hispanic populations and in Ireland, Romania, Britain, and Hungary. These Yearly Meetings renamed themselves to form regions of EFI. Oregon became Northwest Yearly Meeting, Ohio became Friends Church Eastern Region, Nebraska became Rocky Mountain Yearly Meeting, Kansas became Evangelical Friends Church Mid-America Yearly Meeting. Alaskan Friends, set off by mission work from Californian Friends in 1897, and Southwest have also come into EFI (see below). Central Yearly Meeting left FYM in 1924 as they wanted a credal basis to the body and did not want to contribute to the modernist-tainted Earlham College. They have never affiliated with any other Quaker group and practise a conservative world-rejecting Scripture-based Holiness Quakerism. Students at their

Union Bible College have to abide by strict rules (Holden 1988, p. 140) (see p. 222 below). These Friends remain independent and evangelical. Central Yearly Meeting's mission work in the 1920s and 1930s in Bolivia has resulted in more Friends within that particular Friends church (1300) than belong to the originating Yearly Meeting where there are now only 287 Friends.

REUNIFICATION

The ecumenical disposition of Rufus Jones, once he had marginalised the Holiness Revivalist Friends, and the experience of joint service work between Hicksites and Orthodox, led to the reuniting of New England Yearly Meeting in 1945. Canada, New York, and Philadelphia each reunited in the mid-1950s, and Baltimore consolidated. The Canadian experience involved three Yearly Meetings (Genessee Hicksite, Canadian Orthodox, and Canadian Conservative) reuniting. Again, joint service work and connections between young Friends led to 'joint and concurrent' Yearly Meeting sessions before unity was formally achieved. The reunited Yearly Meetings jointly affiliated to Friends General Conference (FGC), the Liberal Quaker umbrella association, and FYM. Baltimore, a 'consolidated Yearly Meeting', gave the choice of affiliation to each Monthly Meeting.

REALIGNMENT

Five Years Meeting, whilst modernist, also experienced divisions of emphasis between more and more permissive modernist evangelicalism and fundamentalism which took over some of the ground held by Revivalist Friends when fundamentalism became strong in the 1920s (following the publication of 'The Fundamentals' of Christian faith). This division has been most evident around the so-called 'pelvic issues' of homosexuality and abortion, in particular same-sex marriage, but also on issues of scriptural literalism and universal salvation. In the 1980s and 1990s, there was the suggestion of 'realignment', of dividing Friends United Meeting (FUM) Yearly Meetings between EFI and FGC but this did not occur. Southwest Yearly Meeting left FUM and became Friends Church Southwest within EFI, with one Monthly Meeting, Whittier, forming the Western Friends Association, to remain affiliated with FUM. At the time of writing, a new hiring policy has just been placed before FUM Meetings asking employees to endorse the hiring policy which bars non-celibate homosexuals and heterosexuals in non-marital sexual relationships. The outcomes and implications are as yet unknown. FUM acts as a parent body to the sixteen Kenyan Yearly Meetings as well as the one in Uganda.

CONSERVATIVE FRIENDS

Sociologically, Conservative schismatics are defined in terms of the body they have left and the time at which they left it. The Conservative tendency of the Wilburite Yearly Meetings was later to form an association with Quakers who had felt the need to conserve the tradition over different issues at different times. In the 1870s and 1880s, at the start of what Kaiser (1994) calls a 'golden age of conservatism' (1874–1917), Western (1877), Kansas (1880), Canada (1881), and Iowa (1883) Yearly Meetings divided over the introduction of pastors. In 1905, a Conservative grouping separated from North Carolina Yearly Meeting over the imposition of a common discipline. This group had tolerated seventy years of Gurneyite and Evangelical theology, unacceptable to Wilburites, in New England and maintained institutions such as Sabbath School inimical to Wilburites. By 1911, however, North Carolina had joined the 'Conservative Circle of Correspondence'. In time, these different brands of Conservatives would find common ground in their christocentric unprogrammed approach to worship and the Quaker tradition. The New England Wilburite Yearly Meeting reunited in 1945 with its Orthodox counterpart, and Canada Conservative (excepting Halcyonia Monthly Meeting) reunited in 1955 with the Hicksite and Gurneyite Yearly Meetings. Kansas joined with Iowa in 1929; Western's last Conservative Monthly Meeting reunited with Western FUM in 1962.

In the early 1990s Ohio Yearly Meeting (Conservative), the last remaining Wilburite Yearly Meeting, initiated a scheme of associate membership for isolated Conservative Friends. Ohio affiliates live worldwide, often in isolation such as in Greece, but under the pastoral care of Ohio Friends. In 1993, those British Friends concerned over the loss of Christianity in London Yearly Meeting held a conference at Fritchley. This consisted of New Foundation Fellowship Friends (those who wished to emphasise the teachings of early Friends), the Quaker Christian Renewal group (a charismatic fellowship), and those with 'primitive' leadings, some already affiliate members of Ohio

Yearly Meeting (Conservative). Those less optimistic about the Christian future of London Yearly Meeting left to form the Yearly Meeting of Friends in Christ, setting up their own newsletter *The Call*. They adopted the 1802 London Yearly Meeting *Queries and Advices*, and forms of plain dress, and hold untimed meetings for worship. They have now formed a connection with Halcyonia Friends, the group originally from Birmingham. In their founding statement from 1993, the Friends in Christ wrote:

After much grief at the apostate condition of London [now Britain] Yearly Meeting, where there are now many who deny the Christian basis of our religious Society and who are not prepared to accept Jesus Christ as their living Saviour, by God's grace we have come together humbly, conscious of our own failings as his children, in the love of our Lord Jesus Christ. (*The Call* 1 (1996), 1)

In 1950, a group of Conservative Friends emigrated from Fairhope, Alabama to Costa Rica in protest at the military economy and the military draft and founded a farming community, Monteverde. The community, now involved in conservation initiatives, continues today.

ST LOUIS

In 1970, the Holiness Friend and missionary Everett Catell set up an All-Friends Conference in St Louis to which, for the first time since the Great Separation, representatives of all US Yearly Meetings were invited. Given not all Yearly Meetings are members of the Friends World Committee on Consultation, this was a rare event. Non-FWCC Yearly Meetings have also had contact with other Yearly Meetings through two World Gatherings of Young Friends, one held in North Carolina in 1985, one in England in 2005.

LIBERAL FRIENDS

Outside of the USA, unprogrammed Quakerism founded by British settlers and expatriates can be found in Australia, New Zealand, West and southern Africa, India, and Hong Kong (Plate 18). For example, Auckland Meeting began in 1885, and by 1900 was a Monthly Meeting under the care of London Yearly Meeting. In 1964, both Australia and New Zealand became their own Yearly Meetings. Quakerism had begun in Norway after 1814 when seamen imprisoned by the British during the Napoleonic wars returned home, and in Denmark in 1875. There are

Plate 18 Friends at Hill House Meeting House, Accra, Ghana, 1988

also Yearly Meetings in Sweden and in the Netherlands dating from the 1930s. Switzerland Yearly Meeting was begun in 1944.

In Korea, Quaker relief work in the 1950s after the Korean War led to a permanent Meeting in Seoul, a phenomenon mirroring the experience in Germany after the First World War, when many of those helped by Friends established Meetings (the Yearly Meeting began there in 1925). In Buzuluk in Russia, Quakers are still held in high regard for their work there after the First World War and this has helped kindle interest in Quaker activities.

DECLINE AND GROWTH

Thus, we find the greatest increase in numbers in the twentieth century. In the older Yearly Meetings numbers rose with the relaxation of the peculiarities and in particular of endogamy, a shift which occurred in the mid-nineteenth century regardless of the type of Quakerism in all save the Conservative Yearly Meetings. The chart constructed by Jennie Levin and Rebecca Berridge (Fig. 3.8) shows the dramatic effects of mission on the

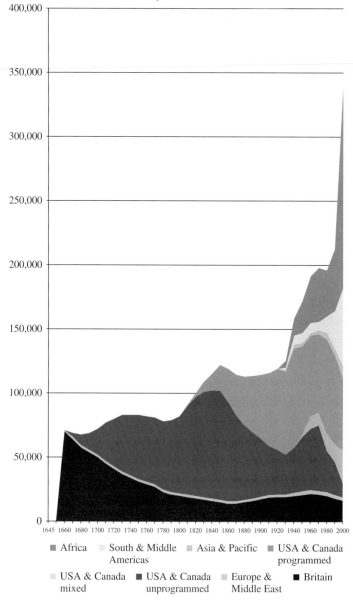

Fig. 3.8 Quakers in time and place: proportions of Quakers in different parts of
the world 1640s–2000

growth of Quakerism and the way in which unprogrammed Quakerism with its different emphasis and historical trajectory accounts for only 15% now of worldwide Quakerism.

The second half of the book looks at the different ideas held by the different branches of Quakerism.

PART II

Worldwide Quakerism today

Introduction

Quakerism worldwide can be divided into two, three, or six types (Fig. 4.1 and Table 4.1). The two types of Quaker in the world are the programmed and the unprogrammed. The terms 'programmed' and 'unprogrammed' refer to the degree to which the content of the worship is planned ahead of the event. In the unprogrammed tradition, only silence and the rite of ending handshake is usually pre-planned, the silence open for whatever ministry is given. In the programmed tradition, most or all of the worship is pre-planned.

Within the unprogrammed tradition there are the Liberal and Conservative traditions whilst programmed Friends can be generally described as Evangelical. Thus we can identify three kinds of Quaker. However, more specifically, present-day Quakerism can be divided into six groupings, relating largely to the history of American schism and their converts and theological allies of each of the branches (Fig. 4.2 and Table 4.2). The types are not wholly distinct and the complex history of schism within the group makes any schema slightly clumsy. However, given most Yearly Meetings have gathered around shared statements of faith or umbrella organisations, it is possible to identify their common ground. The six groupings are as follows.

First, there are unaffiliated Evangelical Yearly Meetings, notably Central in Indiana and Santidad in Bolivia, a Holiness off-shoot of Amigos Central, the original Yearly Meeting created through Mission Work from Central in Indiana. These two have no contact with other Quaker organisations, including each other.

Second, the Yearly Meetings at odds with Friends United Meeting (FUM) (see below), with the exception of Central, formed Evangelical Friends Association in 1965, which became Evangelical Friends International (EFI) in 1989. Their American Yearly Meetings are designated by region, e.g. Friends Church Eastern Region (FCER), but they have begun sizeable groups elsewhere, notably in Bolivia (the largest Yearly

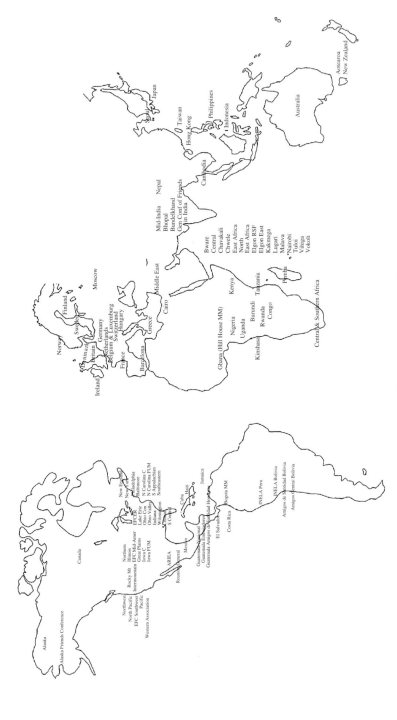

Fig 4.1 Quakers around the world

Table 4.1. *Quaker numbers by continent, 2005 (source: FWCC) ('Affiliated' in this table only refers to FWCC Affiliation)*

Africa
Affiliated Groups

Burundi YM	12,000
Bware YM	7,215
Central & Southern Africa YM	144
Central YM	10,000
Chavakali YM	7,294
Chwele YM	
Congo YM	1,303
Congo (Brazzaville) Worship Group	18
East Africa YM	6,153
East Africa YM (North)	13,000
Elgon East YM	12,000
Elgon RSF	13,000
Hill House MM	12
Kakamega YM	7,000
Kinshasa MM	18
Lugari YM	14,300
Malava YM	12,000
Nairobi YM	7,500
Pemba YM	100
Rwanda YM	3,234
Tanzania YM	3,000
Tuloi YM	4,565
Uganda YM	3,500
Vihiga YM	14,797
Vokoli YM	5,000
TOTAL AFRICA	**157,153**

Asia-West Pacific
Affiliated Groups

Australia YM	949
Bhopal YM	130
Bundelkhand YM	287
GCFI	45
Hong Kong MM	8
Japan YM	185
Mid-India YM	250
New Zealand YM	600
Seoul MM	12
TOTAL AFFILIATED	**2,466**

Unaffiliated Groups

Cambodia YM	2,500
Indonesia YM	3,000
Nepal YM	500
Philippines YM	3,000
Taiwan YM	3,200
TOTAL UNAFFILIATED	**12,200**
TOTAL ASIA-WEST PACIFIC	**14,666**

Table 4.1. (*cont.*)

Europe and Middle East	
Affiliated Groups	
Barcelona MM	8
Belgium & Luxemburg MM	42
Britain YM	15,775
Brummana MM	
Budapest Recognized Meeting	5
Denmark YM	29
Finland YM	20
France YM	71
German YM	338
Ireland YM	1,591
Moscow MM	13
Netherlands YM	115
Norway YM	151
Ramallah MM	
Sweden YM	100
Switzerland YM	104
TOTAL EUROPE & MID-EAST	**18,362**
Americas	
Affiliated Groups	
Alaska Friends Conference	200
Baltimore YM	4,538
Bogotá MM	20
Bolivia Central YM	1,300
Bolivia INELA YM	8,000
Canadian YM	1,154
Cuba YM	373
El Salvador YM	600
Great Plains YM	715
Guatemala Santidad YM	500
Honduras YM	2,000
Iglesia Evangélica Embajadores Amigos	130
Illinois YM	1,100
Indiana YM	4,754
Intermountain YM	1,045
Iowa YM (Con)	548
Iowa YM (FUM)	3,473
Jamaica YM	325
Lake Erie YM	953
México Reunión General Monteverde MM	72
New England YM	4,273
New York YM	3,706
North Carolina YM (C)	400
North Carolina YM (FUM)	10,662
North Pacific YM	877

Table 4.1. *(cont.)*

Northern YM	1,194
Northwest YM	7,751
Ohio Valley YM	812
Ohio YM (C)	541
Pacific YM	1,480
Peru INELA YM	1,200
Philadelphia YM	12,000
South Central YM	315
Southeastern YM	561
Southern Appalachian YM and Association	1,288
Western Association of Friends	530
Western YM	5,304
Wilmington YM	1,977
TOTAL AFFILIATED	**86,671**
Unaffiliated Groups	
Alaska YM	1,000
Bolivia IEUBA	
Bolivia Santidad YM	22,000
Central YM	287
Evangelical Friends Churches	40,000
IE Nacional de Guatemala	20,000
Mexico ARIEA	800
Piedmont Friends Fellowship	
Rocky Mountain YM	1,170
Southwest YM	5,632
TOTAL UNAFFILIATED	**90,889**
TOTAL AMERICAS	**177,560**
AFFILIATED SUBTOTALS	
Africa	157,153
Asia-West Pacific	2,466
Europe & Middle East	18,362
Americas	86,671
International Members	67
WORLD TOTAL AFFILIATED	**264,719**
NON-AFFILIATED SUBTOTALS	
Africa	
Asia-West Pacific	12,200
Europe & Middle East	
Americas	90,889
WORLD TOTAL NON-AFFILIATED	**103,089**
OVERALL TOTALS	
Affiliated	264,719
Non-affiliated	103,089
WORLD TOTAL	**367,808**

Table 4.2. *Quaker numbers by type (Figures rounded up. FUM and FGC
figures both include the 15,000 members of the five jointly affiliated Yearly
Meetings, so total exceeds the Table 4.1 total of about 367,000 by 15,000)*

Unaffiliated Evangelical	22,500	5.9% of total
EFI	114,000	30%
FUM	184,000	48%
Conservative	1,600	0.4%
FGC	34,000	8.9%
Unaffiliated Liberal	26,000	6.8%

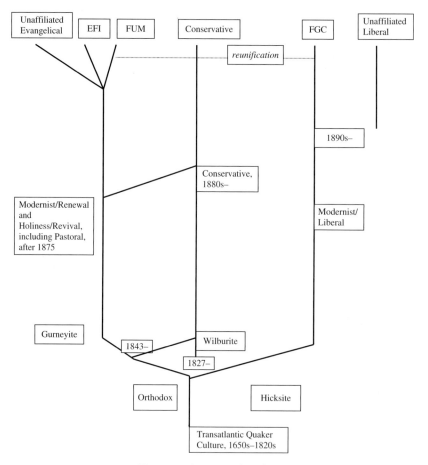

Figure 4.2 Six types of Quakers

Plate 19 Friends church in Santa Cruz, Bolivia

Meeting in the world; Plate 19), Guatemala, Taiwan, Rwanda and Burundi, Congo, Indonesia, the Philippines, and Peru. These Friends represent the Revivalist tendency within Gurneyism but have also been influenced by fundamentalism. Generally, EFI Meetings are not part of Friends World Committee for Consultation (FWCC).

Third, the largest grouping of Quakers consists of those churches within Friends United Meeting or who see it as their parent body, such as Kenyan and most Indian Friends. To recap, this is the organisation that began as Five Years Meeting (FYM) in 1902, having been meeting every five years since the Richmond Conference of 1887. That Conference adopted the Richmond Declaration of Faith, an affirmation of Gurneyite theology and of Quaker peculiarity against water baptism (see p. 117 above). As such, Ohio, which favoured the possibility of water baptism, never joined, and other Yearly Meetings, such as Central, Oregon, and Kansas, would leave in the twentieth century because FYM did not enforce agreement in the Declaration. Whilst Rufus Jones persuaded FYM (FUM from 1963) towards a modernist agenda, Holiness and Fundamentalist Meetings also co-exist within FUM. Attitudes to scriptural inerrancy and homo-sexuality are the areas where there is most tension (see Box 24). FUM Meetings are part of FWCC, FUM is a member of the World Council

---

Box 24 Evangelical modernism

Rufus Jones and his allies brought Five Years Meeting within a modernist outlook in the early years of the twentieth century. This is of course not to say that all Monthly Meetings were of this persuasion and in time many would be influenced by the fundamentalist movement of the 1920s. Others retained a Revival Holiness approach. However, in a way too often overlooked by most commentators of Quakerism, it was modernism, alive and well in both the newly formed Liberal tradition and parts of Quaker evangelicalism by the end of the first decade of the twentieth century, that allowed Jones and others to move so freely amongst different parts of the Quaker world. Hicksism had become modernist in the 1880s (Hamm 2002) and Rowntree and his allies secured its victory within British Quakerism twenty-five years after that. When Jones returned from his trip to Switzerland and his meeting with Rowntree in 1897, it was modernism he had been converted to, not Liberalism. Thus the *American Friend* became a modernist journal. Within the Evangelical tradition, we find both modernist and Holiness (and Fundamentalist) influences and the two are in tension.

Modernists, as Hamm points out, are inclined to renewal, to faith being of the age and in the world (1988, pp. 148–50). Holiness Evangelicalism is rooted in ideas of revival, may be world-rejecting, and prefers a sermon based in devotion rather than reason. When I recently heard a sermon on the rational response to miracles, I knew I was in a modernist Evangelical Friends church. Alongside that rational approach to religion usually sits a more liberal political viewpoint, e.g. on the issues of abortion and homosexuality, although this is not a necessary consequence. Indeed, the way in which the Liberal tradition has maintained unprogrammed worship and Evangelicals have adopted programmed tends to stereotype the form of worship politically and theologically. There is no reason why an unprogrammed Meeting cannot be totally Christ-centred and/or politically conservative and a programmed Meeting pluralistic and/or politically radical. Again, only the outward focus of the programming forces choices over language but it could still be managed within the ideology of the 'absolute perhaps' (see p. 152 above). Freedom Friends in Salem, Oregon are an example of a programmed Christ-centred church which promotes and affirms diversity of sexuality. Friends of Jesus Community in Wichita, whilst Evangelical in origin, have also affirmed the acceptability of homosexuality following a study of Scripture. Both these groups blur the Evangelical/Liberal line.

---

of Churches, and a few FUM Yearly Meetings (principally those which represent reunited Yearly Meetings) are also affiliated with FGC.

Fourth, the rest of Yearly Meetings in the USA are unprogrammed and most belong to Friends General Conference (FGC). Friends General Conference differs from Friends United Meeting in that it provides services rather than leadership to its affiliate Yearly Meetings, in particular book publication and distribution, and an annual gathering for about 2000 Friends. A number of Yearly Meetings, following reunification in the 1940s and 1950s, are affiliated to both FGC and FUM (e.g. Canada), and New England and New York, for example, contain both programmed and unprogrammed Meetings.

Fifth, there are Conservative Friends. These are based mainly in the USA but with isolated members worldwide, many affiliated to Ohio Yearly Meeting (Conservative). Groups are also based in Britain, Greece, and Saskatchewan, Canada (see p. 167 above). Conservative Friends represent an unprogrammed Quietistic or 'primitive' tradition, though some merge Quietistic sentiment with a modernist understanding of Scripture whilst others are evangelical and primitive. There is an independent conservative Meeting at Glenside, Pennsylvania, called the Friends of Truth, and there are other scattered Meetings dedicated to Christian renewal amongst Friends. Many use traditional books of discipline dating from the eighteenth or early nineteenth centuries.

Sixth, there are unaffiliated Liberal Yearly Meetings. Joel and Hannah Bean's College Park Meeting (see Box 16 above) has over 120 years created Pacific, North Pacific, and Rocky Mountain Yearly Meetings and these three, all formalised since the Second World War, have deliberately remained unaffiliated. All the other unprogrammed Yearly Meetings in the world remain unaffiliated. The smaller groups are often set off by expatriates, such as in Hong Kong, or by isolated converts. Outside of Britain and Ireland, Germany is the next biggest European Yearly Meeting, its membership also including Austrian Friends. Small groups exist in a number of other northern European countries (Netherlands, Belgium and Luxemburg, France, Denmark, Sweden, Finland, and Norway), with scattered individuals or very small groups in Belarus, Ukraine, Poland, Slovakia, Spain, and Italy. Ongoing worship groups exist in Hungary, Latvia, Lithuania, Moscow, and Delhi. Larger groups exist in Australia, New Zealand, and central and southern Africa.

This part of the book offers an overview of ideas and practice across the different Quaker traditions. It does so by quoting statements of faith from organisations representative of general types of Quakerism. There is a lack of specifically African and South American material but the Yearly Meetings there are linked to the umbrella organisations whose material is quoted here.

CHAPTER 4

Theology and worship

This chapter begins the overview of worldwide Quaker diversity by considering authority, belief, and worship practice. The section on belief includes sub-sections on God, sin and salvation, eschatology, Christ, and ecclesiology.

AUTHORITY

The variety of primary authority for belief and action lies on an axis between scriptural authority and the authority of inward revelation. Early Friends held inward revelation to be primary but always confirmed by Scripture (see p. 21 above). Evangelical Friends became suspicious of the delusional potential of the inward Light (see p. 95 above), a caution still evident today.

The Evangelical Friends International (EFI) position on authority is primarily scripturally based. The role of the inward Light is to illuminate Scripture, and all doctrines and traditions need to be subject to scriptural authority. Part of EFI, Friends Church Southwest is clearly Bible-centric. The following passage posits the Bible as final authority.

We value the Bible, the written Word of God, as God's revelation and our final authority in all matters of faith and practice. We live in Christ because of its saving message of salvation through Jesus, our Lord and Saviour. This value gives us respect for the authority of Scripture, a love for the teaching and preaching of the Bible and an intense desire to obey its teachings.

Along with the written Word of God we value the Holy Spirit of God, who inspired the Scriptures and illuminates our understanding. We believe that He teaches us to obey all that Jesus commanded, and grants us grace and power to live out the Word of God in daily life. Jesus said, 'You diligently study the Scriptures because you think that by them you possess eternal life. These are the Scriptures that testify about me, yet you refuse to come to me to have life (John 5:39–40).' We value the written Word because it leads us to the living Word, Jesus Christ. This value causes us to worship God in spirit and in truth. Christ, the living Word, teaches us Himself, but never in contradiction of Scripture. We encourage our churches and people to spend time in silent listening to the Holy Spirit during both public and private worship. (*Faith and Practice of Evangelical Friends Church Southwest*, 2001, p. 24)

Within Friends United Meeting (FUM), the idea of the direct authority of Christ the Word is considered primary but is set alongside the ultimate authority of Scripture, which it will never contradict.

The primary authority for Friends is the Holy Spirit who inspired the Scriptures. The Inspirer is greater than the inspired, but all leadings of the Spirit are to be checked with the Scriptures. Leadings are also to be checked with the community of faith. (http://www.fum.org/about/friends.htm#Beliefs, 7 March 2006)

This is a version of the view of seventeenth-century Friends. Fox never prescribed checking leadings against Scripture but claimed he always found them confirmed even though he was not looking to do that (Nickalls 1952, p. 33). The Scriptures did not need to be prescribed as an authority because the inward revelation was so reliable. When early Friends did institute a secondary system of authority, it was the collective (see p. 45 above). The Nayler incident (p. 42 above) did not lead to the use of text as a safeguard but to a means of collective discernment.

The Ohio Yearly Meeting (Conservative) book of discipline includes the following passage implicitly outlining the basis of authority.

Friends place special emphasis on the ever present Holy Spirit in the hearts of men. This power we call the Light Within or the Light of Christ. We believe that a seed of this spirit is in every man. The basis of faith is thus the belief that God endows each human being with a measure of His own Divine Spirit. He leaves no one without witness, but gives the light of His truth and presence to men of all races and walks of life. Love, the outworking of this Divine Spirit, is the most potent influence that can be applied to the affairs of men. The Society of Friends believes this application of love to the whole of life to be the core of the Christian doctrine. As within ourselves we become conscious of the Inner Light or the Christ within and submit ourselves to His leadings, we are enabled to live in conformity to the will of our Heavenly Father. (*The Book of Discipline of Ohio Yearly Meeting*, 1992, p. 4)

It is interesting that a Conservative Yearly Meeting uses the term 'Inner Light' (see p. 133 above) but it is clear that these Friends hold a view close to the early Friends. Through submission to the direct leadings of God within, God's will can be known and followed. Barclay's view of Scripture as a secondary source would be echoed by many Conservative Friends today.

From these revelations of the Spirit of God to the saints have proceeded the Scriptures of Truth, which contain:

a. a faithful historical account of the actions of God's people in divers ages, with many singular and remarkable providences attending them;

b. a prophetical account of several things, whereof some are already past, and some are yet to come;

c. a full and ample account of all the chief principles of the doctrine of Christ, held forth in divers precious declarations, exhortations and sentences, which, by the moving of God's Spirit, were at several times and upon sundry occasions spoken and written unto some Churches and their pastors.

Nevertheless, because they are only a declaration of the fountain and not the fountain itself, therefore they are not to be esteemed the principal ground of all truth and knowledge, nor yet the adequate, primary rule of faith and manners. Yet, because they give a true and faithful testimony of the first foundation, they are and may be esteemed a secondary rule, subordinate to the Spirit, from which they have all their excellency and certainty: for as by the inward testimony of the Spirit we do alone truly know them, so they testify that the Spirit is that Guide by which the saints are led into all truth: therefore, according to the Scriptures the Spirit is the first and principal Leader. (Barclay 2002, pp. 62–3)

For Liberal Friends, experience is primary and sufficient. The following quotation from Francis Howgill in 1665, along with Fox's account of there being 'one, even Christ Jesus', that could speak to his condition (see p. 20 above), can be found at the beginning of the section entitled 'Spiritual Experiences' in the North Pacific Yearly Meeting Discipline.

There was something revealed in me that the Lord would teach his people himself; and so I waited, and many things opened in me of a time at hand … And as I did give up all to the Judgment, the captive came forth out of prison and rejoiced, and my heart was filled with joy, and I came to see him whom I had pierced, and my heart was broken … and then I saw the Cross of Christ, and stood in it … and so eternal life was brought in through death and judgment; and then the perfect gift I received … and the holy law of God was revealed unto me, and was written in my heart. (*Faith and Practice*, North Pacific Yearly Meeting, 1993, p. 15)

These passages are not controversial amongst Friends in themselves. What separates Liberal Friends from the others is that spiritual experience is given primary authority and that no claim is made for scriptural authority. This is a reliance on spiritual experience which is not tied to any text or tradition. Collective discernment provides reliability but no claim is made or sought that revelation is confirmed by Scripture.

Friends find the Jewish and Christian writings which make up the Bible to be a rich and sustaining source of inspiration and a record of God's revelation over many centuries. The Quaker movement began at a time when the Bible had recently come into wide circulation in England, and Friends drew greatly from it. George Fox and others knew the Bible well, studied it earnestly, and quoted it often. The inspiration of the scriptures was affirmed, but a distinction which has remained important to this day was also emphasized by early Friends. In Henry Cadbury's words: 'Divine revelation was not confined to the past. The same Holy Spirit which had inspired the scriptures in the past could inspire living believers centuries later. Indeed, for the right understanding of the past, the present insight from the same Spirit was essential.' Thus, in emphasizing the power which gave forth the scriptures and the accessibility of this same power to us today, Friends have avoided making written records alone a final or infallible test. Instead we are invited to be drawn into that same spirit which gave forth the Bible, both in order to understand its contents and to be led in a continually maturing discovery of the ways of God. (*Faith and Practice*, North Pacific Yearly Meeting, 1993, p. 12)

This is a traditional Quaker view of the use of Scripture from the Liberal Friends of North Pacific. Other Liberal Friends would see this kind of attitude as purely historical. Traditional Quakerism balanced the authority of revelation and of Scripture but at either end of the Quaker spectrum we can find either revelation or Scripture mistrusted or ignored as a source of spiritual authority. Rowntree and Jones assumed a scriptural background amongst Friends, having grown up in Evangelical households. The assumption however gave way to large numbers of those untutored in the Bible joining Liberal Yearly Meetings from an increasingly secular society post-1950. The emphasis on experience was attractive theologically, polit- ically, and psychologically. Personal reaction against the Bible or its seem- ing irrelevance or problems with claims for its authority can be avoided by marginalising Scripture or its authority. British Friends in the 1990s responded that the Bible was best described as any or all of 'the words of God as experienced by its writers' (66.3%), 'the words of God ever open to new interpretation' (45.7%), and a 'useful teaching text' (29.6%) (Dandelion 1996, p. 170).

ECCLESIOLOGICAL AUTHORITY

Different Yearly Meetings also give different levels of authority to the Yearly and Monthly Meetings (see Box 25). Britain Yearly Meeting is almost unique amongst Liberal Yearly Meetings in that its Monthly Meetings are account- able to the Yearly Meeting, which has ultimate authority. Friends Church Southwest in EFI operates a similar system.

Under the Headship of Christ, Evangelical Friends Church Southwest is the highest authority among our churches (and members) in all matters of faith and practice.

Box 25 Monthly Meeting

The Monthly Meeting in Britain is a collection of local Meetings and is not a neighbourhood worshipping community: in America, the local Meeting is called a Monthly Meeting. Both types of Monthly Meeting fulfil similar functions in that they are responsible for local property, for the granting of membership and disownment (termination of membership), the appointment of Elders and Overseers or members of Ministry and Counsel/Worship and Ministry committees. In Britain this means then that the area Meeting, meeting monthly as Meeting 'for Church Affairs' operates as a layer of spiritual and bureaucratic authority over the local Meetings and between them and the Yearly Meeting. In 1965 in Britain, Quarterly Meetings, sitting between Monthly and Yearly Meetings, were renamed General Meetings, their formal duties largely replaced by ones of spiritual nurture. Within forty years, many of these in England had become moribund and had suspended their activity.

Thus, *EFCSW* holds the spiritual and legal power as among its churches to decide all such matters, including without limitation all organizational and operational matters, and its decisions are final. It can counsel, admonish, discipline, dismiss, or close its subordinate churches. It can make administrative decisions and apply church discipline to any of its pastors, staff, elders, members, and attendees. (*Faith and Practice of Evangelical Friends Church Southwest*, 2001, p. 52)

In other Yearly Meetings, the Yearly Meeting has no authority over the constituent Monthly Meetings but merely acts as an umbrella group providing shared services and as a wider gathering. For example, the Southern Appalachian Yearly Meeting and Association book of discipline begins with the lines:

Southern Appalachian Yearly Meeting and Association, a community of local meetings of the Religious Society of Friends, continues to be inspired by the spirit of seventeenth-century English religious reformers who sought to revive primitive Christianity. Our name identifies the geographical center of our widespread monthly (local) meetings and, in traditional Quaker language indicates that we meet annually to conduct our business. The yearly meeting, however, is a cooperative association and exercises no authority, other than moral and advisory, over any local meeting or individual Friend. (*A Guide to Our Faith and Our Practice*, 2000, p. 52)

BOOKS OF DISCIPLINE

The book of discipline, books of discipleship, began in Britain in 1738 with an agreed set of extracts from Yearly Meeting minutes. In 1783, the first

British book of extracts was published and a revision has taken place every thirty years or so. The early book of extracts listed the queries to be answered by men's and women's business meetings (see p. 47 above) as well as minutes of advice and prescription on a whole range of behaviours, as befitted the Quietistic emphasis (see p. 68 above).

Most books of discipline are agreed by the Yearly Meeting and it was at the Yearly Meeting level that schism usually took place. Not all Yearly Meetings have their own book. For example Canadian Friends use the 1959 British *Faith and Practice* but are now working on their own. In 2005 Swiss Friends set up a committee to draft their own book of discipline. The nature and content and thus length of books of discipline vary. For those Yearly Meetings which have a clear sense of doctrine and low levels of prescription of behaviour, the books need only be relatively short. These Yearly Meetings may reprint the Richmond Declaration of Faith (see p. 116 above) or the letter George Fox wrote to the Governor of Barbados in 1671 to summarise Quaker doctrine. Where experience is primary and the search for 'truth' seen to be ongoing, such as Britain, the books are longer as they are more descriptive, and are underpinned by a desire to be inclusive.

These books of discipline express and negotiate unity within Yearly Meetings and historically there have been attempts to create uniform disciplines across groups of Yearly Meetings. The Richmond Declaration can partly be seen in this light. At the same time, individual Friends in Liberal Yearly Meetings can increasingly choose to live by the discipline or not. Meetings can be congregational in their approach to the Yearly Meeting and its book in the same way that individual Friends can now choose to ignore the local Meeting (see p. 150 above). For those still upholding the corporate discipline, the book of discipline is the primary text. In Liberal Yearly Meetings, the focus is on orthopraxis, in Evangelical orthodoxy (see p. 242 below). Kathleen Thomas has suggested that Quakers are the only religious group where their 'sacred text' is written by a committee and replaced in each generation (1993). At the same time, no Yearly Meeting holds their book of discipline actually to be a sacred or inerrant text.

BELIEF

GOD

Belief in God remains fundamental and assumed for most Friends. What varies is the degree of specificity ascribed to the Divine, how far God is external and 'real', and how far the Quaker God is necessarily the God of the Christian Scriptures.

For Evangelical and Conservative Friends, these are not questions. But where Liberal Friends are part of Conservative Yearly Meetings, as their nearest unprogrammed Meeting, and in Liberal Yearly Meetings, the nature of God is an individual choice and theology varies widely.

Thus, we have public Evangelical statements of faith with very specific scriptural references to the nature of God or which are very clear about God's attributes on the one hand, and a Liberal ambivalence about saying anything too specific at a corporate level.

As we have noted (p. 152 above), this corporate ambivalence about theology and personal uncertainty about the content of belief within the Liberal tradition affects the whole of Liberal Quaker theology. Only where items are no longer explicitly or regularly mentioned, such as salvation or eschatology, might we conclude that there is no belief of note or little need for these beliefs amongst those Friends. Elsewhere, we are likely to find a variety of viewpoints all mentioned without any claim to ultimate authority or absolute certainty.

Evangelical Quakerism itself is multi-faceted, with some Friends influenced by the Holiness tradition, others by the Fundamentalist movement, others by modernism (see Box 24). The large percentage of Friends who have come into Quakerism as adults (85% in the Liberal tradition in Britain – Dandelion 1996, p. 331; the percentage for Evangelical and Conservative Friends is unknown) has meant that beliefs from participants' previous affiliations are often brought into Quakerism and can become normative where there is a lack of teaching of the tradition or where the form or content of Quakerism is open to change. For example, Christmas was first celebrated at the Conservative Quaker school at Olney in 1928, and earlier in the Liberal tradition (Carrdus 1993). Some Evangelical Quaker colleges still prohibit 'sociable dancing', and all prohibit alcohol, drugs, pornography, and extra-marital sex (see p. 225 below), reflecting a wider Protestant world-rejecting culture. The collective shaking of hands at the end of unprogrammed worship, an innovation in Britain since the 1970s, has been attributed to the influx of Anglican converts used to sharing the sign of peace. Where Evangelical Friends churches have become or strive to be the local community church, Quaker distinctives may easily disappear in the desire for accessibility. Thus, whilst William Penn claimed the Trinity was unscriptural (although both he and Fox talked of the tri-unity of God), the Richmond Declaration of Faith of 1887 presented a trinitarian formulation as normative within Quakerism.

We believe in one holy (Isa 6:3, 57:15), almighty (Gen 17:1), all-wise (Rom 11:33, 16:27) and everlasting (Ps 90:1–2) God, the Father (Matt 11:25–27), the Creator (Gen 1:1) and Preserver (Job 7:20) of all things; and in Jesus Christ, His only Son, our Lord, by whom all things were made (John 1:30), and by whom all things consist (Col 1:17); and in one Holy Spirit, proceeding from the Father and the Son (John 15:26, 16:7), the Reprover (John 16:8) of the world, the Witness for Christ (John 15:26) and the Teacher (John 14:26), Guide (John 16:13), and Sanctifier (2 Thess 2:13) of the people of God; and that these three are one in the eternal Godhead (Matt 28:19; John 10:30; 17:21); to whom be honor, praise, and thanksgiving, now and forever. Amen (*Faith and Practice of Evangelical Friends Church Southwest*, 2001, p. 34)

From this authoritative document, Evangelical Yearly Meetings have maintained that belief.

We believe in the one holy and loving God, who exists eternally in three persons – Father, Son and Holy Spirit. He is the Creator and Sustainer of the Universe, and the final judge of everyone who lives within it. (Mylander 2004, p. 8)

For those Friends within FUM or who left FYM after its inception, the Richmond Declaration of Faith continues to be a doctrinal starting point. Where Friends churches have adopted the outward elements (see p. 213 below), the section on baptism becomes difficult, but this modernist Evangelical statement still underpins much of Evangelical Quaker theology. The second historical source used by many Evangelical Friends is George Fox's letter to the Governor of Barbados in 1671. His letter to the Governor connects Friends to orthodox Christianity. Some have claimed this as the normative and essential Christianity of Quakerism (e.g. Davie 1997) and it is reprinted in the books of discipline of some Evangelical Yearly Meetings – others view it as a pragmatic composition (Jones 1911, p. 112). For Friends Church Eastern Region (FCER), which was never part of FYM, or Friends Church Southwest, whose position has come to match FCER, these documents are set alongside more orthodox Protestant statements of faith. However, the inward encounter remains a constant throughout this variety.

In the following ten-point statement of faith from the Bolivian Yearly Meeting set off by mission work from Oregon Yearly Meeting, now Northwest, we can see this Protestant emphasis accompanying the Quaker one: Christ is at the heart of the church, revealed through an inward communion without external rite.

DECLARACION DE FE
Los Amigos reconocen y proclaman con enfasis la verdad fundamental y esencial: que Jesucristo es la Cabeza de la Iglesia; El mora en los corazones de los creyentes, sin necesidad de sacramentos y/o ritos externos.

CREEMOS

1. En la trinidad de Dios: Padre, Hijo y Espiritu Santo.
2. En la deidad de Jesucristo nuestro Señor.
3. En la Inspiración plena de las Sagradas Escrituras.
4. En la caida del Hombre y la depravación moral de la humanidad.
5. En la justificación de los pecadores por la fe en Jesucristo y en la sangre que derramo en la cruz.
6. En la santificación de los creyentes por el bautismo del Espiritu Santo.
7. En que la Evangelización del mundo es la mision suprema de la iglesia en esta epoca.
8. En la segunda venida de nuestro Señor Jesucristo.
9. En la resurrección de los muertos, el juicio final de Dios sobre los pecadores y el castigo eterno para los que rechazan a Jesucristo.
   (http://www.quaker.org/christonet/inela/bases_doctrinales.htm, 7 March 2006)

God is triune, Christ divine, the Scriptures given by divine inspiration, humanity sinful. Christ shed his blood as part of an atoning sacrifice, and mission is the primary goal of the church at this time. Christ will come again and the dead will be resurrected and the faithful saved at God's final day of judgement.

Northwest Yearly Meeting of Friends Church affirms as essential Christian truths the following teachings: the sovereignty of God; the deity and humanity of Jesus Christ; the atonement through Jesus Christ by which persons are reconciled to God; the resurrection of Jesus, which assures the resurrection of all true worshipers; the gift of the Holy Spirit to believers; and the authority of the Holy Scriptures.

The Yearly Meeting also endorses traditional statements of Friends, including those emphasizing an inward encounter with God, communion without ritual, an individual responsibility for ministry and service, and striving for peace and justice. In addition, the Yearly Meeting speaks to contemporary issues concerning morality, human relationships, and Christian commitment. Friends hold that an authentic Christian belief results in both an inward faith and an outward expression of that belief. (*Faith and Practice: A Book of Christian discipline, Northwest Yearly Meeting of Friends Church*, 2003, p. 5)

Note this last sentence, emphasising, in line with the earliest Quaker tradition, the interiorisation of the basis of faith and the externalisation of its effects. This is true for most programmed Friends.

The theological tensions within Liberal Quakerism are currently concerned with the nature of God and of religious experience. Non-realist Quaker authors such as David Boulton (2002) and David Rush (2003) suggest that religious belief symbolises our highest human ideals, that such belief does not refer to anything 'real' (hence the term non-realist).

From a realist point of view, the statement 'God exists' is either true or false. Statements made about God are like statements made about your car: they either correspond to reality, the 'facts' or they don't. But, says Cupitt, there's another way of looking at all this: a nonrealist way. From this viewpoint, God is understood not as a real person, power or entity (an intelligence, an energy, a thing like a rock or a daisy) but as a symbol or as an idea. God is a fiction, but a necessary, instrumental fiction. (Boulton 2002, p. 149)

This idea, similar to Feuerbach's view of 'God' as the summation of humanity's political aspirations, lends its current affirmation to the writings of the Anglican Don Cupitt and the Sea of Faith movement in which some Quakers are very active. David Rush's work on non-theistic Friends, which would include non-realists as well as atheists and agnostics, further illustrates this form of Quakerism where a realist God is inappropriate and unnecessary (2003).

However within the liberal-Liberal tradition (see p. 152 above), an implicit semi-realist position is dominant. God is real but statements about God are not facts but interpretations. Indeed, in a paradoxical way, the non-realist statements about God are more certain in their conviction than those of the semi-realists. Additionally, the non-realists, in their certainty, sit uneasily within a liberal-Liberal tradition currently based on a principle of theological perhapsness (see p. 152 above). Like Christian Quakers who feel they have been eldered for their theology, non-theist Friends have sometimes misunderstood their discomfort in terms of theological tension rather than an epistemological tension.

Semi-realists believe that the experience of God is real but that theological statements cannot get close to describing the mystery of the Divine. In this sense, theology is not ultimately 'real' or true in anything other than a symbolic sense. Beliefs are held to be 'true' personally, partially, or provisionally but not true for everyone for all time. This is based on a criticism of the ability of humanity and of language adequately to describe religious and spiritual experience rather than any critique of God (see p. 136 above). Semi-realists are not undermining the existence of something beyond the material although their implicit diversity of explanation and expression does tend towards a pluralism of belief. In this way, the 'something beyond the material' becomes variously described and, in Bruce's terms, part of a 'diffuse belief system' (2003, p. 57). God is variously and alternatively described and God's attributes vary between participants.

For those who are more thoroughly realist in terms of belief and theology, the majority of Friends worldwide, this can appear to look like, in John Punshon's terms, a 'supermarket religion' (1990, p. 23). Self-led eclecticism can appear an overly diffuse form of religion. What is often misunderstood is that, whilst this may be true, belief is not central to Liberal Friends. It is not how Liberal Friends define their Quakerism, but rather and merely an attempt to explain the nature of their *experience*, which is primary. Liberal Friends emphasise the form of Quakerism not because they do not believe anything but because it is the form which leads to the experience which for them is central.

GOD IN THE WORLD/THEODICY

Programmed Quaker worship typically includes time for vocal prayer and prayer requests. Whilst outward, it is not a time of visual programming and might also be found in an unprogrammed Meeting. Modernist Evangelical Friends can be found to rationalise their prayers: for example, 'God, I know we do not ask you to make these things right, but can you help this family feel your love . . .'. God is not asked to intervene directly except in terms of divine love. In less modernist Meetings (see Box 24), God can be asked to intervene or be seen to have acted in the world. World events may be a sign of God's love or God's displeasure.

Some Liberal Friends share the modernist Evangelical outlook, a few the Holiness Evangelical one, and this latter group would have no difficulty in asking God to intervene. For other Liberal Friends, world events are seen to be acts of humanity or acts of nature, both removed from the possibility of divine intervention. Liberal Friends sometimes take a deistic view, in which a higher power may have created the world but then let it regulate itself, through human free will and the laws of physics, etc. In one Meeting, the tsunami disaster of December 2004 was described in this way. 'God would no more stop this book falling to the floor should I drop it than stop the laws of physics and geology from unfolding in this earthquake.' God has given humanity the free will to try to understand such tragedies and to react to them.

A second way around the problem of theodicy (how God can allow suffering) for Liberal Friends is to claim only two of the three traditional attributes of omnipresence, omniscience, and omnibenevolence. In a survey conducted in 1989 amongst British Friends of thirty-two Meetings, 56% claimed God was all-loving, 36% that God was all-knowing, and 19% that God was all-powerful (Dandelion 1996, p. 169). Thus a maximum of 19% could have held to the traditional trinity of divine attributes. Rutherford's survey achieved even lower levels of agreement with these terms in her study of British Friends in 2003 (personal communication).

God as all-loving was the most popular option, and typically in interview British Friends avoided the problem of theodicy by claiming God was all-loving, and perhaps all-knowing, but not all-powerful. Certainly, no Friend I have encountered has claimed that God was all-powerful and all-knowing but not all-loving, although this would also avoid the philo-sophical conundrum. For others, as above, God is beyond these attributes, either unknowable (25% – Dandelion 1996, p. 169) or not the kind of God who has those kinds of attributes. Ideas of 'presence' or 'spirit' are more popular. Finally, there are those for whom God is not real, but the summation of humanity's best hopes and ideals (non-realists), or for whom God does not exist at all (atheists).

The emphasis in the following passage from Friends Church Southwest Quaker, Charles Mylander, is explicit. Humankind inherits sinfulness and sins further.

We believe that God created the human being, male and female, in His own image. When Adam and Eve fell into disobedience and rebellion toward God, they were alienated from Him and the perfect image of God was warped, marred, stained and corrupted. As a result all people inherit a pervasive sinfulness that invades every part of their beings. Further, all people sin by their own willful choices, falling short of both their own personal standards and also of God's moral law. This moral depravity means that everyone is sinful and separated from God and needs to be redeemed and regenerated through Christ by the power of the Holy Spirit. (Mylander 2004, pp. 8–9)

However, Christ's death allows the possibility of salvation from sin through God's grace, and beyond that the possibility of eternal life. To reject Christ is to be assured of eternal death in hell. Good works character-ise saving faith but do not earn it.

We believe that Jesus Christ died on the cross, shedding His blood for us and for our sins and rose again from the dead to make us right with God. A person receives salvation by grace through faith in Jesus Christ as Lord and Savior and not by being good enough to deserve it. To those who receive Christ, God grants forgiveness of sins, the gift of eternal life and ultimately the resurrection of the body to live forever in the new heavens and new earth. Rejecting Jesus Christ and His provisions for salvation and forgiveness of sins results in the penalty of eternal death in hell. The presence of saving faith is revealed by a life lived in obedience to the will of God and results in the good works that God has prepared in advance for us to do. (Mylander 2004, p. 9)

The FUM introductory text begins with an outline of human sin and the possibility of salvation through the atoning work of Christ.

Christians believe that the life, death, and resurrection of Jesus has brought about an atonement (or reconciliation) between humanity and God. Time and again, those who give their lives to Christ find that God has the power to move people from darkness to light (1 Peter 2:1). Throughout the history of Christianity there have been numerous ways of understanding how this works, each of which reflect aspects of biblical truth. The various theories of the atonement are ways of understanding the experience of social and personal evil in light of the forgiveness and redemption that come from God. This points to God's gracious offer of salvation and eternal life. Friends have always been open to expressing their faith in a variety of ways and reject any reliance on creedal affirmations. Nevertheless, Friends share some basic understandings about sin, Christ and the atonement:

1. God created the world, and all that is in it, 'good' and, from the beginning of creation, God intended humanity to live in harmony with creation and one another.
2. Humanity's inability to live that quality of life is objective evidence of human-kind's need for a radical intervention by God. There are many ways of talking about 'original sin' but a key aspect of sin is the ever-repeated choice humans make to exercise self-will rather than to rely upon God for guidance.
3. Outward rules and laws, while useful in reminding us of God's intention, fail to create true goodness either in individuals or in society.
4. God chose to enter into human history in the person of Jesus Christ. As fully human and fully divine, Jesus Christ bridges the gap between humanity and God. Because of sin, Jesus' life led, inevitably, to the cross. The cross, then, becomes both the sign of humanity's rebellion against God, and God's sacrificial love for humanity.
5. Through Jesus' death on the cross God offers forgiveness for sin, and through His resurrection and the gift of the Holy Spirit God. In one of the early expressions of these truths, George Fox (one of the foremost preachers among the early Quakers and the primary organizer of the movement), wrote:

But, I say you are redeemed by Christ. It cost him his blood to purchase man out of the state he is in, in the Fall, and bring him up to the state man was in before his fall. So Christ became a curse to bring man out of the curse and bore the wrath, to bring man to the Peace of God, that he might come to the blessed state, to Adam's state he was in before he fall, and not only thither, but to a state in Christ that shall never fall. And this is my testimony to you and to all people upon the earth. (Richmond 2004, n.p.)

The author reminds readers of the early Quaker claim of being raised up beyond the state of Adam before the fall to the state of Christ. Hell is not mentioned.

Ohio Conservative Yearly Meeting makes no mention of sin or of salvation in its book of discipline but emphasises the transforming power of the Light. For Liberal Friends, the idea of original sin has often been replaced by the idea of original blessing or of some innate divinity. For these Friends, the concept of salvation can be a redundant one. Salvation from what? One of the few references to sin and salvation in the British book of discipline reads as follows:

> Directly I admit that my life might be better than it is. I have a sense of failure and feel a need of help from something or someone outside myself. This sense and this need are to me the meanings of the terms 'sense of sin' and 'need of salvation'. (*Quaker Faith and Practice*, 1995, 26.10)

This is not the original sin of EFI Friends and help in daily life is a different interpretation of salvation. Without a keen sense of eschatological present or future (see below), and a shift away from a purely Quaker-Christian theology, concepts of sin and salvation have been modified within Liberal Quakerism.

ESCHATOLOGY

Present-day views on eschatology vary. Evangelical and Conservative Friends see themselves in the meantime, expecting either an outward or inward second coming depending on the extent to which they maintain a traditional Quaker viewpoint.

The encounter with the risen and Living Christ is often emphasised but not in a final sense. Rather, it is as if Quakers have experienced their own individual Pentecost experience and are still waiting for a more complete or more widespread revelation to come.

> We believe in the Second Coming of our Lord Jesus Christ and all the great events of the end times prophesied in scripture. We refuse to divide fellowship over disputed questions of eschatology that are not clear in the scriptures. We believe in the great resurrection of both the saved and the lost. We believe everyone will stand before Christ in the final judgment to receive their just due. Those whose names are written in the Lamb's book of life will inherit their eternal rewards in the new heavens and the new earth, freed forever from selfishness, sin, demonic influence, control and all evil. The finally unrepentant wicked will suffer the eternal condemnation of hell prepared for the devil and his angels. At that time Christ will reign fully over the restored universe and God the Father will be fully glorified. (Mylander 2004, p. 11)

This passage from Friends Church Southwest Quaker, Charles Mylander, is explicitly meantime, and also explicitly outward in its sense of the endtimes. An outward Christ will come again and all will be judged by Christ. Hell exists in this account, an unusual Quaker reference to a distinct afterlife. Zablon Malenge, writing on Kenyan Quakerism, quotes the Richmond Declaration (see p. 116 above) that a day of judgement will come.

We believe that the punishment of the wicked and the blessedness of the righteous shall be everlasting, according to the declaration of our compassionate Redeemer, to whom the judgement is committed. These shall go away into eternal punishment, but the righteous into eternal life. (Matt 25:46 RSV) (Malenge 2003, p. 82)

A Friends United Meeting introductory text emphasises covenant rather than judgement.

The days are surely coming, says the Lord, when I will make a new covenant with the house of Israel and the house of Judah ... I will put my law within them, and I will write it on their hearts; and I will be their God, and they shall be my people. No longer shall they teach one another, or say to each other, 'Know the LORD', for they shall all know me, from the least of them to the greatest, says the LORD; for I will forgive their iniquity, and remember their sin no more. (Jer 31:31, 33b–34)

The New Covenant has three parts: God promises to write His law on people's *hearts*; everyone gets to know God *directly*; and God declares *forgiveness* of sin. Friends stress that the New Covenant is inward rather than outward. The community of believers is not defined by ethnic or political boundaries but by the changed hearts of its members. God is not declaring more or better rules or ideas, but instead is promising to change people from the inside out. Friends also stress that the New Covenant is unconditional. (Richmond 2004, n.p.)

This statement of faith follows much of early Quaker teaching, including its reliance on Jeremiah 31:31–34. In terms of its eschatological emphasis, however, it draws Quakers back to a Pentecost moment rather than the marriage supper of the Lamb. In other words, the new inward covenant is a new beginning, akin to Pentecost, rather than signal of the culmination of God's plan for humanity. It presents Quakerism as an alternative meantime (see p. 33 above).

All present-day Quakers need to negotiate this lack of belief in a radical and vital unfolding second coming. It is an awkward negotiation because it needs to justify the radical liturgical form of Friends and yet maintain a sustainable meantime position. The radical liturgical form is typically justified, as above, by reference to some new covenant, or dispensation, being placed upon Friends in opposition to the old and now redundant dispensation still being practised by other Christians. But the new dispensation is partial, for its transformation is limited within the context of these meantime theologies. In other words, the new dispensation does not herald the end of time, as it did for Fox, but rather a new way of passing time. It may be seen to be more authentic, more perfect, but these Quaker authors do not claim that it allows those who experience it to be any closer to the New Jerusalem. The following passage from the 1996 epistle of Ohio Yearly Meeting (Conservative) treads this line of maintaining a new dispensation with limited transformative powers.

As the Jews waited hopefully for a messiah, the carpenter's son came proclaiming the acceptable year of the Lord. To many it was blasphemous, but some believed and set about establishing the kingdom of heaven.

As seventeenth century England was mired in deadly controversy over issues of church doctrine and government, the man in leather breeches [George Fox] came proclaiming that Jesus Christ had come to teach his people himself. To many it was blasphemous, but some believed and set about establishing the Society of Friends.

Today, at a time when the world is in great need of spiritual healing, we again proclaim the acceptable year of the Lord, testify to our experience that Jesus Christ is come to teach us himself, and affirm his promise that when two or three are gathered in his name, Jesus Christ is present in the midst of us. To many this is still blasphemous, but some believe and know the joy God offers everyone.

Come and see what our eyes have seen, hear what our ears have heard, taste what our mouths have tasted. For the Lord is good, and his mercies continue forever. Now is the time to begin anew on this beautiful morning of the Gospel Day. Begin deep down inside, where each of us stands guard over the gate of change in our hearts. Are we willing to surrender all to receive all? Then we may join together in that great stream of living water. Now it reaches out – to our families, our meetings and churches, our communities and workplaces until soon old things have passed away and behold, all things are created anew! (*Britain Yearly Meeting Proceedings*, 1997, p. 125)

North Carolina Yearly Meeting (Conservative) quote George Fox's 1671 letter to the Governor of Barbados. This reads in part:

And we do own and believe that He was made a sacrifice for sin Who knew no sin, neither was guile found in His mouth, and that He was crucified for us in the flesh without the gates of Jerusalem, and that He was buried and that He rose again on the third day by the power of His Father for our justification; and we do believe that He ascended into Heaven and now sitteth on the right hand of God . . . He it is that is now come, and hath given us an understanding that we may know Him that is true. And He rules in our hearts by His law of love and life, and makes us free from the law of sin and death. And we have no life but by Him, for He is the quickening Spirit, the Second Adam, the Lord from Heaven, by Whose blood we are cleansed and our consciences sprinkled from dead works to serve the Living God . . .

We do declare that we esteem it a duty incumbent upon us to pray with and for, to teach, instruct and admonish those in and belonging to our families, for whom an account will be required by Him Who comes to judge both quick and dead at the great day of judgment, when every one shall be rewarded according to the deeds done in the body, whether they be good or whether they be evil; at that day we say, of the resurrection both of the good and of the bad, of the just and the unjust: 'When the Lord Jesus shall be revealed from Heaven with His mighty angels, in flaming fire, taking vengeance on them that know not God and obey not the Gospel of our Lord Jesus Christ; who shall be punished with everlasting destruction from the presence of the Lord, and from the glory of His power, when He shall come to be glorified in his saints, and to be admired in all them that believe in that day': II Thess. 1:7–10; II Peter 3:3. (*Faith and Practice: Book of Discipline of the North Carolina Yearly Meeting (Conservative) of the Religious Society of Friends*, 1983, pp. 9–11)

The passage 'He it is that is now come, and hath given us an understanding that we may know Him that is true. And He rules in our hearts by His law of love and life, and makes us free from the law of sin and death' points to a realising eschatology but the subsequent part of the letter emphasises the sinful nature of humanity, the continuing wait for justification and sanctification, and ultimately the wait for the day of judgement. This is not then, ultimately, a realising eschatology, but a Pentecostal meantime experience.

For Liberal Friends, the topic of the second coming is rarely spoken of. When confronted with the second coming message of early Friends, and the possibility that they got it wrong (in that no global transformation followed), some maintain that Friends are still in the vanguard of the second coming and that it is still unfolding. In other words, even whilst not talking about it, Friends are involved in some kind of slowly realising eschatology. God's time is, after all, not the same as human time and the 'twinkling of an eye' (1 Cor 15:52) may be taking more than 350 years. This does not ease relations with other Quakers now firmly in the meantime alongside other Christians or ecumenically (see p. 239 below). Either these Liberal Friends are the vanguard of the true church, holding the unfolding second coming in trust until God wills, or else all other Christians are mistaken for believing they are still in the meantime dispensation and need to catch up, as early Friends claimed. Even where this view is held, it is held privately and usually only offered in response to teaching about the second coming. Certainly the view is not represented in any book of discipline.

CHRIST

This shift into a meantime theology, evident as we have seen from the 1670s, has also affected attitudes to Jesus. As God became more distant and less of a co-agent, so different attitudes to waiting resulted in two contrasting attitudes to the nature of Jesus Christ. Early Friends were charged, for example by Bunyan, of ignoring the historic Christ. Focused on the second coming and filled by an encounter with the inward Christ, they did indeed have little need to remember and rehearse the outward Christ of the first coming. Moore notes how, after the earliest years, Friends strove to answer their critics by emphasising their scriptural allegiances (2001, p. 56). Burrough does this in his answer to Bunyan (Holland 2006).

Quakers are then forever faced with the question of how to treat Christ. As theologies of the meantime become more developed and eventually emerge into post- and pre-millennialism in the nineteenth century, so attitudes to Jesus Christ follow. For the post-millennialists who believe Christ will come again at the end of a thousand-year rule of the saints, Christ provides an example of how the saints are to live and work in their redemptive task. For the pre-millennialists who believe society is so depraved that only Christ himself can usher in the thousand-year rule of the saints, it is the very nature of the atonement that makes this possible.

We believe in the deity and the humanity of our Lord Jesus Christ. He is at the same time fully God and fully man. We believe in His Virgin birth, in His sinless life, in His miracles, in His vicarious and atoning death through His shed blood on Calvary's cross, in His bodily resurrection from the dead, in His ascension, in His being seated (enthroned) at the right hand of the heavenly Father, and in His second coming to earth in power and great glory. (Mylander 2004, p. 8)

The Friends United Meeting text emphasises the inward teacher as well as the atoning sacrifice.

Friends' faith centers on the life, death, resurrection and continuing presence of Jesus Christ. We emphasize the presence of the resurrected Christ and the life transformation that comes from listening to, and following, him. In Christ we have discovered the love of God, God's power to forgive and heal, and God's continuing presence as Teacher and Lord. Therefore, we emphasize listening to the living Word of God – as revealed in Scripture, as well as the Spirit of Christ speaking both within each individual and in the community that makes up the church. We have discovered that when people center their lives in Jesus Christ and practice a listening spirituality, that the community life that results begins to reflect the character of Jesus: gentleness, peace, simplicity, equality, moral purity, integrity, etc. This offers great hope to the world, and it is our joy to share this life with others.

Christians believe that the life, death, and resurrection of Jesus has brought about an atonement (or reconciliation) between humanity and God and their many variations.

... Friends have always been open to expressing their faith in a variety of ways and reject any reliance on creedal affirmations. Nevertheless, Friends share some basic understandings about sin, Christ and the atonement:

1. God created the world, and all that is in it, 'good' and, from the beginning of creation, God intended humanity to live in harmony with creation and one another.

2. Humanity's inability to live that quality of life is objective evidence of humankind's need for a radical intervention by God. There are many ways of talking about 'original sin' but a key aspect of sin is the ever-repeated choice humans make to exercise self-will rather than to rely upon God for guidance.

3. Outward rules and laws, while useful in reminding us of God's intention, fail to create true goodness either in individuals or in society.

4. God chose to enter into human history in the person of Jesus Christ. As fully human and fully divine, Jesus Christ bridges the gap between humanity and God. Because of sin, Jesus' life led, inevitably, to the cross. The cross, then, becomes both the sign of humanity's rebellion against God, and God's sacrificial love for humanity.

Through Jesus' death on the cross God offers forgiveness for sin, and through His resurrection and the gift of the Holy Spirit, God provides the possibility of a new life that reflects the goodness God intended from the beginning of creation. (Richmond 2004, n.p)

Zablon Malenge from Nairobi Yearly Meeting suggests:

Quakers are consecrated to Jesus Christ. The verb 'to consecrate' means to set a place apart for God, to make it holy, by the offering of sacrifice upon it. Friends have been dedicated and consecrated to God by the sacrifice of Jesus Christ. Friends have been called to be God's dedicated people. (Malenge 2003, p. 47)

The passage from North Carolina Yearly Meeting (Conservative), the 1905 addition to the Conservative ranks, mixes modernist Liberal phrases such as 'inner Light' with the transcript of the letter to the Governor of Barbados. Only the references to the wider Christian community suggest this is not a Liberal document.

The experience of the 'Inner Light', or the 'Light of Christ', is the center of the life of Friends and the ultimate source of all our testimonies. The Inner Light is what Friends call 'that of God' in every person which, Friends believe, can be known directly without another's interpretation. The Inner Light gives illumination and clarity to conscience, generating an inward compulsion to follow the leadings of its Spirit. This Spirit is the love of God, implanted in all, overcoming the ambivalence of conscience and leading us to a powerful conviction of God's will for our lives.

The Inner Light is our experience of and connection with God. According to Friends this experience involves a body of convictions about God's nature and His requirements concerning our dealings with all persons. When this body of convictions has consolidated itself in one's inner life and style of outward conduct, it is called 'Truth.' This Truth is a way of following the spirit and not the letter of the law . . .

Friends regard their religion in worship and daily life as being guided by the Inner Light. Thus they have no use for dogma and credal formulas. Quakerism can be described but not defined, since it is an inner vision and outward life style rather than a theological world view. It will often be necessary, however, for Friends to relate their experience to that of the Christian community as a whole, and to satisfy this need in a way compatible with the Light which has been given them.

Friends believe that the same Spirit which guided the ministries of Jesus, the prophets, and the apostles, remains alive and at work in the world today. As Friends so affirm and seek an ever more perfect openness to that Guidance in their daily lives, they have found it preferable to offer no allegiance to either doctrine, dogma, or creed. (*Faith and Practice: Book of Discipline of the North Carolina Yearly Meeting (Conservative) of the Religious Society of Friends*, 1983, pp. 6, 9)

Liberal Quakers who have abandoned meantime theology, as too overtly Christian (see p. 135 above), avoid the dilemma of how to approach the figure of Christ. For those without a Christian emphasis, the question of how to treat Christ is not a central one. For some, it is irrelevant. Where Christ is important, there is a range of views as to the nature and role of Christ, between the usual liberal theological idea of Jesus as example and the more conservative view of the Christ's propitiatory sacrifice and the centrality of the atonement. The liberal-Liberal (see p. 134 above) Britain Yearly Meeting adopted a book of discipline in 1994 which emphasised a relationship with God rather than with Christ. However, Advice Two very near the front of the book reads: 'Bring the whole of your life under the ordering of the spirit of Christ . . . Remember that Christianity is not a notion but a way' (*Quaker Faith and Practice*, 1995, 1.02). What is clear is that Christ is not a central concept for every British Friend (chapter 3).

THE LIGHT WITHIN

The Light Within is the fundamental and immediate experience for Friends. It is that which guides each of us in our everyday lives and brings us together as a community of faith. It is, most importantly, our direct and unmediated experience of the Divine. (*Faith and Practice: A Book of Christian discipline, Philadelphia Yearly Meeting of the Religious Society of Friends*, 2002, p. 16)

The early and various Quaker use of the term Light allows Liberal Friends to avoid doctrinal specificity. The Light operates inwardly, hence the continued emphasis on a liturgy of silence amongst unprogrammed

Friends, but Liberal Friends do not need to specify corporately its theological nature or character. Indeed, as we have seen (p. 152), such vagueness not only is seen to be theologically astute, but also maintains unity. North Pacific Yearly Meeting make this clear in the following passage:

> One central area of belief which has received considerable attention over the years is the relationship of Quakerism to Christianity. Whether one interprets the Quaker movement as a strand within Protestantism or as a third force distinct from both Protestantism and Catholicism, the movement, both in its origin and in the various branches which have evolved, is rooted in Christianity. However, from its inception it has offered both a critique of many accepted manifestations of Christianity and an empathy with people of faith beyond the bounds of Christianity. Some Friends have placed particular emphasis on the Gospel of Jesus Christ, while others have found more compelling a universal perspective emphasizing the Divine Light enlightening every person. One of the lessons of our own history as a religious movement is that an excessive reliance on one or the other of these perspectives, neglecting the essential connectedness between the two, has been needlessly divisive and has drawn us away from the vitality of the Quaker vision at its best.
>
> In yearly meetings such as ours, the concern of Friends is not that members affirm a particular verbal formulation of this faith but that it be a living and transforming power within their lives. Challenged by the words of Jesus as quoted in Matthew 7:21 – 'It is not those who say to me, "Lord, Lord," who will enter the kingdom of heaven, but those who do the will of my Father in heaven' – we do not place emphasis on the naming of God. Instead we encourage one another, in John Woolman's phrase, 'to distinguish the language of the pure Spirit which inwardly moves upon the heart.' In the course of following this spiritual path, many Friends do come to find great depths of meaning in familiar Christian concepts and language, while others do not. (*Faith and Practice*, North Pacific Yearly Meeting, 1993, p. 12)

Within the Liberal tradition the attitude to text, formulated in human language, is as cautious as the attitudes to theology itself. When Rufus Jones and J.W. Rowntree formulated modernist Liberal Quakerism, their emphasis on pure experience was such that they disregarded the earlier Quaker use of Scripture as an implicit test of the truth of revelation (see p. 185 above). For these Liberal Friends, experience was only to be checked by experience and as such the authority of Scripture has fallen within this part of the Quaker family over the twentieth century. This process has been accelerated by pluralism and theological diversity within Liberal Quakerism. Under Jones' influence, the term 'the inward Light' has been replaced by 'inner Light' (see p. 133 above).

ECCLESIOLOGY

In terms of ecclesiology, most Quaker churches and Meetings still maintain a 'flat ecclesiology' based on the 'gospel order' of the 1660s (see Box 6). In other words, the church as the body of believers maintains a mutual and collective accountability and responsibility under the headship of Christ/ leadership of the Spirit. Friends have abolished not the clergy but the laity, they say (*Quaker Faith and Practice*, 1995, 11.01)

We believe that all who truly follow and trust Jesus are the members of one body, and that each local church is a manifestation of that body. We recognize that God calls and equips particular men and women to be leaders in his church, and it is the role of every member to affirm and cooperate with that calling, while maintaining their own responsibilities for service and leadership as well.

We fully affirm that Jesus is the Head of the church, not as a metaphor, but as a matter of practical reality. This makes the church different from all other institutions. While all members are equally part of a local church, the church is not a democracy. Jesus Christ Himself is the leader of each church. This means that decision-making in a local church is primarily a task of spiritual discernment. While it is our task to weigh options and discuss various proposals and ideas, we believe that by humbly and prayerfully submitting our opinions and perspectives to the Holy Spirit's direction, the Lord will guide us to unity regarding His direction for a particular decision. This unity cannot be discerned by voting, nor is it merely human consensus, which is arrived at by compromise and mediating conflicting opinions. Rather, unity in decision-making is a gift our Lord Jesus gives His church when they collectively seek His will as its Head. (Eph 3:6; 1 Cor 12:28; Heb 13:17; Col 1:18; Acts 15, esp. v. 28) (*Faith and Practice of Evangelical Friends Church Southwest*, 2001, pp. 15–16)

Ohio Yearly Meeting (Conservative) speaks of a 'spiritual democracy'.

As all unite before the true Head of the Church, a spiritual democracy becomes a reality. Vocal service in such a meeting, whether prayer or exhortation or teaching, should be uttered under the direct guidance and authority of the Holy Spirit. We fully recognize the importance of intellectual and spiritual training of each member in preparation for any service which may be laid upon him, so that when the commission is given he may serve with his fullest ability as well as with a ready and glad heart. (*The Book of Discipline of Ohio Yearly Meeting*, 1992, p. 4)

Virtually all Friends would agree with the above two passages; some Liberal Friends would 'translate' the term 'Christ' but the lack of human hierarchy and secular democracy is universal. Rather, Friends can see themselves as a theocracy, christocracy, or pneumatocracy.

The presence of unpaid office holders such as Clerks and Elders (see Box 26) and paid staff such as Yearly Meeting Superintendents and/or

---

Box 26 Elders, Clerks, Overseers

'Elders' have been appointed since the beginning of the Quaker movement to help nurture the worship life of Meetings. 'Clerks' help with the administration of the Meeting's business, whilst 'Overseers' have a pastoral role. This latter term has been dropped by some American Meetings because of its connotations with slavery. Throughout American Liberal Quakerism, Committees of Ministry and Counsel work as the Elders, Ministry, and Oversight on pastoral care. Where Meetings have pastors, some of this work falls to them although there would still be Elders and a Clerk to the Meeting or Friends church.

---

pastors still falls within this model. These tasks are seen as particular acts of service or calling within the faith community rather than a mandate of spiritual authority. Payment, within a tradition whose beginnings included an attack on the 'hireling ministry' (see p. 26 above), is to 'release' the individual for their ministry rather than for the ministry itself. Other Quaker employees differentiate between their ministry and their paid work.

In terms of Eldership, some EFI Yearly Meetings allow the Pastor and Elders to take most of the day-to-day decisions regarding the running of the church.

Along with the leadership of pastors and elders we value the priesthood of all believers, the people of God who pray, worship, teach, discern, witness, bless, encourage, love, give and serve. (*Faith and Practice of Evangelical Friends Church, Southwest*, 2001, p. 25)

Friends United Meeting similarly emphasises the priesthood of all believers and the ministry of all alongside its justification of the pastoral system (to generalise, FUM churches rely more than EFI on Monthly Meeting considering the majority of items).

Friends abolished the laity and became a fellowship of ministers. Friends have always recognized that some of their number are more gifted for public ministry than others. These are persons, both men and women, whose gifts of speaking, visitation, and uplifting counsel under the leading of the Spirit, stir up and encourage others in their ministry. Over the years Friends have 'recorded' the gifts of such persons. In addition to ministering helpfully in their local Meetings, recorded Friends ministers have often traveled far and wide in ministry among Quakers and to others. http://www.fum.org/about/friends.htm#Beliefs, 7 March 2006

Meetings may raise their pastors to places of leadership or negotiate their charismatic authority by having a 'Worship and Ministry' committee work alongside them. In some Friends churches, the pastor can be almost invisible in worship, with most of the weekly functions of worship carried out by a rota of those perceived by the church to hold particular gifts, such as music, leadership, or preaching. Sometimes pastors would like to take a less overt role but are prevented by the preferences of the Meeting. One new pastor found he was expected to preach every week for at least the first year in order to give the worship stability and continuity after a period of upheaval in the church.

In the Liberal tradition, these roles exist too. However, unlike the Evangelical tradition, responsibilities are limited to the maintenance of form as opposed to doctrine (see p. 138 above). Elders and Clerks help maintain the silent worship necessary to the spiritual experience at the heart of Liberal Quaker epistemology and authority. Whilst this limits structural authority to matters of form, on which Liberal Quakerism is conservative, it also allows less overt influence from some Friends on other matters. 'Weighty Friends', described as such as their words carry weight, operate an unofficial leadership role, under the cover of corporate discernment and the idea of the priesthood of all believers.

The basic and original understanding of direct revelation (see pp. 20–1 above) underpins this flat ecclesiology. All participate in this intimacy with God, all are part of the priesthood of all believers (not individual priests but all part of the single priesthood of the church in relation to God), and no differentiated system of human authority is thus necessary or appropriate.

COVENANT AND PRACTICE

WORSHIP

Quaker worship, whether unprogrammed (based on silent waiting and prophetic speaking out of the silence) or programmed (with a simple order of service and usually including a period of silent waiting), is a group experience of communion with Christ who is present in the midst of His gathered people. http://www.fum.org/about/friends.htm#Beliefs, 7 March 2006

One of the most visible differences between different kinds of Quakers is in their worship. At its most basic, Liberal Quaker worship may consist of a circle of chairs with a few Friends gathered entirely in silence for an hour. At the other end of the spectrum, a pastoral team and a director of music with a robed choir and piano or multi-piece band, electronically amplified, may lead the worship from a stage, other participants in pews. There may be much movement between elements of the 'service' and a sermon or message will precede or follow on from the open worship. There could be explicit shows of emotion, the laying on of hands for healing, a call to the altar rail or mourners' benches, and expressive participation in the choruses. In some Conservative Meetings, men and women may still sit on different sets of benches on opposite sides of the Meeting House from each other.

However, most Quaker worship still rests on the 1647 revelation of George Fox that there is 'one, even Christ Jesus' that can speak to your condition' (Nickalls 1952, p. 11; and see p. 20 above). The Kenyan Quaker Zablon Malenge puts it thus:

God equips each person so that he or she can hear the Eternal Voice. God can be likened to radio waves that are ever present and are perceptible when human instruments are properly tuned to pick them up. Each of us is a spiritual receiving set. We find God in the silence of our souls. We commune directly with God. Making too much noise in our meetings can distract people from hearing God's voice. People can hear God best in silence (1 Cor 14:1–6). (Malenge 2003, p. 46)

In other words, the personal encounter with Christ underpins both programmed and unprogrammed Quaker worship (see Box 27). As Bill Waggoner suggests:

Programmed worship, when rightly experienced and expressed, is the culmination of the careful, prayerful preparation of our total beings in the worship and praise of God. This conscious planning takes place under the guidance of the Holy Spirit and may include the use of speaking, readings, singing, dancing, musical instruments, silence, and even symbols, such as candles . . . to illustrate the Light. (*Faith in Action*, 1992, p. 3)

Thus the planning is itself Spirit-led. Equally, the plan may not be followed if the pastor feels led in an alternative direction (p. 3). Additionally, in many Evangelical Quaker Meetings, there is still a period of 'open worship' or 'communion after the manner of Friends' towards which all the other programming points. Some pastors see the music, readings, and message as aids to help 'centre' the worshipping community and some Meetings are semi-programmed with equal periods of programmed and unprogrammed worship.

Theologically, programmed worship is clearly Quaker to the extent that the programming is either (i) a means to, (ii) a preparation for, or (iii) a nurturing of direct revelation. For those Friends churches which claim that 'communion after the manner of Friends' or 'Open Worship' is at the heart of worship, this is explicit. As in the unprogrammed tradition, absence ideally leads to a sense of presence. One Friends church bulletin reads on its

---

Box 27 Quaker worship

The following is a classic description of Quaker worship and, reference to 'no vocal service' aside, represents Quaker worship in all its traditions.

We believe that true baptism is the experience of being filled with Divine love which cleanses from all unrighteousness. John said, 'I indeed have baptized you with water: but He shall baptize you with the Holy Ghost' (Mark 1:8). It is the change and purification within, the spiritual fact rather than the outward symbol, which is indeed the true baptism.

Friends place special emphasis on the ever present Holy Spirit in the hearts of men. This power we call the Light Within or the Light of Christ. We believe that a seed of this spirit is in every man. The basis of faith is thus the belief that God endows each human being with a measure of His own Divine Spirit. He leaves no one without witness, but gives the light of His truth and presence to men of all races and walks of life. Love, the out-working of this Divine Spirit, is the most potent influence that can be applied to the affairs of men. The Society of Friends believes this application of love to the whole of life to be the core of the Christian doctrine. As within ourselves we become conscious of the Inner Light or the Christ within and submit ourselves to His leadings, we are enabled to live in conformity to the will of our Heavenly Father.

Growing directly out of this belief in the Inward Light of Christ is our ideal of worship. In our assemblies the Holy Spirit speaks directly to the human soul, and worship is a personal communion with God and a yielding of our wills to the Divine will, for which no form or aid of clergy is necessary. This communion may be realized in a true and vital way though there be no vocal service. A living silence may be so filled with the Divine Presence that all who worship become conscious of it and are drawn together in unity under the power of His love. We concur with George Fox where he states, 'The least member in the church hath an office, and is serviceable; and every member hath need one of another.' (*The Book of Discipline of Ohio Yearly Meeting*, 1992, p. 4)

---

front: 'Worship is a time for *listening to God*. The singing, prayers and message-bearing arise from the practice of listening. These expressions of worship are to keep us centred on Jesus Christ, the Inward Teacher.' There are also leaflets helping those unfamiliar with silent worship understand this form of liturgy. One of the shorter ones reads:

The worship service at First Friends is like many other churches. But at its heart lies a period of silent prayer and devotion which makes it distinctively Quaker.

The silence is both an expression of our faith and a way of helping us to come into the presence of God. Thus, we believe that in the silence we can experience God.

A process begins whereby we seek to escape from the thoughts and cares of everyday life, and listen instead for what God may be saying to us, both individually and as a group. Sometimes we may receive a word to speak for others, sometimes God's word is for us alone. We must always be attentive to the difference.

First, we 'center'. This is a process by which we try to detach ourselves from the sounds of the world around us and the lively thoughts in our minds in order to feel the presence of God within. This is not so much a matter of being silent, as of being still.

Second, there may be spoken or sung ministry arising out of the silence. As the meeting gathers through centering, it is possible that messages will be given. These can come from anybody in the worshipping group. The ministry is most useful when there is plenty of time between spoken contributions for all to absorb and reflect on what has been said.

This open worship aspect of the entire worship experience is important to Quakerism. It underscores the Quaker conviction that every person can experience the Holy directly and any person may be given a message to share. Typically, the open worship deepens the entire worship experience. (First Friends, Richmond, Indiana, Ministry and Oversight Commission, n.d.)

Even where there is no silence, or where the silence is filled by testimony and prayer after the Wesleyan tradition, rather than communion after the Quaker one, the basic understanding of the Quaker liturgical form in all its varieties is the direct unmediated encounter available continually.

We believe that Christ lives in us and we live in Him. Living in this union with Christ we find our true identity in Him. We are crucified, buried, made alive, raised up and seated with Christ at the right hand of the Father. As a result our actual identity is no longer in outward appearances such as performance, looks, intelligence, ability or wealth but rather that each of us is a child of God, a new creation in Christ Jesus. We believe that we can experience Christ directly and intimately without the intervention of human priests or required rituals. Our experience is that we commune with Christ daily as Lord, Savior, Teacher and Friend. (Mylander 2004, p. 9)

Sometimes difference is most apparent to visitors from other traditions. This is an account of Bolivian worship from a North American Liberal Quaker visitor.

All the yearly meetings have programmed worship, with churches and pastors (mostly men, but there are a few women pastors in INELA). Sunday services often run for three hours, with much singing and with separate Bible classes for men and women; in one case there were frequent 'Amen's'. Prayers are generally very

Plate 20   Oscar Lugasa and Jesse Ayuya during a lively programmed worship session, World
Gathering of Young Friends Africa at Kanamai, Mombasa 20–24 October 2005

emotional, often ending with sobbing on the part of the one praying, which was
sometimes solely a pastor and on one occasion the whole congregation praying
individually. (Garver 2001, p. 10)

The point about a predominantly male leadership is particularly true
of programmed Quakerism outside of the USA and to some extent within
the USA as well. In the Liberal tradition, women can outnumber men by
more than three to two, as in Britain (*Proceedings of the Yearly Meeting
2004*), but men still hold a majority of the prestigious roles such as that of
Elder.

In Bolivia and Kenya, worship can take all day (Plate 20). In the USA
programmed worship generally runs to a strict timetable which can sometimes squeeze the time given to open worship towards the end of the
service. Fellowship follows worship and 'Adult First Day School' can
follow that, then fellowship lunch.

Most Friends churches are relatively unadorned to reflect the inward
nature of the encounter. Sometimes an empty cross, as opposed to a
crucifix, is used to denote the risen and living Christ available to all.
Where modern church architecture has provided a 'steeple', it may be
called a 'bell tower' to maintain the connection with early Friends'

criticisms of 'steeplehouses' (see p. 26 above). However where the Friends church has only a nominal connection with the Quaker legacy, this would not be a concern.

(see p. 26 above)

SACRAMENTS

We affirm that every believer receives the Holy Spirit at the point of their conversion, and not as the result of any rite, such as water baptism or the laying on of hands. We believe that the only essential biblical sign that one has been baptized with the Spirit is a transformed life. As the Spirit of Christ dwells within us, He is fully present to lead us and directly teach His will to us. (*Faith and Practice of Evangelical Friends Church Southwest*, 2001, p. 14)

Quakers everywhere continue to uphold the belief in inward baptism and communion.

We affirm that there is only one baptism, in the Holy Spirit, for all believers, and that all believers share a continuing communion or collective experience of Christ's presence. At the same time, we observe that water baptism and the Lord's supper with the elements of bread and wine can sometimes be helpful to believers to experience the already established presence of Christ.

Our perspective comes solely from our desire to conform our practices and beliefs to the Scriptures. We recognize that many Christians view their particular practice as the simple continuation of New Testament observances. We humbly assert that another look at the Bible would suggest otherwise. In the first three gospels Jesus clearly intended for His Jewish disciples to celebrate the Passover from that point onward in memory of His death rather than Israel's Exodus from Egypt. But it is not at all clear that Jesus intended to create a new ritual for all believers. Instead, he appears to be 'christianizing' an already existing practice – which is exactly what we assert that Paul is doing with his regulations for the 'love feast' in Corinth.

We recognize as well that water baptisms occur in the Bible, but we also note that no particular mode is specified. More importantly, water baptism is never established as a required ritual in the New Testament. This leads us to believe that the broader biblical statements about baptism refer to our common baptism in and by the Holy Spirit, and not to the practice of water baptism.

Our study of the Bible leads us to conclude that the practice of the rituals of water baptism and communion with the elements were never meant to be regarded as necessary for the salvation or sanctification of the believer. Again, while we recognize that some may find these practices helpful, we do not believe that the Bible ever considers them necessary acts of obedience or essential aspects of Christian discipleship (Eph 4:5; John 15:4ff; Matt 28:20; John 14:16; Luke 22:7ff; 1 Cor 11:17ff). (*Faith and Practice of Evangelical Friends Church Southwest*, 2001, pp. 14–15)

Whilst permitting speaking in tongues, the above passage from FCSW continues the traditional Quaker line on inward baptism and communion. Friends Church Southwest does permit outward baptism under certain conditions but its 1994 *Elements Statement* makes it clear that it is not encouraging such innovation: 'We believe the best policy will be one that strongly upholds the truth that these ceremonies form no essential part of Christian worship and that the reality to which they point is immeasurably more satisfying' (*Faith and Practice of Evangelical Friends Church Southwest*, 2001, p. 49). This is a situation shared with Kenyan Friends.

The understanding that inward baptism and communion is more legitimate and sufficient is shared by most Friends (see p. 34 above). However, in places, the understanding of inward communion may be more implicit, or left behind, as Quaker churches become community churches. In these cases, sectarian distinctives appear anachronistic as the church attempts to reach a wider congregation. It is in community churches that the Quaker distinctive combination of the emphasis on direct revelation, the priesthood of all believers, the Quaker testimonies including the one to peace, and the inward sacraments may be most easily lost. This has happened in East Africa and South America. Certainly some pastors have been happy to baptise, and some churches, notably in Friends Church Eastern Region, perform outward communion. This may be monthly or once a year. Most typical would be once or twice a year. This links of course to the legacy of David Updegraff in Ohio at the end of the nineteenth century and the efforts of the Waterites or water party to secure permission for water baptism within the Yearly Meeting (see p. 114 above). Whereas the Richmond Declaration of Faith outlawed outward baptism, EFI does not maintain that discipline (and Ohio, now FCER, never accepted the Richmond Declaration in the first place).

John Punshon argues that when Friends begin to move from inward communion to outward communion they are losing an important part of the Quaker tradition (2001, pp. 222–4). Even whilst Robert Barclay altered the basis of inward communion from Fox's understanding of the inward supper as the marriage supper of the Lamb, after Revelation 3:20, to a particular and contested reading of 1 Corinthians 11:26, the move to outward communion is a significant break with the Quaker tradition. At the same time both Barclay and Gurney called Friends to tolerate those who partook in the outward supper, as above all God loves 'a sincere heart' (Gurney 1979, p. 168).

UNPROGRAMMED WORSHIP AND VOCAL MINISTRY

Whereas programmed worship is facilitated by the pastor or pastoral team, unprogrammed worship has no explicit or outward leadership and rules, and guidelines are taught through the book of discipline and leaflets for newcomers (see Box 27). The following extract from Ohio Conservative merges theology and practical guidance.

We meet together in silence and strive to free our minds and hearts for the purpose of spiritual worship. We must then wait in humble reverence for the spiritual ability to worship the Lord of Heaven and Earth in a manner acceptable to Him.

As each soul feels a spirit of supplication answered by the quickening influence of the Holy Spirit, we approach the Throne of Grace; that is to say, we are enabled to enter into an attitude of true worship, in gratitude and praise.

Though the nearness to God may result in spoken ministry or vocal prayer, the distinctive excellence of heavenly favor consists in the direct communication with the Heavenly Father by the inward revelation of the Spirit of Christ.

It is urged that Friends encourage their children and others under their care in the habit of regular and orderly attendance at both First-day and other meetings. Such should be taught, in proportion to their understanding, how to wait in stillness upon the Lord, that they, too, may receive their portion of His spiritual favor through the tendering influence of His Holy Spirit.

Drowsiness and habitual tardiness are not necessarily evidence of a negligent attitude toward the living purpose of our meetings for worship, but because they might appear so, both should be avoided as far as possible, lest they become hindrances to others present.

In preparation for meeting, the individual may find that he becomes quiet in expectation, or he may desire to read Scripture or other devotional material as a quieting discipline. Sometimes First-day school, a discussion group, a family meeting or reading is found helpful in this preparation process.

We appoint an hour to meet for worship. The meeting begins in silence, according to the injunction, 'Be still and know that I am God' (Psalms 46:10). Friends thus allow themselves to become quiet by putting aside words, thoughts of business, cares, and topics of the day.

Not all Friends can become truly quiet instantly or at every meeting. It cannot be done at will; indeed, 'will' too often proves an obstacle. After a time, however, a number of worshippers do seem to be sharing the Presence of a guiding Spirit. Vocal ministry or prayer may or may not occur, springing from the heart of one or more worshippers. Any who feel called by an inward urging of the Holy Spirit to speak are advised to do so, simply and clearly.

As the meeting continues, there comes a time when a Friend, chosen beforehand, feels the appropriate time has come to close the meeting, and shakes hands with his nearest neighbor. (*The Book of Discipline of Ohio Yearly Meeting*, 1992, pp. 5–6)

Deciding to Speak in Open Worship

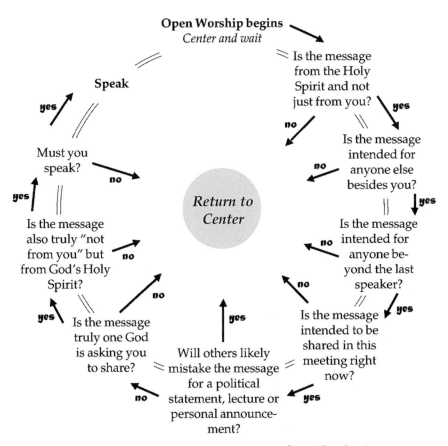

Fig. 4.3 Discerning vocal ministry (courtesy of Stan Thornburg)

Philadelphia Yearly Meeting's (Liberal) discipline contains a similar passage.

There is a renewal of spirit when we turn away from worldly matters to rediscover inward serenity. Friends know from experience the validity of Jesus' promise that 'Where two or three are gathered together in my name, there am I in the midst of them' (Matthew 18:20). Often we realize our hopes for a heightened sense of the presence of God through the cumulative power of group worship, communicated in silent as well as vocal ministry. When we experience such a profound and evident sense of oneness with God and with one another, we speak of a 'gathered' or 'covered' meeting for worship.

Direct communion with God constitutes the essential life of the meeting for worship. Into its living stillness may come leadings and fresh insights that are purely personal, not meant to be shared. At other times they are meant for the Meeting at large to hear. (*Faith and Practice: A Book of Christian Discipline, Philadelphia Yearly Meeting of the Religious Society of Friends*, 2002, p. 19)

Unprogrammed worship is a feature of most North American programmed worship and one Evangelical meeting provides a vocal ministry flowchart for individuals to check whether their message is from God and whether it is to be shared at that point with the whole meeting (Fig. 4.3).

LITURGICAL FORM

Theologically, the differences between Evangelical and Liberal liturgy may be slight. There are other differences between the traditions (see p. 242 below), but programming requires a visual focus from the worshippers in a way which is far more optional in the unprogrammed traditions. For example, Liberal or Conservative Quakers can worship with their eyes shut. Where you have a pastor welcoming you, leading prayers, a choir or handbell group, or a five-piece electric band at the front, or lyrics on an overhead projection, the focus needs to be visual as well. In this sense, parts of the Evangelical liturgical form are more outward than inward, even if the heart-focus or spiritual-focus is inward in the same way. Only when the Meeting enters its open worship or 'inward communion' does that more cataphatic approach diminish. Even then, a busy prayer session, or one full of testimony, may still encourage outward attention. Where Friends churches have been influenced by Wesleyan Holiness, the open worship can become full of vocal prayer and testimony: for it not to would be a sign of spiritual apathy. Elsewhere, the call to inward communion is explicit and based in silence.

Some Friends churches need two periods of open worship, one for testimony, one for communion, and have each clearly delineated. In one Friends church, the twenty minutes of open (unprogrammed) worship are followed by twenty minutes of prayers and prayer requests. When some unprogrammed Meetings are experimenting with untimed or three-hour meetings in order to deepen the experience based in silence (Martin, M., 2003), most Evangelical Friends churches have a maximum of twenty minutes' silent worship. The 'semi-programmed' may have an hour of programming and an hour of unprogrammed worship and the Meeting in Minneapolis divides the two with fellowship time to allow people to choose one or both parts of the worship.

Some Friends churches are 'liturgical' in the sense that they follow the Christian calendar and that the Friends like to hold particular kinds of gatherings at say Christmas and Easter. There may be an advent candle wreath in December, Lenten meetings or disciplines, palm branches brought in by the children on Palm Sunday. Where there are high numbers of children, the desire to educate them and nurture their spirituality can increase the sense of need for the visual and the outward and make the links with the gospel story transparent. One Friends church, for example, has a special Christmas choir for the children as part of its 'Holiday Calendar' activities, another hosts each year an all-age 'Holiday Music and Dessert' close to the time that some of 'the world', and now most Quakers, call Christmas. One Quaker I spoke with managed to attend three Friends churches for worship one 24 December evening, culminating with a midnight service.

MEETING FOR WORSHIP FOR CHURCH AFFAIRS

Throughout the Quaker world, church decisions are taken without voting. The case of the vote concerning Updegraff and water baptism (see p. 116 above) was rare and the format of the Meeting for Worship for Business or for 'Church Affairs' is one of the commonalities between the world family of Friends (see p. 246 below). When divine guidance is found, unity follows, as this extract from Ohio Conservative outlines.

The following method of conducting business has been found equally effective in large or small groups. A business meeting begins, and should also end, in worship. As business is brought before them, Friends try to continue in a spirit of search for divine guidance. It naturally follows that there can be no rightful or satisfactory decision of a matter until there is a large measure of unity in it. Thus our business is decided by the corporate 'sense of the meeting', and not by a majority vote.

As business proceeds Friends speak to it, each according to his best insight. Often the insights of several Friends contribute to a decision more serviceable than any single suggestion. As Friends approach agreement, the Clerk composes a minute declaring what the meeting's will appears to be. When a minute is finally approved, it becomes part of the permanent record. If the meeting fails to reach agreement on an issue, or declines to deal with it, a brief minute is prepared either dismissing it or postponing the decision to a future time. (*The Book of Discipline of Ohio Yearly Meeting*, 1992, pp. 6–7)

Philadelphia Yearly Meeting's discipline parallels the Conservative discipline.

The goal of Friends' decision-making is a Spirit-led sense of the meeting – a crystallization of the search for clarity on the topic under consideration. Even in the face of strong difference of opinion, that goal is achievable when there is spiritual unity.

Our search is for unity, not unanimity. We consider ourselves to be in unity when our search for Truth is shared; when our listening for God is faithful; when our wills are caught up in the presence of Christ; and when our love for one another is constant. A united meeting is not necessarily all of one mind, but it is all of one heart.

We believe that this unity, transcending apparent differences, springs from God's empowering love, and that a Meeting, trusting in the leadership of that love and gathered in its spirit, will enjoy unity in its search for truth. (*Faith and Practice: A Book of Christian Discipline, Philadelphia Yearly Meeting of the Religious Society of Friends*, 2002, p. 22)

One Friend stood up in a British Meeting once and said of a risky financial proposition, 'If we were the Society of Friends, I would oppose this idea, but we are the Religious Society of Friends and I feel strongly moved to support it.' This approach to an extra-rational epistemology characterises the advice to lay aside one's own views and preferences in submission to the process/divine will.

Quaker business meetings have been and continue, across most of the Quaker world, to be rooted within this theological understanding. Matters 'before the Meeting' have their outcomes 'discerned' by the collective using open worship as the medium to 'seek the will of God'. No votes are taken and the 'sense of the Meeting' is recorded by minute, usually agreed by the Meeting in session. The particular mechanics of this process vary widely between Yearly Meetings. In Britain the Clerk (pronounced clark) both manages the process and writes the minute, sometimes aided by an Assistant Clerk, each minute being agreed before the next item is taken. The matter is introduced to the Meeting, and contributions come from 'the body of the meeting' until the Clerk feels able to draft a minute to reflect the sense of the Meeting. In a large or 'busy' meeting, the Clerk will discern who to 'call' to offer the next contribution whilst those contributing discern whether they are really called to do so. The draft minute is read out and put 'before the Meeting', initiating a process which parallels the discussion of the matter and which may take as long if the Clerk has used inaccurate or ambiguous wording.

In other Yearly Meetings, the Clerk (pronounced clurk in the USA) may manage the process whilst the Recording Clerk drafts the minutes. Minutes are not always agreed at the time of the discernment process but are brought back to later sessions. In one Yearly Meeting I visited, those wishing to contribute moved out of their seats and formed a queue in another set of seats until their turn came. The Clerk simply indicated 'next'.

The system is of course open to abuse or unintentional control. The ordering of the agenda, the presentation of items, etc., by the Clerks, can all exert subtle influences. However, those who manage these meetings have no routinised authority beyond their temporary terms of service as part of the priesthood of all believers (see p. 21 above).

OTHER MEETINGS FOR WORSHIP

In terms of marriages and funerals, British Friends are unique in that their original form of marriage is legal in and of itself, following the Hardwicke Act of 1753 (see p. 54 above), and is thus prescribed in its form and wording. Within worship, those marrying take each other by the hand and exchange promises before the Meeting: for example, 'Before God and this Meeting, I take thee, — to be my wife (husband), promising, with God's help, to be unto thee a loving and faithful husband (wife) so long as we both shall live' (*Quaker Faith and Practice*, 1995, 16.39). These phrases are commonly used throughout the Quaker world. However, legal procedure varies between states in the United States, and where Quaker marriage is an adjunct to a legal ceremony elsewhere, its form is left free for Yearly Meetings or individuals to adapt. Weddings may become similar to those found in other churches or self-designed ritual with the couple choosing their own affirmations. Quaker funerals tend to act as celebrations for the life of the deceased as well as a time of farewell and committal. The British Quaker phrase is to 'give thanks for the grace of God as shown in the life of —' and written testimonies perform the same function. In Victorian times, such obituaries published in the *Annual Monitor* would act as 'advice literature', modelling the Christian life for the next generation. Testimonies today implicitly fulfil the same function.

CHAPTER SUMMARY

This chapter has presented examples from the main traditions of Friends on authority, the basic doctrinal issues, and covenant and practice. We find the greatest variation between traditions in theological terms, particularly in relation to perceptions of God and Christ, sin and salvation, and the authority and place of Scripture. The next chapter considers Quaker attitudes and values and contrasting approaches to mission and membership.

CHAPTER 5

Quakers and 'the world'

TESTIMONY

Testimony, as noted above (p. 68), can be defined, historically, as the consequences of the spiritual life as expressed in daily life. For early Friends, this included plain speech and plain dress, the refusal to swear oaths or pay tithes, the interruption of church services, the refusal to mark times and seasons, the enacting of signs, etc. The whole of life was testimony to the inward spiritual experience. In the Quietist period, these consequences became rules, encoded in 'the discipline' of the movement (see p. 66 above). A standard of behaviour was adopted and expected of all bearing the name (and reputation) of the Quaker movement. Gurneyite Quakerism was more world-affirming, and in modernist Evangelical and Liberal Yearly Meetings rules have been replaced by values. At the same time, testimony has often been repackaged. For example, rules about 'plainness' were replaced by the values of 'simplicity'. The 'testimony against war' became 'the peace testimony'. Today, testimony is often presented in terms of five 'testimonies', i.e. to peace, simplicity, equality, integrity, and community or stewardship. Values are interpreted individually (see pp. 139–40 above) within forms of Quakerism which no longer believe the world a spiritually dangerous place. In this section, passages are quoted at length between traditions rather than by subject to avoid this compartmentalisation of testimony. For Evangelical Fundamentalist or Holiness Friends, the world is corrupting and/or depraved and testimony is about following scriptural teaching. This section looks first at a Holiness approach to moral conduct amongst college students, then at Evangelical Friends International (EFI) and Friends United Meeting (FUM) approaches, before turning to Conservative and Liberal ones. What varies is the underpinning of testimony, the content of testimony (particularly on sexuality), and the degree to which it implies continuing separation from 'the world'.

Central Yearly Meeting has little or no contact with the rest of the Quaker world. It broke away from Five Years Meeting in 1926 and represents a Holiness Yearly Meeting. Its Bible College website is very clear about the standards of behaviour expected from its students on and off the campus in and out of term and is quoted at length.

Union Bible College desires that each of its students have a vital, personal relationship with God through faith in Jesus Christ. Since the primary goal of Union Bible College is the preparation of Christian young people for effective service for Christ, it is our purpose to encourage each student to seek the experience of heart holiness. 'Holy' expresses the idea of that which is free from all moral defilement or uncleanness. Therefore, holiness of heart and life means freedom from sin or a cleansing from inherited depravity. We desire that our students bring their lives into more than a pattern of outward conformity to certain principles. We desire that they demonstrate by their conduct an inward purity and a spirit of subjection to Christ's total leadership (Romans 12:1–2).

... The students, staff and faculty are to refrain from using things which are harmful to the mind and body, including alcoholic beverages, illegal drugs, and tobacco (I Corinthians 6:19–20); and from any practice that corrupts morals, including gambling, profane language, and indecent or immoral action, conversation, or writing (Colossians 2:1–10). There is to be no participation in such things as cheating, slang or worldly expressions, and degrading forms of art, music, drama, and literature. The school forbids the playing of cards, mixed swimming, dancing, and the patronage of professional sports events, motion picture theaters, and the viewing of television. Because of the potential spiritual danger to the soul, no television is allowed on campus (Psalm 101:3). We strongly urge discretion in the use of radios and tape and CD players.

... We expect our young people to be friendly and courteous to each other, but petting and other careless relationships between young people are absolutely forbidden. No dating privileges will be given to new students for at least four weeks after enrollment. Our students are to be good stewards of their time and not loiter or be involved in idle conversation (Ezekiel 16:49).

Students are to dress modestly as is becoming to Scriptural Holiness. Both men and women should refrain from wearing gaudy, transparent, tight-fitting, or any other immodest clothing. Jewellery, including bracelets, beads, necklaces, and rings is not permitted (I Peter 3:3–5, I Timothy 2:9–10). Women are not allowed to cut their hair at any time while enrolled at UBC. This includes summer vacation. They are to put their hair up neatly and simply. Women who begin the school year with short hair must let it grow. Absolutely no makeup, cover-up, nail polish, or nail buffer to polish the nails is to be used (I Corinthians 11:2–16). Men are to have their hair cut so as to be off the collar and ears. Conservative hairstyles are to be followed. Men's faces are to be cleanly shaven. Women's skirts/dresses must be well below their knees when they are standing or sitting. Skirts and dresses can be neither tight nor have an open slit. Necklines are to be modest. Clothing is too tight if it does not allow you to take normal steps or walk in a regular fashion. All dresses or skirts should fall below the knee when sitting and standing. Sleeves are to be worn below the elbow (three-quarter-length minimum). Men are not to wear trousers that are too tight or too short. They are required to wear coat and tie to classes, chapel, and school functions when announced. All students are expected to be neat at all times and clean in dress and habits. Students should not follow worldly styles and fads which are not becoming to Christian principles. No student is permitted to wear short sleeves. The school reserves the right to judge if one's appearance is appropriate. (http://www.ubca.org/studentlife.html, 12 August 2005)

The Holiness world-rejecting stance (see p. 80 above) is explicit and unusual, in terms of its numerous proscriptions, in the Quaker world. However, the following extract from EFI clearly delineates the reality of the spiritual enemies of this life.

We believe that in living union with Christ every Christian has the authority to overcome the three major spiritual enemies of this life – the world, the flesh and the devil. The world is the system that is organized to leave God out and to applaud those who violate Christian values. The flesh is the inner weakness within each of us that finds temptation attractive and desires what is evil instead of what is good. The devil is Satan, along with his forces of evil, fallen angels sometimes called demons, that deceive, accuse and harass Christians. Christ has already defeated Satan and all his evil powers at the cross and in the resurrection. Our Lord Jesus is now exalted to the highest place with absolute authority over all His enemies. In Christ we have all the resources we need to win the battle for our minds and overcome the evil one. These resources include God's Spirit, God's Word, God's Works, and God's people. (Mylander 2004, p. 10)

The Friends Church Southwest discipline outlines the basis of testimony in terms of the transformation of sanctification, or the latter part of the convincement process (see p. 23 above).

We believe that when a person receives Jesus Christ in faith, a genuine transformation takes place in both the person's status before God and in his or her very nature. We believe this happens because God makes the repentant believer righteous. Our righteousness before God is not the result of any meritorious actions on our part, but neither are we righteous merely because God considers us to be so. We believe God radically transforms us in salvation, actually making us righteous before Him and at the very core of our selves. We receive a new life, one that is now entirely capable of faith, obedience, and love. This new life transforms and restores our relationship with our Lord, enabling us to know and experience Jesus in our daily lives.

We believe this transformation is not completed when we receive Jesus. From the moment of our conversion until our glorification, God is continually at work in us, conforming us to the image of His Son. This grace-filled work of the Holy Spirit that makes us Christ-like in character and conduct is often called sanctification – it is God making us holy as He is holy. (*Faith and Practice of Evangelical Friends Church Southwest*, 2001, p. 17)

Thus, spiritual progress underpins a righteous life. Unlike the Central Yearly Meeting extract, the Friends Church Southwest discipline is affirming of a particular stance rather than proscriptive in tone. The following extract on truth and truth-telling offers an example.

Friends have a testimony about how we are to speak. Following Jesus' command Friends decline to use oaths of any kind, even in legal settings, preferring to use a simple affirmation (Matthew 5:33–37; James 5:12). In earlier times, Friends refused to use the second person plural, 'you', to address an individual of higher rank or social status, using the singular form, 'thee' or 'thou' to address all individuals.

Friends have had an earlier testimony about how we are to speak. Following Jesus' command, they refused to take oaths, and recognizing the essential equality of all people, they refused to use the formal form of address. They addressed all with the informal 'thee' and 'thou.'

At the heart of this testimony was a belief that language was given to us to communicate truth. Taking an oath implied that somehow one's other words were not always as true; an abasement of language and an implied dishonesty. Formal address required bowing to a social convention based on a passing human reality, and not on the eternal values of the Kingdom of God.

We believe the Lord is calling us to redeem our speech. Words were given to us to tell the truth. We should be very aware of the constant temptation to exchange clarity for what presents best and simplicity of speech for calculated expressions. When we disagree, we can and should express ourselves clearly and honestly, but we must be careful not to dishonor those with whom we disagree. Most of all, we must embrace the positive use of words. The Scriptures command us to bless, encourage, and honor each other. More than avoiding the misuse of words, the Lord is calling us to put speech to work for the gracious and beneficial purposes for which He created it. (*Faith and Practice of Evangelical Friends Church Southwest*, 2001, pp. 18–19)

Friends Church Southwest lists the following areas of witness arising out of the Christian life: Ministry, Peace, Justice, Simplicity, Integrity. On peace, Southwest states:

With regard to military service we encourage prayerful and conscientious study and obedience to our Lord's call to peacemaking. While each person must live out his or her understanding of Scripture, the time-tested Friends' counsel is to decline to serve, or where the state allows, to give alternative service. In keeping with the teachings and example of Jesus, we are each called to oppose war and violence, to alleviate suffering, work for reconciliation, and promote justice in the name of our Lord Jesus Christ and the power of His love (Matt. 26:51–54; Luke 6:27–36; Romans 12:14–21; 1 Cor. 6:7; 1 Tim. 2:1–8; 1 Peter 2:19–24; Is. 2:4). (*Faith and Practice of Evangelical Friends Church Southwest*, 2001, p. 16)

This list, mirrored in Conservative and Liberal disciplines (see below), has the additional elements, typical for Evangelical Friends, of respect for human life, and for the body, sexuality, and the home. This Yearly Meeting, typical of EFI, is opposed to abortion, euthanasia, and sex outside of heterosexual marriage. For example:

As a gift of God, a marriage covenant provides the framework for intimate companionship and is the only appropriate context for sexual fulfilment and procreation. (*Faith and Practice of Evangelical Friends Church Southwest*, 2001, p. 21)

Divorce is permitted but 'God hates divorce' (p. 21).

In cases of domestic violence or abuse separation may be necessary and appropriate for the safety and health of the individual or family. In times of physical or emotional separation, as well as divorce, God's desire is for transformation and reconciliation. (p. 21)

In common with Friends worldwide, Friends Church Southwest hold a concern about wealth and materialism. The discipline suggests a role as stewards rather than owners, that Friends need to be concerned about the way wealth is accumulated often at the expense of others:

in subtle ways the values of our economic system undermine or contradict biblical values. The Bible tells us we are valuable because we are made and loved by God. Our economy assigns value according to what we produce or the power and wealth we possess. (p. 22)

In terms of politics, the Friends Church Southwest discipline reminds Friends that they should seek to follow God's law above all, and that God's kingdom extends beyond national concerns:

our primary citizenship is in God's Kingdom. We are always to seek first the values and benefit of God's Kingdom over our country of residence or nationality, especially when the values and purposes of the Kingdom might clash with those of our nation. (p. 24)

In Kenyan Quakerism, Yearly Meetings have proscribed polygamy (see p. 156 above), (Malenge 2003, pp. 72–3). Malenge also writes against prostitution and abortion. Family planning is recommended (Malenge 2003, pp. 73–5).

The following extract from FUM literature emphasises the personal stance within the world, that of 'dying to the self' as the basis of individual and collective testimony.

Friends understand that Christ's baptism is best understood as the inward experience of 'dying' to one's own will. This is the necessary precondition to being able to listen to and obey the living teachings of Jesus Christ. It is by daily dying to self-will that the believer is enabled to live a new life of righteousness.

Paul wrote about this in his letter to the Romans:

Do you not know that all of us who have been baptized into Christ Jesus were baptized into his death? Therefore we have been buried with him by baptism into death, so that, just as Christ was raised from the dead by the glory of the Father, so we too might walk in newness of life . . .

But if we have died with Christ, we believe that we will also live with him. We know that Christ, being raised from the dead, will never die again; death no longer has dominion over him . . .

But thanks be to God that you, having once been slaves of sin, have become obedient from the heart to the form of teaching to which you were entrusted, and that you, having been set free from sin, have become slaves of righteousness. (Rom 6:3–4, 8, 17–18, NRS)

Friends understand that inward yielding to the will of God is the way of the cross, which is the power of God.

It is an essential part of the witness of Friends that Christ frees people *from the power of sin* in their lives and does not merely save people in their sins. Friends joyfully proclaim that it is possible to know the will of God, and to do it. (Richmond 2004, n.p.)

Interestingly, in contrast with the EFI Yearly Meeting discipline extracts, the content is less specific.

Over the years, Friends have born a corporate witness to the power of Christ to bring us – in George Fox's terms – into the state that Adam and Eve were in before the fall. It is this power of Christ that each of the Friends 'testimonies' testify to. From a culture dominated by materialism and greed, Friends testify that Christ leads us into a life of simplicity. From a culture of social inequality, Friends testify that Christ leads us to practice the equality of all. From a culture of sexual promiscuity and exploitation, Friends testify that Christ leads us to chastity and fidelity in marriage. From a culture which seeks security and meaning through violence and war, Friends testify that Christ leads us to forgiveness, nonviolence and peacemaking. From a culture where exaggeration and falsehood dominate discourse, Friends testify that Christ leads us to speak truth plainly. From a culture where individualism is exalted, Friends testify that Christ leads us into communities of love and accountability. (Richmond 2004, n.p.)

Ohio Yearly Meeting (Conservative) holds similar views to Evangelical Friends but the language connects with the Quaker tradition rather than scripture. The commonalities are clear however.

4th Query. Believing our bodies to be the temple of God, are we concerned to attain a high level of physical and mental health? To this end are our lives examples of temperance in all things? Do we avoid and discourage the use and handling of intoxicants, tobacco, and improper use of drugs?

5th Query. Are we sensitive to the needs of those around us who may be in less fortunate circumstances? Do we prayerfully consider how we can share one another's burdens when the need arises? Do we counsel lovingly and prayerfully with those members whose actions in any phase of life give us grounds for concern?

6th Query. Do we live in the life and power which takes away the occasion of all wars? Do we, on Christian principles, refuse to participate in or to cooperate with the military effort? Do we work actively for peace and the removal of the causes of war? Do we endeavor to cultivate good will, mutual understanding, and equal opportunities for all people?

7th Query. Do we observe simplicity in our manner of living, sincerity in speech, and modesty in apparel? Do we guard against involving ourselves in temporal affairs to the hindrance of spiritual growth? Are we just in our dealings and careful to fulfill our promises? Do we seek to make our Christian faith a part of our daily work? (*The Book of Discipline of Ohio Yearly Meeting*, 1992, p. 22)

Similar to the list of contents of the 1802 British discipline (see p. 68 above), the Ohio Yearly Meeting (Conservative) Advices combines items pertaining to everyday life and the sustenance of the soul with the sustenance of corporate identity. Ohio Yearly Meeting (Conservative) records the following on marriage:

Friends regard marriage as a continuing religious sacrament, not merely a civil contract. We believe that marriage is an ordinance of God, appointed for the help and blessing of both partners and for the right upbringing of the next generation. Divorce and broken homes are a blight to our country, and great care needs to be exercised that the union be on the right foundation. Even when the marriage relationship fails to achieve its highest possibilities and unhappiness develops, we believe that by patient and prayerful determination these obstacles may be overcome. (*The Book of Discipline of Ohio Yearly Meeting*, 1992, p. 38)

Ohio also record their long-held testimony against war and violence, for racial equality, and simplicity. In the tradition where plain dress may still be worn, they say the following on dress:

Pertaining to dress, our principle is to let decency, simplicity, and utility be our guide. When one is truly trying to seek first the Kingdom of God he will not be a slave to fashion. Since we believe our bodies are the temples of the living God, we should dress simply and modestly. As in dress, so in all our phases of living, we should each one of us strive to follow the dictates of the Light of Christ within. (pp. 49–50)

And Ohio Yearly Meeting (Conservative) urge:

total abstinence from the use or handling of any intoxicants, not only on the ground that our bodies are the temples of the Holy Spirit, but also on the principle set forth by the Apostle, 'If meat make my brother to offend, I will eat no flesh while the world standeth, lest I make my brother to offend.' (1 Cor 8:13) (p. 50)

North Carolina Yearly Meeting (Conservative), Gurneyite in its foundation (p. 167 above) but the most Liberal of the Conservative Yearly Meetings, given that modernist connection and its current membership, is less prescriptive in its general advices. Its discipline includes the following on simplicity.

The heart of Quaker ethics is summed up in the word 'Simplicity.' Simplicity is forgetfulness of self and remembrance of our humble status as waiting servants of God. Outwardly, simplicity is shunning superfluities of dress, speech, behavior, and possessions, which tend to obscure our vision of reality. Inwardly, simplicity is spiritual detachment from the things of this world as part of the effort to fulfill the first commandment: to love God with all of the heart and mind and strength.

The testimony of outward simplicity began as a protest against the extravagance and snobbery which marked English society in the 1600's. In whatever forms this protest is maintained today, it must still be seen as a testimony against involvement with things which tend to dilute our energies and scatter our thoughts, reducing us to lives of triviality and mediocrity.

Simplicity does not mean drabness or narrowness but is essentially positive, being the capacity for selectivity in one who holds attention on the goal. Thus simplicity is an appreciation of all that is helpful toward living as children of the Living God. (*Faith and Practice: Book of Discipline of the North Carolina Yearly Meeting (Conservative) of the Religious Society of Friends*, 1983, p. 7)

Liberal Friends emphasise the loss of self far less. Rather they place agency at the heart of right living. Philadelphia also emphasises home life, peace, equality, simplicity, stewardship, and right sharing. Whilst their section on stewardship mirrors Friends Church Southwest's idea that our wealth is on loan from God, Philadelphia's section on right sharing emphasises the environmental rather than covenantal concerns.

We recognize that the well-being of the earth is a fundamental spiritual concern. From the beginning, it was through the wonders of nature that people saw God. How we treat the earth and its creatures is a basic part of our relationship with God. Our planet as a whole, not just the small parts of it in our immediate custody, requires our responsible attention. As Friends become aware of the interconnectedness of all life on this planet and the devastation caused by neglect of any part of it, we have become more willing to extend our sense of community to encompass all living things. We must now consider whether we should lay aside the belief that we humans are acting as stewards of the natural world, and instead view human actions as the major threat to the ecosystem. Friends are indeed called to walk gently on the earth. Wasteful and extravagant consumption is a major cause of destruction of the environment. The right sharing of the world's remaining resources requires that developed nations reduce their present levels of consumption so that people in underdeveloped nations can have more, and the earth's life-sustaining systems can be restored. The world cannot tolerate indefinitely the present rate of consumption by technologically developed nations.

Friends are called to become models and patterns of simple living and concern for the earth. Some may find it difficult to change their accustomed lifestyle; others recognize the need and have begun to adopt ways of life which put the least strain on the world's resources of clean air, water, soil, and energy.

A serious threat to the planet is the population explosion and consequent famine, war and devastation. Called on to make decisions to simplify our lives, we may find that the most difficult to accept will be limiting the number of children we have.

Voluntary simplicity in living and restraint in procreation hold the promise of ecological redemption and spiritual renewal. (*Faith and Practice: A Book of Christian Discipline, Philadelphia Yearly Meeting of the Religious Society of Friends*, 2002, p. 81)

Philadelphia, typical of Friends General Conference (FGC) and Liberal Yearly Meetings more widely, takes an alternative view to Friends Church Southwest on sexuality, emphasising integrity and the nature of relationship over a 'preset moral code'. It does not list a view on medically assisted suicide but does mention AIDS (2002, p. 72). Mention is made of the moral choice involved in having children. On abortion, Philadelphia Friends recognise divided attitudes rather than prescribe a single view. This is also typical of Liberal Quakerism. In Britain the adoption of the 1994 book of discipline took place over two weekends. At the first, an appeal went out for more passages on abortion and the final text contains six. Rather than a single view, this liberal-Liberal Yearly Meeting chooses to share a variety of experience to help those dealing with the issues. On sexuality, Philadelphia Yearly Meeting suggests:

In our personal lives, Friends seek to acknowledge and nurture sexuality as a gift from God for celebrating human love with joy and intimacy. In defining healthy sexuality, Friends are led in part by our testimonies: that sexual relations be equal, not exploitative; that sexual behavior be marked by integrity; and that sex be an act of love, not of aggression. Sexuality is at once an integral and an intricate part of personality. Our understanding of our own sexuality is an essential aspect of our journey toward wholeness. Learning to incorporate sexuality in our lives responsibly, joyfully, and with integrity should be a lifelong process beginning in childhood.

Friends are wary of a preset moral code to govern sexual activity. The unity of the sacred and the secular implies that the sacramental quality of a sexual relationship depends upon the Spirit as well as the intentions of the persons concerned.

Our faith can help us to examine relationships honestly, with the strength to reconcile the often conflicting demands of the body, heart, and spirit. Even with its respect for individual leadings, Quakerism does not sanction license in sexual behavior. Precisely because our sexuality is so powerful, seeking the divine will becomes all important. The obedience thus called for is more personal, perhaps more difficult than adherence to an external code. For many Friends, 'celibate in singleness, faithful in marriage' has proven consonant with the divine will. Sexual activity, whether or not it includes intercourse, is never without consequence. Current global population trends and concern for the equitable distribution of resources require us to ask what good stewardship of the earth entails for our decisions about sex and childbearing. Friends approve the concept of family planning and endorse efforts to make pertinent education and services widely available. We are in unity about the value of human life, but not about abortion. We are urged to seek the guidance of the Spirit, to support one another regarding how to end the situations contributing to abortion, and to discern how to act as individuals, family members, and Meetings. (pp. 70–1)

Thus, on the Liberal side of the Quaker spectrum, we find a more world-accepting stance, but one that is equally counter-cultural in terms of its attitudes to materialism and consumption. It is more accepting of homo-sexuality and does not condemn abortion. Rather it lays down the criteria of integrity rather than judge particular choices. It acknowledges different family relationships and divorce. Evangelical Quakerism has a different view on these and proscribes homosexuality and abortion. All of Quakerism accepts testimony to peace, simplicity, integrity, equality, and civic duty (as long as it does not contradict God's will) as normative outcomes of the spiritual life even if these are not prescribed in the Liberal tradition. Central Yearly Meeting Friends are most separated from 'the world' whilst the Conservative Yearly Meetings continue their own version of the 'hedge' (see p. 62 above).

MISSION, MEMBERSHIP, AND DIVERSITY

MISSION

The final verses of the book of Matthew read:

And Jesus came and speak unto them, saying, All power is given unto me in heaven and in earth. Go ye therefore, and teach all nations, baptizing them in the name of the Father, and of the Son, and of the Holy Ghost: Teaching them to observe all things whatsoever I have commanded you: and lo, I am with you always, even unto the end of the world.
    Amen (Matt 28:18–20)

Box 28 Congregation accountability questions

The following is extracted from the Friends Church Southwest book of discipline as an example of one Quaker group's present-day focus for accountability. It is interesting to compare it with the list prepared by George Fox in 1670 (see p. 46 above).

1. Have we witnessed effectively for Christ through our church's events, programs, retreats, camps, and organized evangelistic efforts? Have we assimilated new believers into our fellowship and helped them grow in the faith and knowledge of our Lord Jesus Christ?

2. Have we built loyalty for placing weekly worship as a higher priority than pleasure, youth sports, business or recreation? Have we encouraged our people to worship and serve in one congregation rather than becoming consumers of programs offered by different churches?

3. Has our congregational life together revealed an intense desire to obey the written and living Word of God?

4. Have we spent time in silent listening to the Holy Spirit in both personal and corporate worship?

5. Have we prayed publicly and often for God to send out workers from among us into His harvest fields?

6. Have we honored and protected those neglected by society–the unborn, poor, prisoners, orphans, widows, abandoned, disabled, disadvantaged, addicted, institutionalized, homeless, hungry? Since we cannot do everything, have we done something?

7. Have we taught and practiced spiritual disciplines–Bible reading, prayer, fasting, witnessing, service, worship, silence, solitude?

8. Have we honored our pastors and staff with love and appreciation, making their ministry a joy, not a drudgery?

9. Have we honored the counsel of our elders and pastors? When we were not in unity, did we find the mind of Christ through discussion and prayer rather than through politicking and voting?

10. Have we encouraged and built each other up, speaking only what is helpful? Have we resolved conflict effectively by avoiding gossip and encouraging critics to talk with the right person in the right spirit?

11. Have we encouraged people in the church to use their spiritual gifts and to work together in teams for the cause of Christ?

12. Have we called for dedication to God of our time, talent and treasure, offering control of our money and our resources to Christ?

13. Have we prayed for those in authority? Have we encouraged people to vote and to carry out civic responsibilities in the name of Christ?

14. Have we taught and practiced non-violence? Have we placed the kingdom of God above the kingdom of this world, honoring the convictions of those who are conscientious objectors to war? Have we made every effort to live in peace with everyone, including those who have hurt us or with whom we disagree?

(*Faith and Practice of Evangelical Friends Church Southwest*, 2001, pp. 28–9)

The risen Christ tells the disciples what they must do. This is known as the Great Commission and it informs mission work by Christians worldwide. EFI Missions Movement claims:

Our purpose and passion is to lead our people worldwide to live so close to Jesus Christ that we will worship, serve and obey God as faithful witnesses. We live and die for the cause of fulfilling the Great Commission in the spirit of the Great Commandment. We exist to fuel a worldwide multiplication movement of worshipping, God-glorifying Evangelical Friends Churches through evangelism, leadership development and missionary-sending. (http://www.friendsmission. com/welcome.htm, 7 March 2006)

Friends Church Southwest include the following in their book of discipline:

We value Christ's Great Commission to preach the gospel to every creature and to disciple all the nations. We believe the Great Commission begins at home, where we live, work, play and participate – and extends to every nation, culture and people group worldwide. We go in Christ's authority and with His presence. This value causes us to invest in cross-cultural missions, disciple making, church planting, pastoral training, and sending out missionaries and workers into the harvest.

Along with the Great Commission we value the Great Commandment to love God with all our heart, soul, mind and strength and to love our neighbors as ourselves. This value causes us to honor and protect every individual – high and low, rich and poor, unborn and disabled, mentally ill and terminally ill, exceptional and institutionalized. We seek to obey the often-repeated commands in Scripture to love one another and to do good. (*Faith and Practice of Evangelical Friends Church Southwest*, 2001, p. 25)

FUM is equally involved in educational and evangelical mission work. It is this work which has led to the growth of Quakerism worldwide in the last 150 years (chapter 3). It is an integral part of evangelical theology.

Conservative Friends are not involved in mission, feeling their particular calling is to nurture the spiritual welfare of those already within the Yearly Meeting. Conservative Friends still record Ministers, unlike most Liberal Yearly Meetings, and issue travelling minutes to those with leadings to travel amongst Friends. There is nothing in the Ohio or North Carolina Yearly Meetings (Conservative) disciplines about outreach or mission.

Liberal Quakerism can be ambivalent about 'outreach', partly through fear of being seen to proselytise, partly out of hesitation about overly championing Quakerism. The amount of energy put into this activity varies enormously between Meetings. The perceived distinction between outreach and traditional mission work is made clear in the following extract from a British Quaker.

Outreach is for me an invitation to others to join us in our way of worship and response to life which are so important to us that we wish to share them. At the simplest level this means supplying information about meetings, Friends to contact, and basic beliefs, all of which should be given accurately, clearly and if possible attractively. In the second stage outreach offers to others, through meetings, personal contact and literature, the experience and truth which Friends have found for themselves through three centuries and which impel us just as strongly today. It is different from some forms of evangelism in that it does not use mass emotional appeal, idiosyncratic demands or autocratic compulsion but only the persuasion of insight, humanity and good sense. It does not depend on rewards or threats, but on the active acceptance of those who see it as truth. (*Quaker Faith and Practice*, 1995, 28.09)

Of course, many involved in mission work would echo these sentiments. Not only is the experience of Liberal Quakers less of transformation than was the case for early Friends, but the stakes are less high. Salvation is not of upmost concern for Liberal Friends and they are not corporately convinced of its necessity or its existence (chapter 4). Thus, unlike the first Friends, who felt an urgency behind their mission work, modern Liberal Friends hold no reason as to why anyone should come to Meeting other than it may be personally helpful. This is obviously in stark contrast to the mission statements above, living and dying for the cause of the Great Commission.

One of the modern equivalents of organised mission work is the continued practice of travelling in the ministry (see p. 64 above) (Abbott and Parsons 2004). This practice continues in all traditions of Quakerism but its effects may be most profound where organised mission or systematic adult education is lacking.

MEMBERSHIP

The Church is the company of the people in whom Christ dwells.
(http://www.fum.org/about/friends.htm#Beliefs, 7 March 2006)

For all branches of Quakerism, the church is the body of believers. What varies is what the church is seen to be for, what the believers are required to believe, and the processes by which commitment is measured and publicly accepted. An EFI text states:

We believe the church is composed of all people who through repentance and faith receive Jesus Christ as Lord and Savior and become His devoted followers in fellowship with like-minded believers. This church, universal in scope, unites all true Christians in spirit to love one another, live holy lives and proclaim the gospel to all the world. It has local expressions in individual congregations and in families of churches called denominations or movements. Our denomination is called Friends, from the words of Jesus, 'You are my friends if you do what I command you.' (John 15:16 NIV) The church gathers to worship God, encourage believers, preach the gospel, teach the Bible, equip the saints, serve the needy, and pray for God's best. The church then fans out into the community and the world to demonstrate the love of Christ and the presence of His reign in the daily routines and crises of life. As a body the church uses its material, organizational and spiritual resources to obey its Head, Jesus Christ, until His coming kingdom finds fulfillment in His return. (Mylander 2004, pp. 10–11)

Friends Church Southwest states:

Evangelical Friends receive into membership only those who declare and live out their faith in Christ Jesus as their personal Savior and Lord, and who are in agreement with the teachings of faith taught in the Scriptures and held by Evangelical Friends Church Southwest.

    ... Membership is *not* for those who are outside of Christ. Membership is *not* a means to salvation, but it is helpful for a Christian to declare commitment to Christ and to the local church. It means personal agreement with basic Christian beliefs as practiced by the local congregation of the body of Christ. When a group of Christians commit themselves to membership and to loyalty to the church, it enables them together to accomplish more for the glory of God. (*Faith and Practice of Evangelical Friends Church Southwest*, 2001, pp. 75, 76)

Friends Church Southwest includes the following expectations in its discipline:

- I will endeavor to attend worship regularly and participate in other meetings of the church.
- I will contribute cheerfully to the expenses of the church and for the spreading of the Gospel to the world.
- I will serve with my time, talent and spiritual gifts in ministry to others as God instructs, watching over others in care and prayer and offering aid when they are in sickness or distress.
- I will seek to be loving and courteous in speech, to be slow to take offense and to be always ready for reconciliation. It is my desire to cooperate with the leadership of our church and the proceedings of Evangelical Friends Church Southwest.
- I will endeavor to maintain regular times of personal prayer and Bible study, to provide my children with Christian instruction and to seek the salvation of others.
- I will endeavor to live above reproach in the world, to be just in my dealings and exemplary in my conduct and to avoid practices harmful to my personal witness and to the testimony of our church.
- I understand that my name may be removed from membership if I discontinue attending for a period of twelve months. If I move beyond commuting distance

from this church, I will seek the Lord's guidance about uniting with another church where I can carry out the spirit of this fellowship and the principles of God's Word. (*Faith and Practice of Evangelical Friends Church Southwest*, 2001, pp. 75–6)

Kenyan Yearly Meetings require a two-stage doctrinal test for membership. As God's chosen people, becoming a Quaker involves more than becoming a Christian (Malenge 2003, p. 65). 'Class One' involves six months of study in Bible, Christian instruction and basic Quakerism. Successful completion, which involves appearing before a panel of Elders and Clerks at monthly meeting level, akin to the catechism in other churches (Malenge 2003, p. 65), results in 'Associate membership'. 'Class two' takes a further nine months of Bible study and Quaker studies: 'The syllabus covered includes Quaker history, Church government, Organizational structure, Church leadership, Quaker Faith and Practice which includes stewardship and finance' (Malenge 2003, p. 65). Completion involves being interviewed by a panel of Elders and Clerks under the clerkship of the General or Regional Superintendent.

Ohio Yearly Meeting (Conservative) has developed four kinds of membership: 'birthright', 'waiting', 'affiliate', and 'full'. Birthright membership lasts until age twenty-five, by which time the individual will have chosen another form of membership or none. 'Waiting' membership is an expression of commitment but where an individual is not ready to assume full and active membership: here they 'must be open to the experience of the Divinity of Christ and must have an understanding of the necessity to surrender oneself to the Will of God as shown to us by the Power of Christ within us' (http://www.ohioyearlymeeting.org/discipline.htm, 7 March 2006)

Britain Yearly Meeting states:

Like all discipleships, membership has its elements of commitment and responsibility but it is also about joy and celebration. Membership is a way of saying to the meeting that you feel at home, and in the right place. Membership is also a way of saying to the meeting, and to the world, that you accept at least the fundamental elements of being a Quaker: the understanding of divine guidance, the manner of corporate worship and the ordering of the meeting's business, the practical expression of inward convictions and the equality of all before God. In asking to be admitted into the community of the meeting you are affirming what the meeting stands for and declaring your willingness to contribute to its life. (*Quaker Faith and Practice*, 1995, ch. 11)

Like all Liberal Yearly Meetings, the British emphasis is not doctrinal but relies more on adherence to the way in which the group is religious.

(We return to this distinction between Evangelical and Liberal Friends in chapter 6.) The Britain Yearly Meeting discipline states:

When early Friends affirmed the priesthood of all believers it was seen as an abolition of the clergy; in fact it is an abolition of the laity. All members are part of the clergy and have the clergy's responsibility for the maintenance of the meeting as a community. This means helping to contribute, in whatever ways are most suitable, to the maintenance of an atmosphere in which spiritual growth and exploration are possible for all. It means contributing to the meeting by giving time and energy to events and necessary tasks, and also being willing to serve on various regional or yearly meeting committees and other groups. There is a special responsibility to attend meetings for church affairs, for it is here that the meeting enacts its faith. Membership also entails a financial commitment appropriate to a member's means, for without money neither the local meeting nor the wider structure can function. (*Quaker Faith and Practice*, 1995, ch. 11)

Waiting members in Ohio Yearly Meeting (Conservative) can serve on some committees but do not usually take part in business meetings. A similar distinction has been made in Britain in the past between 'Attenders' and 'Members'. 'Attenders' was a category fully developed in the twentieth century when 'Recognised Attenders' started to be counted alongside Members and have their names included in membership lists. For a time, they were not expected to give financially or serve on committees but those distinctions have been blurred now. Many Attenders feel fully committed without the need to join formally, as per Putnam (2000), and concessions to financial giving and office holding have made some of the distinctions between Members and Attenders, except those felt by the individual, redundant.

The origin of formal membership was in the list of settlement of the eighteenth century. This listed which Friends were eligible for poor relief from which Meetings (p. 63 above). That was all. Membership in terms of belonging was already clear by the behaviour of the Friend, the use of plain language and plain dress. Disownment preceded formal membership because it was already clear who claimed to be a Quaker. Listing everybody geographically incidentally resulted in a more formal membership system, more closely regulated since the dropping of visible outward markers of Quakerism. Putnam's analysis of the decline of joining in the twentieth century (2000) may mean the idea of membership falls out of favour again. In Britain, Young Friends General Meeting, representing those aged eighteen to thirty, have twice had a concern for the abolition of formal membership. In 2001, Britain Yearly Meeting allowed local Meetings to experiment with different forms of acquiring membership and one Monthly Meeting abolished 'paper membership' in favour of listing those involved in the life of the meeting.

Thus, the meaning and expectations of membership, never a spiritual rite of passage and of course unaccompanied by water baptism, has been developed locally and pragmatically in the context of each Yearly Meeting's theology and practice. Where doctrine or behaviour is clearly prescribed by the Meetings, agreement is required by the Yearly Meeting. Where an attitude is at the heart of a Yearly Meeting, then this is required.

Affiliate membership is unique to Ohio Conservative.

This form of membership provides one way for persons living at a distance from established meetings of Ohio Yearly Meeting to be formally affiliated with us. Affiliate membership is intended to provide spiritual support from and connection to Ohio Yearly Meeting for Friends who lie outside our normal geographic area and who feel a sense of spiritual isolation. This is not meant to discourage those who, living at a distance, wish to participate as full members in the business of our meetings. (*The Book of Discipline of Ohio Yearly Meeting of the Religious Society of Friends (Conservative)*, 1992, p. 9)

Affiliate membership was adopted in the late twentieth century as a way of increasing fellowship amongst Conservative Friends, many of whom found themselves in areas served only by Liberal Yearly Meetings or by none. It accommodates a form of dual affiliation or membership. This is unique in Quaker circles and still does not allow full dual membership. Dual membership of Quakers and another faith or church is generally allowed within the Liberal tradition, although the difficulty of maintaining both is acknowledged (e.g. *Quaker Faith and Practice*, 1995, 10.31) and it is not widespread.

All Yearly Meetings maintain a system of terminating membership or of publicly distancing the meeting from the claims or behaviour of an individual. The discipline of Friends Church Southwest states:

Church discipline is the process of confronting Christians in the church who err in doctrine or who engage in conduct that violates scripture, as determined by the elders, seeking their repentance and restoration to fellowship. The purpose of church discipline is twofold. First, it is to carry out the ministry of reconciliation in restoring a Christian brother or sister caught in sin (Gal. 6:1). The goal is not to expose the sin, but to win back the offender. Second, it is to maintain the spiritual health of the church (Acts 5:1–11; Heb. 12:10–12; 1 Cor. 5:1–5).

The Bible specifically names disorderly conduct, divisiveness, sexual immorality, false teaching, drunkenness, abusive speech, swindling and idolatry as issues requiring church discipline (Rom. 16:17–18; 1 Cor. 6:9–11; 2 Thess. 3:6–15; 1 Tim.

1:20, 2 Tim. 2:17–18; Rev. 2:14–16). This list is not all-inclusive. (*Faith and Practice of Evangelical Friends Church Southwest*, 2001, p. 85)

The Free Quakers were disowned for taking up arms (see p. 52 above) and Updegraff's campaign for water toleration centred on the ability of ministers to maintain their Quaker status and receive outward baptism (see p. 114 above). Paying extra attention to those in more public roles has continued into the twentieth and twenty-first centuries. Pastors have been asked to desist from drinking alcohol in public or from divorce.

In Liberal Yearly Meetings, discipline is less likely to be focused on behaviour outside of the Meeting House. Since the 1860s, Meetings have been less inclined to 'interfere' in the 'private' lives of Friends. Elders no longer visit Friends in their homes unexpectedly or police their consumption and lifestyle. Indeed, with freedom of dress and speech and marriage, Quakers could be invisible and unaccountable outside of the Meeting House. For those who still place their Quaker identity as primary, this may feel unsettling. For others, it fits with increasingly permissive levels of attendance and the consequences of attendance. Testimony, as noted above, becomes an optional aspiration within the Liberal tradition following the centuries of codifying the earlier consequences of personal transformation. A British Friend was disowned in the early 1990s, for example, for writing publicly as a Quaker that Muslims and homosexuals would burn in hell. The Meeting needed to state publicly that it was not in unity with such sentiment.

DIVERSITY

Quakers have never been very strong on cultural diversity within their Meetings. Black Friends outside of Africa are still relatively uncommon and most Quakers in 'the north' come from middle-class educated backgrounds regardless of their tradition. Where Friends churches have become community churches, their membership may be drawn from a wider social grouping.

The tensions over homosexuality have meant that in certain Friends churches, 'out' lesbian and gay participants have not been allowed to join formally or take up positions of responsibility such as being part of a pastoral team or minister of music. Different from disownment, this is a new kind of sanction, where a portion of the population are explicitly excluded from applying for Quaker membership, or from service as part of the priesthood of all believers.

Couples asking for Meetings for Worship to celebrate same-sex relationships or gay and lesbian marriages have created further tensions. These tensions run throughout Evangelical and, to some degree, Conservative Quakerism. Liberal Quakerism, freed from textual authority and politically liberal, has had less difficulty accepting lesbian, gay, bisexual, and transgender members and offering celebrations of commitment for loving monogamous relationships. They argue that the content of the relationship or its nature is of more importance than the sex or sexuality of those involved (e.g. *Quaker Faith and Practice*, 1995, ch. 22). This does not mean there is wholehearted and open acceptance of lesbians and gays but it is generally not a corporate tension any longer.

Across the traditions there is the criticism that Friends are comfortable with their limited diversity. No longer the only true church, Quakers do not need to be all things to all people, and legitimate paths to salvation are available elsewhere. The organisational temptation is to send those who do not easily fit to one of those elsewhere churches and continue to recruit their own social type. The sectarian impulse to be the gathered remnant remains in some cases, as we can see in Liberal ambivalence about outreach. One of the advantages of having pastors is that the responsibility for these concerns is focused and accountable. Where everyone has the responsibility, it can mean that no one has.

ECUMENISM

An FUM introductory text reads:

Belief in the Light of Christ leads to a special kind of Christian universalism. The requirement – and opportunity – to respond to the Light pertains to everyone, and those who are obedient to the inward Light of Christ will be saved. This is not to say that 'everyone will be saved,' because God also grants everyone freedom to turn away from God's witness in their heart.

There are important consequences of this belief in the universal saving Light of Christ. Amongst these are:

1. The essential character of God is love. Jesus' salvation is available to everyone without exception.
2. Everyone must come to a decision of obedience in his or her inward relationship with God.
3. We can appeal to this Light in those whom we meet. We have confidence that there is no one in whom God has not already placed a witness.

This Inward Light is Jesus Christ. Therefore, Friends believe that while the community of salvation extends beyond the boundary of any religious affiliation, the Christian church of which Friends are a part is the outward fellowship of those who make a personal profession of faith in Jesus Christ. (Richmond 2004, n.p.)

This is the traditional line taken by early Friends. It is not in itself ecumenical however: it simply states that those who do not know the name of Christ may be saved. For early Friends, those who preached wrong doctrine were more guilty than the innocent.

Evangelical Friends may or may not be involved in ecumenical dialogue. For some, their Protestant counterparts may feel more like natural allies than Liberal Quakers. FUM is affiliated to the World Council of Churches, as are some individual Yearly Meetings. Others have declined the membership because it requires adherence to a credal basis. Within Britain, Quakers were offered a non-credal basis for membership of the national ecumenical bodies and successfully applied to join. Locally, Meetings may or may not have been able to negotiate such an agreement.

Within the Liberal tradition, ecumenism, which is technically concerned with the whole people of God, not just Christians, incorporates an interfaith approach, where all religions are seen as potentially legitimate paths 'up the mountain' to God. Indeed, for those who have not made peace with their previous Christian affiliations, interfaith work can be more attractive than interchurch ecumenism. Ignorance of the specific details of other faiths can sometimes help in this way too. For christocentric Friends, interfaith work is less of a priority except on issues of testimony and social witness: they are less interested in 'mutual irradiation' (Steere 1971).

At the same time, Quakers have always defined themselves *vis-à-vis* the established church and Christianity in general (Collins 1996). Now that the experience of the unfolding second coming has receded, Friends emphasise the liturgical consequences of that initial Quaker experience as distinctive from their Christian counterparts. Where Friends do not want to emphasise this distinctiveness, they play down the differences or eradicate them from their practice. Thus Updegraff pushed for the toleration of water baptism, and some Quaker churches look and feel very mainstream Protestant. Ecumenism is intuitive in these situations. Liberal Friends who suggest that they are still experiencing the unfolding second coming (see p. 200 above) challenge their own preference for an implicit ecumenism by inherently differentiating between their realising eschatology and the meantime stance of the churches in general. These Quakers are either a vanguard of the whole Christian church, 'ahead' of other Christians, or separated from them as still or again the only true church (Dandelion et al. 1998, p. 221).

CHAPTER SUMMARY

As we have seen throughout the first part of the book, Quakers have continually changed their relationship with 'the world'. These modifications have centred on what or who exactly counts as 'the world' and what attitude Quakers should take towards 'the world'. The first Friends considered all who were not Quaker to be part of apostasy and in need of Quakerism (see p. 33 above). Second and third generations were less charged with bringing the world to Quakerism and more concerned with protecting Quakerism from the world (see p. 49 above). Evangelical Friends were both more relaxed about the world and more interested in joining with parts of it to achieve common purposes, such as reform and mission. In most ways and in most traditions, Quakers joined the world in the nineteenth century. Little, outside of pacifism, separates present-day Quakers from other religionists in their outlook on the world. What varies between Quakers is the degree and specificity of testimony and the degree to which it is counter-cultural. For most now, 'the world' is small: less counts as being apostate or inherently sinful. Certainly, in all its traditions, Quakerism is again optimistic about its ability to challenge those areas of moral fragility or wrong.

The degree to which Quakers are world-rejecting or world-accommodating (see p. 80 above), coupled with their view on how far they feel they are the sole true church, directly affects their attitude to mission, membership, and ecumenism. Today's Quakers generally work in coalition with others of like-minded values and beliefs where purposes are held in common. Networks and allies differ between different traditions of Quakers and working together can prove more challenging. The next chapter looks at internal Quaker diversity and commonality and charts the future prospects for the group.

CHAPTER 6

The Quaker family

TENSIONS AND COMMONALITIES

Does anything unite this diverse group beyond our common love and humanity? Does anything make us distinctively Quaker? I say yes. Each of us has different emphases and special insights, but wherever Friends are affirming each other's authentic experience of God, rather than demanding credal statements, we are being God's faithful Quakers. Wherever we are seeking God's will rather than human wisdom, especially when conflict might arise, we are being faithful Quakers. Wherever we are affirming the total equality of men and women, we are being God's faithful Quakers. Wherever there is no division between our words and our actions, we are being faithful. Whenever we affirm that no one – priest, pastor, clerk, elder – stands between us and the glorious and mystical experience of God in our lives, we are faithful Friends. Whether we sing or whether we wait in silence, as long as we are listening with the whole of our being and seeking the baptism and communion of living water, we will be one in the Spirit. (*Quaker Faith and Practice*, 1995, 29.16)

This section looks at the differences between Friends worldwide and then the commonalities. Table 6.1 lists thirteen areas in which Liberal and Evangelical Friends have different or distinct approaches from each other.

The first difference is the way Liberal and Evangelical Friends define themselves. Evangelical Friends tend to find their identity in doctrine whereas Liberal Friends define themselves in terms of their 'behavioural creed' (see p. 136 above), the way in which they operate as a religious group. Liberal Friends will mention their form of worship as a defining characteristic rather than the theology underpinning it (see p. 138 above).

Experience is primary and sufficient for Liberal Friends as a source of spiritual authority. Conservative Friends require a blend of revelation and Scripture whereas Evangelical Friends emphasise Scripture above revelation.

Liberal and Conservative Friends identify primarily as Quaker. For Evangelical Friends, they may see themselves as Christians primarily, who happen to be Quaker.

Table 6.1. *Key differences between Liberal and Evangelical Friends*

Liberal	Evangelical
Defined in terms of method/form	Defined in terms of belief
Experience as primary	Scripture and spiritual experience as primary
'Quaker' identity primary	'Quaker' can be secondary to 'Christian'
Christian, post-Christian and non-Christian, e.g. Buddhist, non-theist	Christian
Semi-realism and non-realism	Realism
Truth only personal, partial, or provisional	Final and complete and whole Truth possible
Theology always a 'towards' kind of activity; The 'absolute perhaps'	Theology as true, not just story
Unprogrammed worship (form not open to change)	Programmed or semi-programmed worship (led by Holy Spirit)
No visible leadership	Pastors
Restraint of emotion	Restraint variable church by church
Outreach	Mission
Quakerism seen as unimportant	Christianity seen as salvific
Politically liberal on sexual morality	Traditional teaching on sexual morality
More exclusive?	More inclusive?

Following these first three characteristics, non-Christians are accommodated within Liberal Quakerism. Doctrine is marginalised within the Liberal tradition and a wide diversity of theology exists. For Evangelical Friends, Quakerism is clearly and solely Christian, a position shared by the more conservative of the Conservative Friends.

For Liberal Friends, God is semi-realist or non-realist (see p. 193 above). For Conservative and Evangelical Friends, God is real. The 1985 World Gathering of Young Friends epistle commented on the differences of language reflecting deeper differences:

Our differences are our richness, but also our problem. One of our key differences is the different names we give our Inward Teacher. Some of us name that Teacher Lord; others of us use the names Spirit, Inner Light, Inward Christ or Jesus Christ. It is important to acknowledge that these names involve more than language; they involve basic differences in our understanding of who God is, and how God enters our lives. (*Quaker Faith and Practice*, 1995, 29.17)

Liberal Friends thus do not believe theology to be necessarily 'true' (see p. 152 above). Equally, under their doctrine of progressivism (p. 132), and of continuing revelation, any truth can only be personal, partial, or provisional. Conservative and Evangelical Friends believe theology is true and that final and complete truth can be found. They do not share the doctrine of progressivism with Liberal Friends.

Liberal Friends operate an 'absolute perhaps' attitude to believing (see p. 152 above). In other words, they are absolutely sure that their theology will be provisional or partial, a 'belief story' (Dandelion 1996, p. 300). They can only be certain of uncertainty. Conservative and Evangelical Friends believe in the possibility and actuality of certainty.

Liberal and Conservative Friends operate unprogrammed worship and are pragmatically and theologically (respectively) conservative about change to form. Evangelical Friends have demonstrated freedom in their attitude to form, and have moved to a programmed and a pastoral system, whilst arguing that each service is still led by the Spirit, not the pastor (see p. 208 above).

There is no visible leadership in the unprogrammed tradition whereas pastors and others lead the worship in the programmed one.

Liberal and Conservative Friends display a restraint of emotion in their Meetings, which may or may not be mirrored in programmed Meetings. Levels of emotion and its expression vary church by church.

Salvation is still a primary concern for Evangelical Friends, as is the Great Commission (see p. 230 above). Salvation features less in Conservative Quaker theology and is not a key component of Liberal Quaker theology. As such, and coupled with an ambivalent attitude towards Scripture, mission is unimportant. 'Outreach' is treated with ambivalence.

Liberal Friends are also liberal in terms of sexual and family morality and political issues generally. Conservative and Evangelical Friends hold more traditional Christian views on sexual and family morality, although Conservative Friends may place a greater priority on peace issues, than say abortion, when it comes to choosing how to vote, for example in a presidential election.

Given their adherence to Quaker distinctives, Liberal and Conservative Friends may be more exclusive than Evangelical Friends. Their emphasis on form over belief, and the way their worship is so different from mainstream liturgies, may present a greater threshold for the newcomer to cross and a greater commitment to a particular form of participation. In other words, Liberal and Conservative Friends make higher demands of participants and can be considered more sectarian (see p. 80 above), except where Evangelical Friends are highly world-rejecting or, possibly, where their liturgical form includes a long period of open worship. The

Liberal attitude to salvation, as above, may result in a lack of proactive recruitment.

The differences over primary identity and the nature of theology seem the most important here. Partly the attitude to theology defines the Liberal tradition in its liberal-Liberal variant (see p. 152 above). Equally, together with questions of sexual morality, these differences provide the biggest stumbling block to Evangelical Friends seeing Liberal Quakers as Friends. Indeed some Evangelical Friends will not use the term Quaker as it is so associated with a liberal attitude to belief and behaviour.

In contrast to these differences, there appear three main areas of commonality: the emphasis on inward encounter, business method, and testimony.

First, all the Quaker traditions continue to emphasise the primacy of direct encounter. Foundational in 1647, it remains fundamental to defining Quaker and Friend today. All that differs is how Friends describe the encounter and how they interpret it. A Friend from Philadelphia Yearly Meeting had this experience of programmed worship in Africa:

Ushered firmly but with great welcome to our seats, we squeezed together on backless wooden benches, like beads on a necklace, while others poured in behind us and did likewise. In all the activity, it took me twenty minutes to realize everyone on our side of the room was female, everyone on the other side was male, and all the 200-some faces except ours were black. However, just like Meeting at home, a little kid kept crawling over our laps to get from one person to another, while everyone patiently helped him get there. Unlike meeting at home, every seat was filled, and we were constantly urged to squeeze tighter to make room. Within a few minutes, there was an overflow of faces in the doorway behind us, with more arriving all the time and trying to fit inside.

I couldn't understand a word that was said in the Kiswahili service, but the spirit was big and strong, and I wished it could have reached across the globe. As we sat, the room rapidly became warm, I could feel the people beside me breathing in and out against my ribs, and Julia nudged me periodically to point out the Bible verse being read or to tell me 'Pray' or 'Stand up.' I knew at least one of the men up front was the pastor, but instead of his giving a single sermon, several people took turns telling their stories of faith. In between testimonies and Bible readings, we sang hymns that sounded vaguely familiar but surprisingly straightforward in bouncy Kiswahili.

I was also surprised to find myself fighting off tears throughout the entire service. Why? I was surrounded by awareness of all the people from home who were with me in spirit, and how very much I wanted them to know and see and feel and hear the people who were with me in that room. I couldn't have explained our crazy family of Quakers to anyone at that moment, except to say there is a place where faith comes from that words don't reach very well, and I believe that is our common ground. (Elliott 1991, p. 7)

While the Liberal emphasis on experience and the mystery beyond language (see p. 142 above) is accommodated by the lack of understanding of the native tongue, this author is also clear that common ground exists between the Quaker traditions. The World Gathering of Young Friends 1985 epistle stated:

We have often wondered whether there is anything Quakers today can say as one. After much struggle we have discovered that we can proclaim this: there is a living God at the centre of all, who is available to each of us as a Present Teacher at the very heart of our lives. (*Quaker Faith and Practice*, 1995, 29.17)

Second, following on from the commonality of inward communion is the similarity of business practice. Friends worldwide attempt to seek the will of God without voting (see p. 217 above).

Third, Quakers have maintained a testimony against war from their earliest days. Fox refused a captaincy in the army whilst in jail in Derby and Margaret Fell presented her written testimony to Charles II in 1660. At the same time, Quakers have always fought. In the American Civil War, many Quakers joined the fight against slaveholding. In World War I one third of eligible Quaker men joined up (see p. 162 above). In the Second World War, perhaps up to 50% of eligible Quaker men joined up in the USA. This did not result in mass disownments. What was important was sincerity of conscience. At the same time, the different Quaker branches have all maintained the testimony against war. The death in Iraq of the Quaker peacemaker Tom Fox, in March 2006, brought responses from across the Quaker traditions. Having said this, the more Friends churches identify as Christian as opposed to Quaker, the more permissive the teaching in this area. Where pastors have come in from other traditions, they may have mixed allegiances. Some feel that obedience to the needs of the nation come above individual conscience.

However, most Quakers hold to the same elements of testimony generally, as the first section of chapter 5 illustrates.

This list of three commonalities reflects more on the distinctive form of Quaker worship and its outcomes rather than on doctrine. In this way it is easier for Liberal and Conservative Friends to feel themselves part of a Quaker family. Such dialogue is also easier for Liberal and Conservative Friends, keen to retain Quaker distinctiveness, to prioritise.

However, whilst a large number of Evangelical Friends worldwide are not members of Friends World Committee for Consultation (FWCC), the family resemblance of Quakers throughout the world is clear. The ongoing dialogue at the world gatherings of Young Friends, outside of FWCC politics, reveals a desire and ability to dialogue which, even in its struggle, suggests a family relationship. The epistle for the World Gathering of Young Friends 2005 reads:

We were united not so much in the expression of our faith as in our common desire to be unified and by the power of the Spirit amongst us during these 9 days. We were challenged to put aside the labels we hide behind, programmed, unprogrammed, liberal, evangelical, and come together as Friends of the Truth, seeking together for the common truth behind our language. We have not finished this process. We are only at the beginning of a long path, but the love and joy we have felt in being in this place together have allowed us to come this far, and we pray that they will lead us further yet. (*World Gathering of Young Friends, Epistle, 2005*)

FUTURE PROSPECTS

Since the latter half of the twentieth century, in line with all liberal religion in Europe and in line with all voluntary organisations in 'the north', numbers have fallen in the Liberal tradition. In Britain, for example, the 1959 highpoint of 23,000 declined to 15,000 in 2005. Decline has been particularly sharp since the 1990s and attempting polynomial regression from 1990 results in a projected endpoint for Quakerism in Britain of 2032 (Chadkirk 2004, p. 116). This is in line with Methodists in Britain (Bruce 2003, p. 61). Other analysis offers a later date of 2037 (Stroud and Dandelion 2004, p. 121) or suggests regional/national variation within the wider British picture, with some rural English, and the Scottish, General Meetings increasing in size whilst the more urbanised General Meetings decline (Burton 2005, pp. 249–55).

Heelas and Woodhead *et al.* in their study of Kendal, a small town in the north of England, suggest that religion, activity focused on the transcendence of the individual, is in decline, whilst the 'spiritual milieu', where the focus is on the subjective, is increasing (Heelas *et al.* 2005). Quakers in Britain sit on the cusp between the two, but the implicit transcendence of the rhetoric of their praxis ultimately classifies them as a religion; certainly it seems so in the eyes of those in the spiritual marketplace who increasingly prefer something even more individualised, personal, and private. The advent of on-line meetings for worship may afford new ways of popular engagement.

Work on church conversion has suggested that 'seriousness' is a major attraction for those who 'switch' or convert (Dandelion 2002). Typically, people leave liberal denominations and join more conservative ones as the lesser permissiveness signals greater seriousness. In this, it might be expected that Liberal Quakerism would lose out to stricter churches who appear more serious. Having said that, 47% of converts into British Quakerism come from no prior religious affiliation (Heron 1992, p. 13). They have been agnostics or atheists or practising their faith alone. In this sense, Quakerism as an organised religion appears more serious, and is attractive whilst also being permissive enough not to demand immediate confessions of a particular rendering of faith. Liberal Quakerism should do well in these terms. Additionally, whilst Liberal Quakerism is permissive in terms of belief content, it is not permissive in terms of its form ('the behavioural creed' – see p. 136 above) or in terms of how it requires participants to believe ('the absolute perhaps' – see p. 152 above). It is implicitly sectarian, making high demands on its members on both of these counts. In these terms, it should also do well in terms of recruitment. The bigger question is the degree to which large numbers, especially in Europe (Davie 2002), are still looking for organised collective seriousness or whether they are happy believing without belonging (Davie 1994) or not believing and not belonging (Voas and Crockett 2005).

In the USA, the situation is different. Secularisation is less advanced and liberal religion is faring better. Sandy Springs Meeting in Virginia is an example of a flourishing Liberal Quaker Meeting which has now set off a number of satellite Meetings.

For Evangelical Friends, numbers in the USA (as opposed to the huge growth in, say, Kenya) have not risen as much as some would have hoped. The connection between the Friends churches and the Quaker tradition where it is still explicit or implicit may counter the possibility of attracting huge waves of seekers who hope for something less formal or more innovative (Roof 1993; Sargeant 2000), or of 'generation x' who are drawn to liturgical reappropriation or innovation, as identified by Flory and Miller (2004). Only where Friends churches explicitly aim to reconstruct themselves as community churches with little or no connection to what may appear an anachronistic tradition or one still laden with pacifist, voteless decision-making, and open-worship oddity, can they be sure to have an open chance in the marketplace. Yorba Linda Friends Church, according to the *Los Angeles Times*, hosts 3500 worshippers each weekend, operating buses from the local malls to the church (Schrader 1997). Other, more traditionally Quaker, Evangelicals argue that the doctrine of Christ the Light allows the work of the cross to be affirmed cross-culturally without losing the historic centrality of incarnation, atonement, and resurrection. John Punshon's *Reasons for Hope* (2001) is a call for Evangelical Friends to reclaim their rich and sufficient evangelical Quaker heritage.

Further schism may occur, although groups that break away may also prefer a separate identity. However, major schisms seem a feature of the past. This is because there is no longer a single Quaker hegemony to protest against. Quakerism is already broken up through its Yearly Meetings and no one Yearly Meeting has authority over another. For some Friends, the splits have been positive, allowing each emphasis to flourish unhindered. Other Friends see the branches as complementary, each branch contributing something to a bigger picture.

FUM, which does maintain authority over its constituent Monthly Meetings, could face further schism if it takes an assertive line on a controversial issue. A new umbrella group of modernist and politically tolerant evangelicals could emerge over the issue of homosexuality or abortion. Equally, East African and Bolivian Quakerism are likely to emerge as the new ground for leadership of the Quaker movement: this may also take Quakerism in a more conservative direction. At present the political reality hampers an equality of worldwide Quaker leadership, but increased encounter, more publications in Spanish and Kiswahili, and more funds, will all empower this majority-Quakerism. Liberal Yearly Meetings can expect mission activity to help them rediscover their Christian Quakerism for as long as they are considered within the pale. If Liberal Yearly Meetings continue to drop in size, it will be measure of how strong the Quaker family identity is as to how much of any released assets, for example from the sale of unused Meeting Houses, is given to Quakers elsewhere or whether the fear of evangelicalism amongst the Liberals precludes this. My sense is that different agendas will remain stronger than unconditional giving, even within 'the family', whilst most Quakers remain in ignorance of, and isolation from, the nature of Quaker diversity. In the Pacific Northwest women from programmed and unprogrammed Quakerism have been meeting for a number of years, informally and formally, and have come to build real bonds of friendship and understanding. In some ways, this reflects the work in the early twentieth century amongst Young Friends and service organisations which led to the reunification of some Yearly Meetings. The World Gatherings of Young Friends have also contributed to the greater recognition of family across the traditions. In the meantime, Quakerism remains a growing faith worldwide and one still vastly under-researched.

Important dates in Quaker history

(Adapted, with permission, from *Historical Dictionary of the Friends (Quakers)*, edited by Margery Post Abbott, Mary Ellen Chijioke, Pink Dandelion, and John Oliver, 2003.)

1534	Henry VIII breaks with Rome.
1611	King James I Authorised Version of the Bible widely distributed.
1624	Birth date of George Fox.
1642	Beginning of the English Civil War.
1647	George Fox has the opening that 'there is one, even Christ Jesus, that can speak to thy condition'.
1649	Execution of King Charles I; Oliver Cromwell and the Puritans govern in England.
1652	George Fox's vision on Pendle Hill of a great people to be gathered.
1654	'Valiant Sixty' missionary work.
1656	James Nayler's entry into Bristol and trial by Parliament. First Friends arrive in North America. Others set off for the Vatican and the Sultan of Constantinople.
1658	Death of Oliver Cromwell.
1659–61	Four Quakers hanged, on Boston Common; anti-Quaker laws enacted in Virginia, USA.
1660	Death of James Nayler. Restoration of King Charles II.
1661	First General Meeting held in Newport, Rhode Island, start of New England Yearly Meeting, the oldest such body in the world.
1662	'Quaker Acts' forbid Quakers to meet in England.
1668	First Quaker schools in England. London Yearly Meeting established.
1670	Trial of William Penn and William Meade establishing rights of juries.

1671–73	George Fox travels in America.
1672	Baltimore Yearly Meeting established.
1675	Quakers acquire West Jersey, USA.
1676	Robert Barclay's *Apology* published. Meeting for Sufferings organised in London.
1681	William Penn obtains charter for Pennsylvania; Philadelphia Yearly Meeting established.
1683	First Friends' school in North America.
1688	Germantown Meeting in Pennsylvania protests against slavery.
1689	Toleration Act in England passed. Death of Robert Barclay.
1691	Death of George Fox.
1694	Publication of George Fox's *Journal*.
1696	New York Yearly Meeting established.
1698	North Carolina Yearly Meeting established.
1702	Margaret Fell dies.
1722	Recording of Ministers established in Britain.
1737	Lists of Settlement create a formal list of members.
1739–48	Methodist Revival in England.
1756	Quakers relinquish control of Pennsylvania legislature.
1758	Philadelphia Yearly Meeting condemns slaveholding by Friends.
1783	First 'Book of Extracts' (book of discipline) published in Britain.
1796	York Retreat, the first modern mental hospital, is founded by Friends in Britain.
1808	John Dalton states atomic theory.
1813	Elizabeth Fry begins prison reform work at Newgate prison in England. Ohio Yearly Meeting established.
1816	First Peace Society in England founded by William Allen and Joseph T. Price.
1817	Friends Asylum, the first modern mental hospital in the USA, founded in Frankford, Pennsylvania.
1821	Benjamin Lundy begins publication of *The Genius of Universal Emancipation*, an antislavery periodical. Indiana Yearly Meeting established.
1825	Edward Pease opens the Stockton and Darlington Railway, the first passenger railway in England.
1827–28	The Great Separation in North America into Hicksite and Orthodox branches.

1833	Joseph Pease elected to the British Parliament. John Greenleaf Whittier published.
1835	Isaac Pidgeon and family become first Quakers to settle west of the Mississippi River. Isaac Crewdson and the 'Beaconites' leave London Yearly Meeting.
1837	Joseph John Gurney travels to America.
1843	John Bright enters British Parliament. Indiana Yearly Meeting of Anti-Slavery Friends separates from Indiana Yearly Meeting.
1845	The Gurneyite–Wilburite separation in New England.
1846	Levi Coffin settles in Cincinnati, Ohio, and becomes known as 'president' of the Underground Railroad.
1846–47	Quaker famine relief in Ireland.
1847	Adult School and Home Mission movements in Britain become established.
1848	Lucretia Mott initiates organisation of the first women's rights convention in Seneca Falls, New York.
1852	Friends Temperance Union formed in Britain.
1854	Gurneyite–Wilburite separation in Ohio.
1859	Endogamy discontinued in Britain.
1860	Conference held at Ackworth, England, for active consideration of new forms of foreign missionary work by Friends.
1862	American Quakers undertake relief and educational work for freed slaves.
1865	Provisional Committee of Foreign Gospel Service established in England.
1866	Rachel Metcalf sent by British Friends to undertake missionary work in India. Home Mission Association established by the women of Indiana Yearly Meeting.
1867	Canadian Yearly Meeting established.
1868	Fritchley General Meeting separates from London Yearly Meeting, rejoining in 1968.
1869	American Friends undertake supervision of Native American agencies in Nebraska, Kansas, and Indian Territories. Sybil and Eli Jones sent by New York Yearly Meeting as missionaries to Ramallah, Palestine, and help establish school for girls there.
1870	David Duncan Controversy in Manchester, England.
1870–71	British Quaker relief work in Franco-Prussian War. Indiana Yearly Meeting Foreign Missionary Association established.

1871–95	Gulielma Purdie of North Carolina and Samuel A. Purdie of New York sent as missionaries to Mexico, initially by Indiana Yearly Meeting.
1873	First Quaker meeting on the Pacific coast, in San Jose, California.
c.1875	Introduction of 'pastoral system' among American Friends.
1875	Illinois Yearly Meeting established.
1882	John Bright resigns from British cabinet in protest against bombardment of Alexandria, Egypt. Theophilus Waldmeier establishes girls' school in Brummanha, Lebanon, then Lebanon Hospital for Mental Diseases.
1884	Publication of *A Reasonable Faith* in England.
1885	Joseph and Sarah Cosand of Kansas sent by Philadelphia Yearly Meeting (Orthodox) to open a mission in Japan.
1886	Iowa Yearly Meeting is first formally to accept pastoral system.
1887	Richmond Declaration of Faith adopted by most Gurneyite North American Yearly Meetings.
1891	Women's Foreign Missionary Society of Western Yearly Meeting established.
1892	Lenna M. Stanley sent by Ohio Yearly Meeting to China.
1896–1937	Esther Baird sent by Ohio Yearly Meeting as missionary to India.
1895	Manchester Conference held in England, with Summer Schools held in subsequent years, culminating in opening of Woodbrooke in 1903.
1897	Robert and Carry Sams sent by California Yearly Meeting to Alaska. Rufus Jones and J. W. Rowntree meet in Switzerland.
1900	Friends General Conference (FGC) established.
1902	Five Years Meeting (FYM, renamed Friends United Meeting (FUM) in 1965) established.
1903	Willis R. Hotchkiss, Arthur B. Chilson, and Edgar Hole sent by FYM to East Africa.
1909	First fully united men's and women's London Yearly Meeting.
1914	War Victims Relief Committee established by British Friends. Friends Ambulance Unit created to provide care for soldiers and civilians injured in World War I.
1917	American Friends Service Committee (AFSC) established.
1919–24	Friends undertake feeding programme for German children at request of Herbert Hoover; programme then expands into Poland, Russia, and other European countries.

1920	All Friends Conference held in London and publishes *Friends and War.*
1921	Emma Morrow and Walter Lanstom sent by Central Yearly Meeting to Bolivia.
1924	Central Yearly Meeting, Westfield, Indiana, withdraws from Five Years Meeting.
1926	Oregon Yearly Meeting withdraws from Five Years Meeting. British Friends Service Committee formed.
1930	American Quaker study centre, Pendle Hill, established.
1933	AFSC begins work camp programmes for youth.
1936	Wider Quaker Fellowship established.
1937–39	Non-partisan relief work in Spanish Civil War.
1937	Second World Conference of Friends held in Swarthmore, Pennsylvania. Friends World Committee for Consultation (FWCC) founded.
1939–46	Quaker war relief in Europe and Asia.
1940	Civilian Public Service camps for conscientious objectors to war established by US Government and administered by AFSC.
1943	Friends Committee on National Legislation (FCNL) established.
1945	Reunion of Yearly Meetings separated in 1845 to form the modern New England Yearly Meeting.
1947	Nobel Peace Prize awarded to AFSC and Friends Service Council (Britain) on behalf of the Religious Society of Friends.
1946	East Africa Yearly Meeting formed, the first such body in Africa.
1947–70	Association of Evangelical Friends meets regularly.
1952	Third World Conference of Friends held in Oxford, England.
1955	Meetings divided by 1827 separation rejoin, forming united Yearly Meetings in New York, Canada, and Philadelphia.
1960	Opening of Earlham School of Religion.
1961	South Central Yearly Meeting established.
1962	Lake Erie Yearly Meeting and Southeastern Yearly Meeting established.
1963–64	Establishment of Evangelical Friends Alliance (becoming Evangelical Friends International (EFI) in 1990).
1967	Fourth World Conference of Friends held in Greensboro, North Carolina, USA.
1968	Separated Yearly Meetings in the Middle Atlantic states form the consolidated Baltimore Yearly Meeting.

1969	Creation of Central Alaska Friends Association and Piedmont Friends Fellowship.
1970	St. Louis Conference on The Future of Friends sponsored by Committee of Concerned Friends for Renewal initiates 'Faith and Life Movement'; Evangelical Friends Church in Guatemala established as an independent body.
1974	Bolivian Friends Yearly Meeting established. Friends Disaster Service (U.S.) formed.
1979	Southern Appalachian Yearly Meeting and Association established.
1985	First World Gathering of Young Friends held at Guilford College, North Carolina, USA.
1990	First International Theological Conference of Quaker Women held at Woodbrooke Quaker Study Centre in England.
1991	Fifth World Conference of Friends on Three Sites held at venues in Kenya, The Netherlands, and Honduras.
1993	Fellowship of Quakers in the Arts formed. Formation of a new Conservative Yearly Meeting, 'Friends in Christ'. Opening of the Iglesia de los Amigos Evangelicos (Evangelical Friends Church) in the metropolitan area of Mexico City.
1994	Friends Church Southwest Yearly Meeting brings its entire organization and missions program under the umbrella of EFI.
1995	London Yearly Meeting changes its name to Britian Yearly Meeting.
1996	Sixth Consultation on Mission and Service held in Uganda.
1999	EFI-Africa Region opens the Great Lakes School of Theology at Bujumbura, Burundi.
2005	Second World Gathering of Young Friends, held at Lancaster University, England.

Further reading

In terms of books in print or widely available, I would recommend the following as further reading.

The Braithwaite/Jones 'Rowntree History Series' is difficult to better. Braithwaite is particularly reliable and wonderfully detailed and referenced (*The Beginnings of Quakerism*, 1912, *The Second Period of Quakerism*, 1919). Jones' volume on *The Later Periods of Quakerism* (1921) is also well written and insightful. Rosemary Moore's *The Light in their Consciences* (2000) is the most thorough study of nuances of Quaker theology in the 1650s, whilst Doug Gwyn's pioneering trilogy of work on early Friends (*Apocalypse of the Word*, 1986; *Covenant Crucified*, 1995; *Seekers Found*, 2000) are also essential reading. Richard Bauman's *Let Your Words Be Few* (1973) is equally outstanding. The work of Geoffrey Nuttall (*The Holy Spirit in Puritan Faith and Experience*, 1946) and Hugh Barbour (*The Quakers in Puritan England*, 1964) remains highly significant. Richard Bailey's *New Light on George Fox and Early Quakerism* (1992) offers an alternative approach, as do the materialist histories of Christopher Hill (*The World Turned Upside Down*, 1972) and Barry Reay (*The Quakers and the English Revolution*, 1985). Contrasting theories of Quakerism are presented in Dandelion's *The Creation of Quaker Theory* (2004a).

Good biographies of the three early Quaker leaders now exist: Larry Ingle has written on George Fox in *First among Friends* (1994); Bonnelyn Kunze on *Margaret Fell and the Rise of Quakerism* (1994), with Margaret Fell's letters now compiled by Elsa Glines (*Undaunted Zeal*, 2003); Leo Damrosch has written excellently on James Nayler in his *The Sorrows of the Quaker Jesus* (1996). Rosemary Moore has edited a reprint of *The History of the Life of Thomas Ellwood* (2004).

Early Quaker women are written about in Phyllis Mack's *Visionary Women* (1992), Christine Trevett's *Quaker Women Prophets in England and Wales* (2000), and Catie Gill's *Women in the Seventeenth-Century Quaker Community* (2005). Kate Peters' volume on *Print Culture and the Early Quakers* (2005) is also important in terms of Quaker women's history.

The Cambridge version of *Fox's Journal* edited by Nigel Smith is now available in Penguin (1998). The first edition of Barclay's *Apology* has been transcribed and published by Quaker Heritage Press (2002). Hugh Barbour's and Arthur Roberts' *Early Quaker Writings* has justifiably been recently republished (2004).

Rufus Jones' *Quakers in the American Colonies* (1911) is comprehensive on early American Quaker history. Michael Heller's *A Tendering Presence* (2003) is a scholarly collection of articles on John Woolman; Jack Marietta's *The Reformation of American Quakerism* (1984) is worth tracking down for insights into eighteenth-century Quakerism. Thomas Hamm's *The Transformation of American Quakerism* (1988) is a key text in understanding the schisms of nineteenth-century American Quakerism whilst Carole Spencer's *Holiness: The Soul of Quakerism* offers a contrasting view of Quakerism as Holiness throughout its history (2007).

Thomas Kennedy's *British Quakerism 1860–1920* (2001) is a both monumental yet eminently readable account of late Victorian British Quakerism and the Liberal renewal. It makes up for the scarcity of the excellent *Victorian Quakers* by Elizabeth Isichei (1970). James Walvin's *Quakers, Money and Morals* is the standard work on Quaker business history in Britain (1997).

John Punshon's *Reasons for Hope* (2001) offers an evangelical perspective on Quakerism; Margery Post Abbott and Peggy Parsons have edited a powerful collection across Quaker traditions on 'travelling in the ministry' (*Walk Worthy of Your Calling*, 2004); and Pink Dandelion has addressed worship across the traditions in his *The Liturgies of Quakerism* (2005). Jackie Leach Scully and Dandelion have edited *Good and Evil: Quaker Perspectives*, also a book crossing the Quaker traditions (2007). Emma Lapsansky and Anne Verplanck have produced an important volume on *Quaker Aesthetics* (2003). Wilmer Cooper's *A Living Faith* (2001) has been usefully republished.

Quaker Studies and *Quaker History* are both refereed journals, whilst *The Journal of the Friends Historical Society* and *Quaker Religious Thought* are also excellent sources of academic insight. *The Historical Dictionary of the Friends (Quakers)* (Abbott *et al.* 2003) provides comprehensive and well-researched entries on worldwide Quaker history and theology. John Punshon's *Portrait in Grey* (1984) is an excellent short history with a greater emphasis on biography than this volume.

We can live in the hope that the theses by Sally Padgett on Margaret Fell (2003), Esther Mombo on Kenyan Quaker women (1998), Michele Tarter on celestial inhabitation (1993), Brian Phillips on the Quaker renaissance, 1895–1910 (1989), Kathryn Damiano (1988) and Sylvia Stevens (2004) on eighteenth-century Friends, and Michael Graves on early Quaker sermons (1972) will be published in book form. Work by Peter Collins and other sociologists of British Quakerism is due out in collected form in 2009.

Books of discipline are available from all Yearly Meetings and are increasingly available on the web, as are increasing numbers of earlier Quaker writings. Both Earlham College and Quaker Heritage Press have very helpful on-line resources in this regard.

References

A Clear Distinction between the Old Covenant, or Old Testament, and the New Covenant, or Testament (1708) [1680], in G. Fox, *Gospel Truth Demonstrated in a Collection of Doctrine Books, Given Forth by that Faithful Minister of Jesus Christ, George Fox*, London: T. Sowle, pp. 746–76.

A Distinction between the Two Suppers (1991), Gloucester: George Fox Fund.

A Guide to Our Faith and Our Practice (2000). Bristol, TN: Southern Appalachian Yearly Meeting and Association.

A Testimony from the Brethren, who were met together in London in the Third Month 1666, to be communicated to faithful Friends and Elders in their counties, by them to be read in their several meetings, and kept as a testimony amongst them (1666), reprinted in A. R. Barclay (ed.), *Letters of Early Friends*, London: Harvey and Darton, 1841, pp. 318–24.

Abbott, M. P., Chijioke, M. E., Dandelion, P. and Oliver, J. (eds.) (2003), *The Historical Dictionary of the Friends (Quakers)*, Lanham, MD: Scarecrow.

Abbot, M. P. and Parsons, P. S. (eds.) (2004), *Walk Worthy of Your Calling: Quakers and the Travelling Ministry*, Richmond, IN: Friends United Press.

Advices and Queries (1995), London: Britain Yearly Meeting.

Allen, R. C. (2003), ' "A most industrious well-disposed people." Milford Haven Quakers and the Pembrokeshire Whaling Industry c.1791–1821', in Patricia O'Neill (ed.), *Nation and Federation in the Celtic World*, Sydney: University of Sydney Press, pp. 64–94.

Allott, S. (1994), *John Wilhelm Rowntree, 1869–1905, and the Beginnings of Modern Quakerism*, York: Sessions.

Ambler, R. (1989), *Creeds and the Search for Unity*, London: Quaker Home Service.

Ayoub, R. (2005), 'The Persecution of "an Innocent People" in Seventeenth-Century England', *Quaker Studies* 10, pp. 46–66.

Ayoub, R. and Roeltgen, D. (n.d.), 'Lexical Agraphia in the Writing of George Fox', unpublished manuscript.

Bacon, M. H. (2003), 'Lucretia Mott', in Margery Post Abbott, Mary Ellen Chijioke, Pink Dandelion and John Oliver (eds.), *The Historical Dictionary of the Friends (Quakers)*, Lanham, MD: Scarecrow, pp. 186–7.

Bailey, R. (1992), *New Light on George Fox and Early Quakerism: The Making and Unmaking of a God*, San Francisco: Mellen Research University Press.

(2004), 'Was Seventeenth Century Quaker Christology Homogeneous?', in P. Dandelion (ed.), *The Creation of Quaker Theory: Insider Perspectives*, Aldershot: Ashgate, pp. 61–82.

Barbour, H. (1964), *The Quakers in Puritan England*, New Haven and London: Yale University Press. Reprinted with a new preface by the author, Richmond, IN: Friends United Press, 1985.

(1994), 'Early Quakerism as a Perfectionist Movement of Awakening', in D. N. Snarr and D. L. Smith-Christopher (eds.), *Practiced in the Presence: Essays in honor of T. Canby Jones*, Richmond, IN: Friends United Press, pp. 1–14.

(2004), 'Sixty Years in Early Quaker History', in P. Dandelion (ed.), *The Creation of Quaker Theory: Insider Perspectives*, Aldershot: Ashgate, pp. 19–31.

Barbour, H. and Roberts, A. O. (2004), *Early Quaker Writings 1650–1700*, Wallingford, PA: Pendle Hill.

Barclay, R. (1676), *Anarchy of the Ranters*, London.

(2002) [1678], *Apology for the True Christian Divinity*, Glenside, PA: Quaker Heritage Press.

(1876), *The Inner Life of the Religious Societies of the Commonwealth: Considered Principally with Reference to the Influence of Church Organization on the Spread of Christianity*, London: Hodder and Stoughton.

Bauman, R. (1983), *Let Your Words Be Few: Symbolism of Speaking and Silence amongst Seventeenth-Century Quakers*, Cambridge: Cambridge University Press.

Baxter, R. (1655), *The Quakers Catechism*, London.

Bell, M. (1988), 'Mary Westwood – Quaker Publisher', *Publishing History* 23, pp. 5–66.

Bell, S. H. (1995), 'George Fox's Hill of Vision', *Friends Quarterly*, July, pp. 306–20.

Benson, L. (1968), *Catholic Quakerism: A Vision for All Men*, Philadelphia, PA: Philadelphia Yearly Meeting.

Berger, Peter L (1967), *The Sacred Canopy: Elements of a Sociological Theory of Religion*, Garden City, NY: Doubleday.

Bernet, C. (2004), 'Between Quietism and Radical Pietism: The German Quaker Settlement Friedensthal', *Woodbrooke Journal* 14, Birmingham: Woodbrooke.

Bill, B. (1983), *David Updegraff: Quaker Holiness Preacher*, Richmond, IN: Friends United Press.

Book of Extracts (1783), London: London Yearly Meeting.

Boulton, D. (1995), 'Which Hill of Vision? The Case for Pendle', *Friends Quarterly*, October, pp. 364–71.

(2002), *The Trouble with God: Religious Humanism and the Republic of Heaven*, Ropley, Hants: John Hunt Publishing.

Braithwaite, W. C. (1912), *The Beginnings of Quakerism*, London: Macmillan.

(1919), *The Second Period of Quakerism*, London: Macmillan.

(1955), *The Beginnings of Quakerism*, revised edn, Cambridge: Cambridge University Press.

Brodie, J. and Brodie A. (1993), *Seeking a New Land: Quakers in New Zealand*, Wellington: New Zealand Yearly Meeting.

Bruce, S. (2003), 'The Demise of Christianity in Britain', in G. Davie, P. Heelas and L. Woodhead (eds.), *Predicting Religion: Christian, Secular, and Alternative Futures*, Aldershot: Ashgate, pp. 53–63.

Burrough, E. (1656), *A Trumpet Sounded Forth Out of Sion*, London: Giles Calvert.
  (1657), *A Standard Lifted Up*, London: Giles Calvert.
  (1672), *Memorable Works of a Son of Thunder*, no publication details.

Burton, P. (2005), 'Keeping the Light Shining? The End of British Quakerism Revisited', *Quaker Studies* 9, pp. 249–56.

Cantor, G. (2003), 'How Successful Were Quakers at Science?', *Quaker Studies* 7, pp. 214–26.

Carrdus, A. (1993), 'The Quaker Unchristmas', *The Friend* 151, pp. 1659–60.

Carroll, K. (1962), *John Nichols and the Nicholites*, Easton, MD: Easton Publishing Company.
  (1970), *John Perrot, Early Quaker Schismatic*, London: Friends Historical Society.

Chadkirk, B. (2004), 'Will the Last (Woman) Friend to Leave Please Ensure the Light Remains Shining?', *Quaker Studies* 9, pp. 114–19.

Clark, D. and Smith, J. (1895), *David B. Updegraff and His Work*, Cincinnati, OH: Knapp.

Clark, P. (2003), 'Quaker Women in South Africa during the Apartheid Era', unpublished MPhil thesis, University of Birmingham.

Collins, P. J. (1996), '"Plaining": The Social and Cognitive Practice of Symbolisation in the Religious Society of Friends (Quakers)', *Journal of Contemporary Religion* 11, pp. 277–88.

Cooper, W. A. (1994), 'The Legacy of Rufus M. Jones', in D. N. Snarr and D. L. Smith-Christopher (eds.), *Practiced in the Presence: Essays in Honor of T. Canby Jones*, Richmond, IN: Friends United Press, pp. 15–35.
  (2001), *A Living Faith: An Historical and Comparative Study of Quaker Beliefs*, Richmond, IN: Friends United Press.

Cowie, I. (1990), 'On Not Having a Creed', *The Staffordshire Quaker*, September, p. 7.

Crawford, P. (1993), *Women and Religion in England, 1500–1720*, London and New York: Routledge.

Creasey, M. A. (1962), '"Inward" and "Outward": A Study in Early Quaker Language', *Journal of the Friends Historical Society*, Supplement No. 30, pp. 1–24.

Cross, F. L. and Livingstone, E. A. (eds.) (1997), *The Oxford Dictionary of the Christian Church*, Oxford: Oxford University Press.

Damiano, K. (1988), 'On Earth as It Is in Heaven: Eighteenth Century Quakerism as Realized Eschatology', unpublished PhD thesis, Union of Experimenting Colleges and Universities.

Damrosch, L. (1996), *The Sorrows of the Quaker Jesus: James Nayler and the Puritan Crackdown on the Free Spirit*, Cambridge, MA: Harvard University Press.

Dandelion, P. (1996), *A Sociological Analysis of the Theology of Quakers: The Silent Revolution*, Lampeter: Edwin Mellen Press.

(2002), 'Those Who Leave and Those Who Feel Left: The Complexity of Quaker Disaffiliation', *Journal of Contemporary Religion* 17, pp. 213–28.

(ed.) (2004a), *The Creation of Quaker Theory: Insider Perspectives*, Aldershot: Ashgate.

(2004b), 'Implicit Conservatism in Liberal Religion: British Quakers as an 'uncertain sect', *Journal of Contemporary Religion* 19, pp. 219–29.

(2005), *The Liturgies of Quakerism*, Aldershot: Ashgate.

Dandelion, P., Gwyn, D., Muers, R., Phillips, B. and Sturm, R. E. (2004), *Towards Tragedy/Reclaiming Hope: Literature, Theology and Sociology in Conversation*, Aldershot: Ashgate.

Dandelion, B. P., Gwyn, D. and Peat, T. (1998), *Heaven on Earth: Quakers and the Second Coming*, Birmingham and Kelso: Woodbrooke and Curlew.

Davie, G. (1994), *Religion in Britain since 1945: Believing without Belonging*, Oxford: Blackwell.

(2002), *Europe: The Exceptional Case. Parameters of Faith in the Modern World*, London: Darton, Longman and Todd.

Davie, M. (1997), *British Quaker Theology since 1895*, Lewiston, NY: Edwin Mellen Press.

Davies, A. (1988), 'Talking in Silence: Ministry in Quaker Meetings', in N. Coupland (ed.), *Styles of Discourse*, London: Croom Helm, pp. 105–37.

Densmore, C. (2003), 'Native Americans', in M. P. Abbott, M. E. Chijioke, P. Dandelion and J. Oliver (eds.), *The Historical Dictionary of the Friends (Quakers)*, Lanham, MD: Scarecrow, pp. 190–2.

Dewsbury, W. (1689a), *A Faithful Testimony of that Ancient Servant of the Lord*, London.

(1689b), *Collected Works: The Faithful Testimony*, n.p.

Dixon, S. and Shaw, G. (2005), 'Sources, Patterns and Myths: A Comparative Study of Quaker Sufferings in London and the East Riding of Yorkshire, 1654–1699', paper presented at Quaker Studies Research Association Annual Conference, Birmingham, England, August.

Doherty, R. W. (1967), *The Hicksite Separation: A Sociological Analysis of Religious Schism in Early Nineteenth-Century America*, New Brunswick, NJ: Rutgers University Press.

Dorland, A. G. (1968), *The Quakers in Canada: A History*, Toronto: Ryerson Press.

Elliott, M. K. (1991), 'Beads on a Necklace', *Friends Journal* 37 (12), p. 7.

Endy, M. B., Jr. (1981), 'The Interpretation of Quakerism: Rufus Jones and His Critics', *Quaker History* 70, pp. 3–21.

Extracts from the Minutes and Advices of the Yearly Meeting of Friends Held in London from Its First Institution (1802), second edition, London.

Ezell, M. J. M. (1993), *Writing Women's Literary History*, Baltimore, MD: Johns Hopkins University Press.

Faith and Practice (1993), Corvallis, OR: North Pacific Yearly Meeting of the Religious Society of Friends.

Faith and Practice: A Book of Christian Discipline, Northwest Yearly Meeting of Friends Church (2003), Newberg, OR: Northwest Yearly Meeting.

Faith and Practice: A Book of Christian Discipline, Philadelphia Yearly Meeting of the Religious Society of Friends (2002), Philadelphia, PA: Philadelphia Yearly Meeting.

Faith and Practice: Book of Discipline of the North Carolina Yearly Meeting (Conservative) of the Religious Society of Friends (1983). Ahoskie, NC: North Carolina Yearly Meeting (Conservative).

Faith and Practice of Evangelical Friends Church Southwest (2001), Whittier, CA: Evangelical Friends Church Southwest.

Faith in Action: Encounters with Friends. Report from the Fifth World Conference of Friends, 1991 (1992), London: FWCC.

Flannery, A. (ed.) (1975), *Vatican Council II: The Conciliar and Post-conciliar Documents*, Dublin: Dominican Publications.

Flory, R. and Miller, D. (2004), 'The Embodied Spirituality of Post-Boomer Generations', paper presented at the British Sociological Association Sociology of Religion Study Group Annual Conference, 29 March–1 April, Bristol, England.

Fox, G. (1891), *The Journal of George Fox*, Bicentenary edition, 2 vols., London: Friends Tract Association.

Freiday, D. (1967), *Barclay's Apology in Modern English*, Manasquan, NJ: privately published.

    (2003) 'Robert Barclay', in M. P. Abbott, M. E. Chijioke, P. Dandelion and J. Oliver (eds.), *The Historical Dictionary of the Friends (Quakers)*, Lanham, MD: Scarecrow, pp. 19–20.

Frost, W. J. (2003), 'From Plainness to Simplicity: Changing Quaker Ideals for Material Culture', in Emma J. Lapsansky and Anne A. Verplanck (eds.), *Quaker Aesthetics: Reflections on a Quaker Ethic in American Design and Consumption*, Philadelphia, PA: University of Pennsylvania Press, pp. 16–40.

Garver, N. (2001), 'Quakers in Bolivia', *Friends Journal* 47/2, pp. 10–13.

Giles, H. and Powesland, P. F. (1975), *Speech Style and Social Evaluation*, London: Academic Press.

Gill, C. (2001), 'Women in the Quaker Community: A Literary Study of Seventeenth-Century Political Identities', unpublished PhD thesis, Loughborough University.

    (2005), *Women in the Seventeenth-Century Quaker Community: A Literary Study of Political Identities, 1650–1700*, Aldershot: Ashgate.

Glines, E. (2003), *Undaunted Zeal: The Letters of Margaret Fell*, Richmond, IN: Friends United Press.

Graham, E. (1996), ' "Lewed, Profane Swaggerers" and Charismatic Preachers: John Bunyan and George Fox', in H. Wilcox, R. Todd and A. MacDonald (eds.), *Sacred and Profane: Secular and Devotional Interplay in Early Modern British Literature*, Amsterdam: Vrije Universiteit University Press, pp. 309–18.

Graham, E., Hinds, H., Hobby, E. and Wilcox, H. (eds.), (1989), *Her Own Life: Autobiographical Writings by Seventeenth-Century Englishwomen*, London: Routledge.

Graves, M. P. (1972), 'The Rhetoric of the Inward Light: An Examination of Extant Sermons Delivered by Early Quakers, 1671–1700', unpublished PhD thesis, University of Southern California.

Greenwood, O. (1978), *Signs of Life: Art and Religious Experience*, London: FHSC.

Gregory, J. (2004), '"Some account of the progress of truth as it is in Jesus": The White Quakers of Ireland', *Quaker Studies* 9, pp. 68–94.

Grubb, E. (1908), *Authority and the Light Within*. London: James Grubb.

Grundy, M. P. (2007), 'Learning To Be Quaker: Spiritual Formation and Religious Education among Early Friends', *Quaker Studies* 11, forthcoming.

Gurney, J. J. (1979) [transcript of *Observations on the Distinguishing Views and Practices of the Society of Friends*, seventh edn, 1834], *A Peculiar People: The Rediscovery of Primitive Christianity*, Richmond, IN: Friends United Press.

Gwyn, D. (1986), *Apocalypse of the Word: The Life and Message of George Fox, 1624–1691*, Richmond, IN: Friends United Press.

—— (1995), *Covenant Crucified: Quakers and the Rise of Capitalism*, Wallingford, PA: Pendle Hill.

—— (2000), *Seekers Found: Atonement in Early Quaker Experience*, Wallingford, PA: Pendle Hill.

Hamm, T. D. (1988), *The Transformation of American Quakerism: Orthodox Friends 1800–1907*, Bloomington, IN: Indiana University Press.

—— (1995), *God's Government Begun: The Society for Universal Inquiry and Reform, 1842–1846*. Bloomington, IN: Indiana University Press.

—— (2002), '"A Protest against Protestantism": Hicksite Friends and the Bible in the Nineteenth Century', *Quaker Studies* 6, pp. 175–94.

—— (2003), *The Quakers in America*, New York: Columbia University Press.

—— (2004), 'George Fox and the Politics of Late Nineteenth-Century Quaker Historiography', in P. Dandelion (ed.), *The Creation of Quaker Theory: Insider Perspectives*, Aldershot: Ashgate, pp. 11–18.

Hawkes, A. C. (2003), 'Progressive Friends', in M. P. Abbott, M. E. Chijioke, P. Dandelion and J. Oliver (eds.), *The Historical Dictionary of the Friends (Quakers)*, Lanham, MD: Scarecrow, pp. 228–9.

Heelas, P., Woodhead, L., Seel, B., Szerszynski, B. and Tusting, K. (2005), *The Spiritual Revolution: Why Religion Is Giving Way to Spirituality*, Oxford: Blackwell.

Heller, M. (ed.) (2003), *The Tendering Presence: Essays on John Woolman*, Wallingford, PA: Pendle Hill.

Heron, A. (1992), *Caring, Conviction, Commitment: Dilemmas of Quaker Membership Today*, London: Quaker Home Service.

Hewitt, J. (1990), 'Embracing Uncertainty', *The Friend* 148, pp. 757–8.

Hill, C. (1972), *The World Turned Upside Down: Radical Ideas during the English Revolution*, Harmondsworth: Penguin.

Hinds, H. (1996), *God's Englishwomen: Seventeenth-Century Radical Sectarian Writing and Feminist Criticism*, Manchester: Manchester University Press.

Hobby, E. (1989), *The Virtue of Necessity: English Women's Writing 1649–88*, Ann Arbor, MI: University of Michigan Press.

(1995), 'Handmaids of the Lord and Mothers in Israel: Early Vindications of Quaker Women's Prophecy', in T. N. Corns and D. Loewenstein (eds.), *The Emergence of Quaker Writing: Dissenting Literature in Seventeenth Century England*, London: Frank Cass, pp. 88–98.

Holden, D. (1988), *Friends Divided: Conflict and Division in the Society of Friends*, Richmond, IN: Friends United Press.

Holland, R. J. (2006), 'The Debate between John Bunyan and Edward Burrough, 1656–7', unpublished MPhil thesis, University of Birmingham.

Holton, S. S. (1994), 'From Anti-Slavery to Suffrage Militancy: The Bright Circle, Elizabeth Cady Stanton and the British Women's Movement', in C. Daley and M. Nolan (eds.), *Beyond Suffrage: International Feminist Perspectives*, Auckland: Auckland University Press, pp. 213–33.

(1996), *Suffrage Days: Stories from the Women's Suffrage Movement*, London and New York: Routledge.

(2005), 'Family Memory, Religion and Radicalism: The Priestman, Bright and Clark Kinship Circle of Women Friends and Quaker History', *Quaker Studies* 9, pp. 156–75.

Holton, S. S. and Allen, M. (1997), 'Offices and Services: Women's Pursuit of Sexual Equality within the Society of Friends 1873–1907', *Quaker Studies* 2, pp. 1–29.

Horle, C. W. (1988), *The Quakers and the English Legal System 1660–1688*, Philadelphia, PA: University of Pennsylvania Press.

Hubbard, G. (1992), *Quaker by Convincement*, revised edn, London: Quaker Home Service.

Huber, K. (2001), 'The Spirituality of Buddhist Quakers', unpublished MPhil thesis, University of Sunderland.

Ingle, H. L. (1986), *Quakers in Conflict: The Hicksite Reformation*, Knoxville, TN: The University of Tennessee Press.

(1994), *First among Friends: George Fox and the Creation of Quakerism*, Oxford: Oxford University Press.

(2001), 'Richard Nixon: Exemplary 20th Century Quaker', unpublished lecture, Pendle Hill, Wallingford, PA, 21 May.

Isichei, E. (1967), 'From Sect to Denomination among English Quakers', in B. R. Wilson (ed.), *Patterns of Sectarianism: Organisation and Ideology in Social and Religious Movements*, London: Heinemann, pp. 161–81.

(1970), *Victorian Quakers*, Oxford: Oxford University Press.

Jiseok, J. (2004), 'Quaker Peace Testimony: Ham Sokhon's Ideas of Peace and Korean Reunification Theology', unpublished PhD thesis, University of Sunderland.

Jones, R. M. (1911), *Quakers in the American Colonies*, London: Macmillan.

(1921), *The Later Periods of Quakerism*, 2 vols., London: Macmillan.

Kaiser, G. (1994), *The Society of Friends in North America*, Chart, seventeenth edn, Sumneytown, PA: privately published.

Kaplan, J. (ed.) (1982), *Whitman: Poetry and Prose*, New York: Library of America.

Kashatus III, W. C. (1990), *Conflict of Conviction: A Reappraisal of Quaker Involvement in the American Revolution*, Lanham, MD: University Press of America.

Keiser, M. (2001), 'Touched and Knit in the Life: Barclay's Relational Theology and Cartesian Dualism', *Quaker Studies* 5, pp. 141–64.

Kelly, T. (1944), *The Gathered Meeting*, London: Friends Home Service Committee.

Kennedy, T. C. (1989), 'Why did Friends Resist? The War, the Peace Testimony and the All-Friends Conference of 1920', *Peace and Change* 14 (4), pp. 355–71.

—— (2001), *British Quakerism 1860–1920: The Transformation of a Religious Community*. Oxford: Oxford University Press.

Kunze, B. Y. (1994), *Margaret Fell and the Rise of Quakerism*, Palo Alto, CA: Stanford University Press.

Lacock, R. (2001), 'The Quakers in Gloucester 1655–1737'. Unpublished MPhil thesis, University of Birmingham.

Lapsansky, E. J. and Verplanck, A. A. (eds.) (2003), *Quaker Aesthetics: Reflections on a Quaker Ethic in American Design and Consumption*, Philadelphia, PA: University of Pennsylvania Press.

Larson, R. (1999), *Daughters of Light: Quaker Women Preaching and Prophesying in the Colonies and Abroad, 1700–1775*, New York: Alfred A. Knopf.

Leichty, D. (1990), *Theology in Postliberal Perspective*, London: SCM.

Lloyd, A. (1950), *Quaker Social History, 1669–1738*, London: Longmans.

Lowndes, W. (1980), *The Quakers of Fritchley 1863–1980*, privately published.

Lunn, P. (1997), '"You Have Lost Your Opportunity": British Quakers and the Militant Phase of the Women's Suffrage Campaign 1906–1914', *Quaker Studies* 2, pp. 30–56.

Mack, P. (1989), 'Gender and Spirituality in Early English Quakerism, 1650–1665', in E.P. Brown and S.M. Stuard (eds.), *Witnesses for Change: Quaker Women over Three Centuries*, New Brunswick: Rutgers University Press, pp. 31–63.

—— (1992), *Visionary Women: Gender and Prophecy in Seventeenth-Century England*, Berkeley, CA: University of California Press.

Malenge, Z. I. (2003), *Quakerism in the Perspective of Friends Church in Kenya*, Nairobi: Dianas Books Library Services.

Maltz, D. N. (1985), 'Joyful Noise and Reverent Silence: The Significance of Noise in Pentecostal Worship', in D. Tannen and M. Saville-Troike (eds.), *Perspectives on Silence*, Norwood, NJ: Ablex Publishing, pp. 113–37.

Manasseh, P. (2000), 'Quaker Relief Work and the Brynmawr Experiment', *Woodbrooke Journal* 7, Birmingham: Woodbrooke.

Marietta, J. D. (1984), *The Reformation of American Quakerism, 1748–83*, Philadelphia, PA: University of Pennsylvania Press.

Martin, L. (2003), 'Female Reformers as the Gatekeepers of Pietism: The Example of Johanna Eleonora Merlau and William Penn', *Monatshefte* 95 (1), pp. 33–58.

Martin, M. (2003), *Invitation to a Deeper Communion*, Wallingford, PA: Pendle Hill.

McFadden, D. and Gorfinkel, C. (2004), *Constructive Spirit: Quakers in Revolutionary Russia*, Pasadena, CA: International Productions.

Mendlesohn, F. (2002), *Quaker Relief Work in the Spanish Civil War*, Lampeter: Edwin Mellen Press.

Mingins, R. (2004), *The Beacon Controversy and Challenges to British Quaker Tradition in the Early Nineteenth Century: Some Responses to the Evangelical Revival by Friends in Manchester and Kendal*, Lampeter: Edwin Mellen Press.

Ministry and Oversight Commission (n.d.), 'About Silent Worship', Richmond, IN: First Friends.

Mombo, E. M. (1998), 'A Historical and Cultural Analysis of the Position of Abaluyia Women in Kenyan Quaker Christianity: 1902–1979', unpublished PhD thesis, University of Edinburgh.

(2003), 'East Africa (Kenya, Tanzania, Uganda)', in M. P. Abbott, M. E. Chijioke, P. Dandelion and J. Oliver (eds.), *The Historical Dictionary of the Friends (Quakers)*, Lanham, MD: Scarecrow, pp. 77–80.

Moore, R. (2000), *The Light in Their Consciences: The Early Quakers in Britain 1646–1666*, University Park, PA: Pennsylvania State University Press.

(2004), *The History of the Life of Thomas Ellwood*, Walnut Creek, CA: Altamira Press.

Moulton, P. (ed.) (1989), *The Journal and Major Essays of John Woolman*, Richmond, IN: Friends United Press.

Mylander, C. (ed.) (2004), *Welcome to Friends*, Whittier, CA: Evangelical Friends Church Southwest.

Nayler, J. (1716), *A Collection of Sundry Books, Epistles and Papers*, London: Sowle.

Newman, E. (2005), 'John Brewin's Tracts: The Written Word, Evangelicalism and the Quakers in the Mid Nineteenth Century England', *Quaker Studies* 9, pp. 234–48.

Newton, S. P. (2003), 'Temperance', in M. P. Abbott, M. E. Chijioke, P. Dandelion and J. Oliver (eds.), *The Historical Dictionary of the Friends (Quakers)*, Lanham, MD: Scarecrow, pp. 278–80.

Nickalls, J. (1952), *The Journal of George Fox*, Cambridge: Cambridge University Press.

Niebuhr, H. R. (1975) [1929], *The Social Sources of Denominationalism*, New York: New American Library.

Nixon, R. (1978), *The Memoirs of Richard Nixon*, London: Book Club Associates.

Nuttall, G. F. (1946), *The Holy Spirit in Puritan Faith and Experience*, Oxford: Basil Blackwell. Reprinted with new introduction by P. Lake, Chicago: University of Chicago Press, 1992.

O'Donnell, E. A. (1999), 'Woman's Rights and Woman's Duties: Quaker Women in the Nineteenth Century, with Special Reference to Newcastle Monthly Meeting of Women Friends', unpublished PhD thesis, University of Sunderland.

Oliver, J. (2003), 'Malone, Emma Isabel Brown (1860–1924) and John Walter (1957–1935)', in M. P. Abbott, M. E. Chijioke, P. Dandelion and J. Oliver (eds.), *The Historical Dictionary of the Friends (Quakers)*, Lanham, MD: Scarecrow, pp. 163–4.

O'Shea, U. J. (1993), *Living the Way: Quaker Spirituality and Community*, n.p.: The Religious Society of Friends (Quakers) in Australia Incorporated.

Otto, R. (1923), *The Idea of the Holy: An Inquiry in the Non-rational Factor of the Idea of the Divine and Its Relation to the Rational*, trans. J. W. Harvey, Oxford: Oxford University Press.

Padgett, S. B. (2003), 'The Eschatology of Margaret Fell (1614–1702) and Its Place in Her Theology and Ministry', unpublished PhD thesis, University of Durham.

Peters, K. (2005), *Print Culture and the Early Quakers*, Cambridge: Cambridge University Press.

Penington, I. (1996), *The Works of Isaac Penington: A Minister of the Gospel in the Society of Friends*, vol. III., Glenside, PA: Quaker Heritage Press.

Phillips, B. D. (1989), 'Friendly Patriotism: British Quakerism and the Imperial Nation, 1890–1910', unpublished PhD thesis, University of Cambridge.

(2004), 'Apocalypse without Tears: Hubris and Folly among Late Victorian and Edwardian British Friends', in P. Dandelion, D. Gwyn, R. Muers, B. Phillips and R. Sturm, *Towards Tragedy/Reclaiming Hope: Literature, Theology and Sociology in Conversation*, Aldershot: Ashgate, pp. 57–76.

Pickvance, J. (1989), *A Reader's Companion to George Fox's Journal*, London: Quaker Home Service.

Pilgrim, G. (2002), 'The Quakers: Towards an Alternate Ordering', in G. Davie, P. Heelas and L. Woodhead (eds.), *Predicting Religion: Christian, Secular and Alternative Futures*, Aldershot: Ashgate, pp. 147–58.

(2004), 'Taming Anarchy – Quaker Alternate Ordering and "Otherness"', in P. Dandelion (ed.), *The Creation of Quaker Theory: Insider Perspectives*, Aldershot: Ashgate, pp. 206–25.

Proceedings of the Yearly Meeting of the Religious Society of Friends (Quakers) in Britain 2004 (2004), London: British Yearly Meeting.

Punshon, J. (1984), *Portrait in Grey: A Short History of the Quakers*, London: Quaker Home Service.

(1989), *Letter to a Universalist*, Pendle Hill Pamphlet No. 285, Wallingford, PA: Pendle Hill.

(1990), *Testimony and Tradition: Some Aspects of Quaker Spirituality*, London: Quaker Home Service.

(2001), *Reasons for Hope: The Faith and Future of the Friends Church*, Richmond, IN: Friends United Press.

Putnam, R. D. (2000), *Bowling Alone: The Collapse and Revival of American Community*, New York: Simon and Schuster.

Pyper, H. S. (1998), 'Resisting the Inevitable: Universal and Particular Salvation in the Thought of Robert Barclay', *Quaker Religious Thought* 29 (1), pp. 5–18.

Quaker Faith and Practice: The Book of Christian Discipline in the Yearly Meeting of the Religious Society of Friends (Quakers) in Britain (1995), London: Britain Yearly Meeting.

Reay, B. (1985), *The Quakers and the English Revolution*, London: Temple Smith.

Richmond, B. (2004), *The Christian Faith of Friends*, Richmond, IN: Friends United Press.

Roof, W. C. (1993), *A Generation of Seekers: The Spiritual Journeys of the Baby-Boom Generation*, San Francisco: HarperCollins.

Rowntree, J. S. (1859), *Quakerism, Past and Present*, London: Smith, Elder and Co.

Rowntree, J. W. (1906), *Essays and Addresses*, London: Headley Bros.

Rush, D. (2003), 'They Too Are Quakers: A Survey of 199 Nontheist Friends', *Woodbrooke Journal* 11, Birmingham: Woodbrooke.

Sargeant, K. H. (2000), *Seeker Churches: Promoting Traditional Religion in a Nontraditional Way*, New Brunswick, NJ: Rutgers University Press.

Sauls Errand to Damascus (1653), London.

Schrader, E. (1997), 'Quakers: Evangelical Churches Hold Glitzy Services', *Los Angeles Times*, 17 August.

Schrauwers, A. (1993), *Awaiting the Millennium: The Children of Peace and the Village of Hope 1812–1889*, Toronto: University of Toronto Press.

Schweitzer, A. (1968) [1909], *The Quest for the Historical Jesus*, New York: Macmillan.

Scott, J. (1980), *What Canst Thou Say? Towards a Quaker Theology*, London: Quaker Home Service.

Scully, J. L. and Dandelion, P. (eds.), (2007), *Good and Evil: Quaker Perspectives*, Aldershot: Ashgate.

Sharpless, I. (1911), 'The Quakers in Pennsylvania', in R. M. Jones, (eds.), *Quakers in the American Colonies*, London: Macmillan, pp. 415–580.

Siler, E. C. (1887), 'The Pastoral Question', *Christian Worker* 17, pp. 397–401.

Simon, S. (2003), 'A Response', *Friends Journal* 49 (5), pp. 18–21.

Skidmore, G. (ed.) (2005), *Elizabeth Fry, a Quaker life: Selected Letters and Writings*, Lanham, MD: Altamira Press.

Smith, N. (1998), *George Fox: The Journal*, Harmondsworth: Penguin.

Spencer, C. (2001), 'James Nayler: Antinomian or Perfectionist?', *Quaker Studies* 6, pp. 106–17.

    (2004a), 'Holiness: The Quaker Way of Perfection', in P. Dandelion (ed.), *The Creation of Quaker Theory: Insider Perspectives*, Aldershot: Ashgate, pp. 149–71.

    (2004b), 'Quakerism as Holiness: An Historical Analysis of the Theology of Holiness in the Quaker Tradition', unpublished PhD thesis, University of Birmingham.

    (2007), *Holiness: The Soul of Quakerism*, Milton Keynes: Paternoster.

Spielhofer, S. (2001), *Stemming the Dark Tide*, York: Sessions.

Steere, D. (1971), *Mutual Irradiation: A Quaker View of Ecumenism*, Pendle Hill Pamphlet 175, Wallingford, PA: Pendle Hill.

Stevens, Sylvia (2004), 'A Believing People in a Changing World: Quakers in Society in Northeast Norfolk, 1690–1800', unpublished PhD thesis, University of Sunderland.

Stroud, C. and Dandelion, P. (2004), 'British Quakers and a New Kind of End-time Prophecy', *Quaker Studies* 9, pp. 120–5.

Sykes, Marjorie (1997), *An Indian Tapestry: Quaker Threads in the History of India, Pakistan, and Bangladesh from the Seventeenth Century to Independence*, York: Sessions.

Taber, F. I. (1992), 'Paradoxical Understandings to Hold in Creative Tension', *Friends Journal* 38 (7), pp. 16–17.

Taber, W. P., Jr (1978), 'Worship in the Conservative Tradition', in F. B. Hall (ed.), *Quaker Worship in North America*, Richmond, IN: Friends United Press, pp. 75–86.

Tarter, M. L. (1993), 'Sites of Performance: Theorizing the History of Sexuality in the Lives and Writings of Quaker Women, 1650–1800', unpublished PhD thesis, University of Colorado.

(1995), 'The Milk of the Word of God', in C. Fager (ed.), *New Voices, New Light: Papers from the Quaker Theology Roundtable*, Wallingford, PA: Pendle Hill.

(2001), 'Quaking in the Light: The Politics of Quaker Women's Corporeal Prophecy in the Seventeenth-Century Transatlantic World', in J. M. Lindman and M. L. Tarter (eds.), *A Centre of Wonders: The Body in Early America*, Ithaca, NY: Cornell University Press, pp. 145–62.

(2004), '"Go North!" The Journey towards First-Generation Friends and their Prophecy of Celestial Flesh', in P. Dandelion (ed.), *The Creation of Quaker Theory: Insider Perspectives*, Aldershot: Ashgate, pp. 83–98.

The Book of Discipline of Ohio Yearly Meeting of the Religious Society of Friends (Conservative) (1992), Barnsville, OH: Ohio Yearly Meeting of Friends.

The Harmony of Divine and Heavenly Doctrines: demonstrated in sundry declarations on variety of subjects. Preach'd at the Quaker meetings in London … (1723), second edn, London: J. Sowle.

The Priesthood of the Ordained Ministry (1986), London: Board of Mission and Unity of the Church of England.

Thomas, K. (1993), 'The Quaker Book of Discipline: A Sacred Text by Committee?', in Jon Davies and Isabel Wollaston (eds.), *The Sociology of Sacred Texts*, Sheffield: Sheffield Academic Press.

To Lima with Love. Baptism, Eucharist and Ministry: a Quaker Response (1986), London: Quaker Home Service.

Tolles, F. B. (1948), *Meeting House and Counting House: The Quaker Merchants of Colonial Philadelphia, 1682–1763*, Chapel Hill, NC: University of North Carolina Press.

Tonsing, B. K. (2002), *The Quakers in South Africa: A Social Witness*, Lampeter: Edwin Mellen Press.

Tousley, N. C. (2003), 'The Experience of Regeneration and Erosion of Certainty in the Theology of Second-Generation Quakers: No Place for Doubt?', unpublished MPhil thesis, University of Birmingham.

Trevett, C. (1991), *Women and Quakerism in the Seventeenth Century*, York: Ebor Press.

(2000), *Quaker Women Prophets in England and Wales 1650–1700*, Lampeter: Edwin Mellen Press.

(2001), '"Not Fit To Be Printed": The Welsh, the Women and the Second Day's Morning Meeting', *Journal of the Friends Historical Society* 59, pp. 115–44.

Tuke, Henry (1801), *The Faith of the People Called Quakers in Our Lord and Saviour Jesus Christ*, London: Phillips and Fardon.

(1806), *Principles of Religion, as Professed by the Society of Christians, Usually Called Quakers*, York: R. and J. Richards.

Vann, R. T. (1969), *The Social Development of English Quakerism, 1655–1755*, Cambridge, MA: Harvard University Press.

Vining, E. G. (1958), *Friend of Life: A Biography of Rufus Jones*, Philadelphia, PA: Lippencott.

Voas, D. and Crockett, A. (2005), 'Religion in Britain: Neither Believing nor Belonging', *Sociology* 39, pp. 11–28.

Wallis, R. (1984), *The Elementary Forms of the New Religious Life*, London: Routledge and Kegan Paul.

Walliss, J. (2002), *The Brahma Kumaris as a Reflexive Tradition: Responding to Late Modernity*, Aldershot: Ashgate.

Walvin, J. (1997), *The Quakers: Money and Morals*, London: John Murray.

Ward, B. (2005), 'Broadcasting Truth to Power: The American Friends Service Committee and the Early Southern Civil Rights Movement', *Quaker Studies* 10, pp. 87–108.

Warren, E. (1992), 'Ranters and Quakers', paper presented to the course on 'Unity and Diversity in the Society of Friends', Charney Manor, Oxfordshire, November.

West, J. (1940), *The Friendly Persuasion*, New York: Harcourt Brace.

West, R. (2001), 'What I Learned from Rachel Hicks', *Friends Journal* 47 (7), pp. 10–12.

White, D. (1659), *Friends, you that are of the Parliament, hear the word of the Lord*, n.p.

Wilbur, J. (1832), *Letters to a Friend on some of the Primitive Doctrines of Christianity*, London: Harvey and Darton.

Wilcox, C. (1995), *Theology and Women's Ministry in Seventeenth Century English Quakerism: Handmaids of the Lord*, Lampeter: Edwin Mellen Press.

Wilson, B. R. (1970), *Religious Sects*, London: Weidenfield and Nicolson.

Wisbey, H. A., Jr (1964), *Pioneer Prophetess: Jemima Wilkinson, the Publick Universal Friend*, Ithaca, NY: Cornell University Press.

Zielinski, S. (1975), *Psychology and Silence*, Pendle Hill Pamphlet No. 210, Wallingford, PA: Pendle Hill.

Index